UPROOTING
RACISM

HOW
WHITE PEOPLE
CAN WORK FOR
RACIAL
JUSTICE

PAUL KIVEL

new society
PUBLISHERS

Cover: Digital composite—Diane McIntosh;
images: birds ©iStock (493221057); texture ©iStock (474736866).
P. 91 © beermedia; p. 129 © Christopher Jones;
p. 177 © glisic_albina; p. 243 © StudioAraminta / Adobe Stock

Printed in Canada. First printing September 2017.

Inquiries regarding requests to reprint all or part of *Uprooting Racism*
should be addressed to New Society Publishers at the address below.
To order directly from the publishers, please call toll-free (North America)
1-800-567-6772, or order online at www.newsociety.com

Any other inquiries can be directed by mail to:

New Society Publishers
P.O. Box 189, Gabriola Island, BC V0R 1X0, Canada
(250) 247-9737

LIBRARY AND ARCHIVES CANADA CATALOGUING IN PUBLICATION

Kivel, Paul, author
Uprooting racism : how white people can work for
racial justice / Paul Kivel.—Revised and updated 4th edition.

Includes bibliographical references and index.
Issued in print and electronic formats.
ISBN 978-0-86571-865-4 (softcover).—ISBN 978-1-55092-657-6
(PDF).—ISBN 978-1-77142-252-9 (EPUB)

1. Racism—United States. 2. Race awareness—United States.
3. Whites—Race identity—United States. 4. United States—Race
relations. I. Title.

E184 A1 K58 2017   305.800973   C2017-904268-8
                                              C2017-904269-6

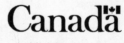

New Society Publishers' mission is to publish books that contribute
in fundamental ways to building an ecologically sustainable and just
society, and to do so with the least possible impact on the environment,
in a manner that models this vision.

Praise for *Uprooting Racism*

With current context, deepened history and new chapters, Paul Kivel's revised and updated *Uprooting Racism* offers visionary and practical tools for white people to reflect, share, learn, show up and act. Given all we have at stake in building a racially just society, this is both a timeless and urgent work. Like my copy of a previous edition, this one will be dog-eared from use, and my wallet thinner as I will gift copies of this book over and over.

—Pam McMichael, Highlander Center, Executive Director, 2005–2016

Paul Kivel...presents a powerful yet accessible vision, informed by research and reflection on racism in the US.... This book provides the best concrete guidance for the new or perplexed would-be white ally that I have ever seen in print. For the individual explorer, the self-study exercises are amazing. As a resource for the educator or trainer's library, *Uprooting Racism* is indispensable and unique. I have personally used many of the exercises in the book in my own teaching. Paul's support and guidance for educators and trainers in his books and on his website is outstanding.

—Victor Lee Lewis, Progressive Life Coach,
founder/director of the Radical Resilience Institute,
Co-Editor with Hugh Vasquez of Lessons from "The Color of Fear."

Uprooting Racism gives the student, activist and practitioner something for their social justice tool box. The expanded edition is challenging, informative and practical. You'll finish the book and want to get right to work.

—Dr. Eddie Moore Jr., Founder/Director, The White Privilege Conference

Uprooting Racism continues to be a powerful and wonderful book, a major contribution to our understanding of racism as white people.... Not only does Kivel address tough issues related to whiteness and racism,...he also identifies specific ways that whites can be allies for change—all done with honesty, forthrightness, respect, and from the heart. For any white person who is sincere about working for social justice, here's the source.

—Judith H. Katz, Ed. D., author,
White Awareness: Handbook for Anti-Racism Training and
The Inclusion Breakthrough: Unleashing the Real Power of Diversity

Paul Kivel writes with clarity and depth in a style that is adequately complex for understandings of racism in our time. He uses his writing power to illuminate all the systems, inner and outer, which lead to inequitable distribution of power, respect, money, safety, security, and opportunity in the world....

—Peggy McIntosh, founder and co-director, National SEED Project on Inclusive Curriculum, author, *White Privilege: Unpacking the Invisible Knapsack*

Uprooting Racism is a fact-filled resource for teachers and parents to use in educating ourselves and our young people about the history and the hidden costs of racism in our communities. Kivel presents simple, meaningful actions we can all take to build a more just and healthy society.

—Jackie Shonerd, parent and Coordinator for Conflict Resolution Programs, Oakland, (CA) Unified School District

As a woman of color actively engaged in social justice movements for over 25 years, I have often longed for a book like *Uprooting Racism* to help white people understand the institutional, systematic, and persistent character of racism in our world. Paul Kivel has written a handbook to critically examine racism in our lives, and in our work for peace and justice.

—Luz Guerra, activist, consultant/writer

...the 'how-to manual' for whites to work with people of color to create an inclusive, just world in the 21st century. *Uprooting Racism* succinctly describes how intricately racism is tied to all institutions and our daily lives.... It should be in the toolbox of anyone who is working for an anti-racist society.

—Maggie Potapchuk, Senior Program Associate, Network of Alliances, Bridging Race and Ethnicity (NABRE), a program of the Joint Center for Political and Economic Studies

Those of us who commit to the life-long journey of being anti-racist whites need lots of help. The revised edition of *Uprooting Racism* offers a clear vision of the journey's destination, an invaluable and accessible map and a set of tools for the steps we must take to get there.... I recommend it highly and plan to use it in my own work.

—Louise Derman-Sparks, co-director, of the Early Childhood Equity Alliance. Author, *Teaching/Learning Anti-Racism: A Developmental Approach*

Uprooting Racism is a uniquely sensitive, wise, practical guide for white people struggling with their feelings about race.

—Howard Zinn, author, *A People's History of the United States*
(Praise from previous edition)

To my family—Micki, my love

Ariel, SAM, Ryan, Amanda, Leticia, Kesa,

Niko, Mateo and Anahi, my inspiration

And to all those fighting for justice

Contents

Part II: The Dynamics of Racism

Part III: Being Allies

Part IV: The Effects of History

Part V: Fighting Institutional Racism

Part VI: Democratic, Anti-Racist Multiculturalism

Lists, Diagrams, and Exercises

PART V: Fighting Institutional Racism

PART VI: Democratic, Anti-Racist Multiculturalism

Acknowledgments

I acknowledge and offer thanks to the creative spirit that is the source of life and connects us to each other and to all life. I offer thanks to the earth that nurtures and sustains us, the Chochenyo and Karkin Ohlone peoples whose land I am a settler on, and all those whose work makes my life possible.

North America has a long and distinguished history of white people who have fought against racism and racial violence. This history began in the days of Antonio de Montesinos and Bartolomé de Las Casas, Spanish priests who documented and protested against the atrocities Columbus and other early colonizers committed against Native Americans in the West Indies. It continues today with white people fighting against hate crimes, police brutality, housing and job discrimination, and recent attacks against immigrants and poor people of color. These efforts have been inspired by the constant, unrelenting fight by people of color and Native Americans for survival, for justice, and for an end to the political, economic, and cultural exploitation they continue to experience in the United States.

My deepest gratitude goes to the multitudes of people of color who have challenged racism in both small and large ways over the centuries, and who have demonstrated by their lives that the lies of racism are untrue, inhumane and violate the integrity of each person who colludes with injustice.

I am also proud to be Jewish and to be part of the historic struggle of Jewish people to survive waves of anti-Jewish oppression and create our lives anew in the framework of freedom and justice Judaism provides. I want to acknowledge my Jewish foreparents and the many Jews who are still on the front lines of the battle for racial justice because they understand the connections between anti-Jewish oppression (anti-Semitism) and racism.

There are many people who have inspired my work and writing, most of whom I have never met. I have read their words, heard their songs, witnessed their actions, and strive to be true to their vision.

I want to acknowledge specifically those who I have learned from and who have supported my work in the last few years. They are Bill Aal, Margo Adair, Martin Cano, Jim Coates, Hari Dillon, Steve Falk, Isoke Femi, Margot Gibney, Luz Guerra, Sonia Jackson, Francie Kendall, David Landes, Nell Myhand, Namane Mohlabane, Daphne Muse, Ayana Morse, Kiran Rana, Bill Rosenfeld, John Tucker, Akaya Windwood, Shirley Yee, and my mother, Betty Jean Kivel.

I also thank my wonderful "Jews schmooze" group: Alina Evers, Chaya Gusfield, Julie Nesnansky, Adee Horn, Ariel Luckey, Aurora Levins-Morales, Ilana Schatz, Richard Shapiro, and Penny Rosenwasser.

Several people reviewed earlier editions of the book and gave me support and feedback. Special thank-yous to Robert Allen, Kostas Bagakis, Allan Creighton, Victor Lewis, Nell Myhand, Yeshi Neumann, Barry Shapiro, and Hugh Vasquez.

It was my great pleasure and challenge over the years to work with Robert Allen, Nefera Amen, Allan Creighton, Victor Lewis, Jackie Shonerd, Harrison Sims, and others at the Oakland Men's Project and Nell Myhand, Hugh Vasquez, and Shirley Yee at the Todos Institute. I have learned much from their passion for justice, their gentle caring and their fierce dedication to freedom.

My family has been particularly inspiring and supportive in many ways. My deepest love and appreciation go to Ariel Luckey, SAM Luckey, Ryan Luckey, Amanda Luckey, Leticia Rigatti Luckey, Kesa Kivel, Dana Kivel, and our grandchildren Niko, Mateo, and Anahi. My life-partner, Micki, has been a loving support, insightful editor, wonderful co-parent and shares my vision of a just world.

My appreciation also goes to the staff at New Society Publishers who provided strong and consistent support to this project from their initial enthusiasm for the book through the final editing and production, and on to this now fourth edition. Ingrid Witvoet and Sue Custance are the guiding light for the revised edition. Betsy Nuse has provided excellent editing, and the beautiful cover design is by Diane McIntosh. EJ Hurst, Sara Reeves, and Jean Wyenberg also provided essential support.

Preface to Previous Editions

Before I wrote this book, I accumulated a long list of reasons why it was an important project. Racism is pervasive, its effects devastating, the need to fight against it urgent. People of color are being blamed for our social problems and attacked on all fronts. Recent immigrants, African Americans, youth of color, Native Americans, and Muslims are just some of the current targets of white anger. The civil rights and social justice gains of the 1960s and 70s are being rolled back.

I could also see the huge impact racism had on my relationships with other people, what my children learned in school, how we dealt with economic issues at the state and federal level and what sports and music I paid attention to. Racism is everywhere, influencing us at every turn. There is no shortage of immediate reasons why writing a book like this one needed to be done.

In workshops my coworkers and I were facilitating, participants were eager to talk about these issues and anxious to become involved. Somehow, few of them were able to translate their understanding of the issues and their commitment to ending racism into concrete community action. When they asked me for resources, I could point them to no guides for critical thinking and social action. What was available about racism or white people was theoretical—interesting, important, but not practical.

With all this in mind, I sat down to write this book. I suddenly accumulated a long list of reasons why I couldn't do it. I wasn't qualified. The subject was too big. The issue was too important. How could I add anything new? The connections between racism, religious oppression, gender, and economic issues were too complex.

People of color have addressed all the issues much more powerfully than I could. Other white people would call me racist. The entire task felt formidable, scary, fraught with problems, and I felt ill-equipped to carry it out successfully.

I procrastinated. I hoped someone else would do it. "There must be someone else who knows more, writes better, or knows how to say it the right way." "There's certainly someone who could do it without making mistakes or looking foolish." These thoughts went through my mind as I waited for someone else to step forward.

Then one day I recognized these feelings. They were the same feelings white people experience in our workshops—the same "reasons" they give for not doing more to stop racism. When confronting the reality of racism, white people become sad, angry, overwhelmed, numb, anxious, and passive. When faced with the need to intervene, speak up or take action against racism, we become tentative, waiting for someone more qualified to step up.

There is no one else who can take your place or do your part. I realized it was crucial for me to write what I could; that was my responsibility. Yes, I didn't know all the answers; I wouldn't be able to cover everything; some people might not like what I wrote. But a book like this needed to be written, and I was in a position to write it.

I'm sure you will experience many feelings as you read this book. Let them guide you, but don't let them stop you. It is easy to become overwhelmed by our feelings, by how much there is to do, and by how confusing and risky it seems. I'm asking you to tap into another set of feelings—understanding and compassion for people of color; outrage at injustice; courage, passion, and commitment to building a democratic, multicultural, and just society. Concentrate on what it is we can do, how we can make a difference.

Whenever I become overwhelmed thinking about how much there is to do, I remind myself of a saying by Rabbi Tarfon. I hope it will guide you as well.

It is not upon you to finish the work.
Neither are you free to desist from it.

Preface to the Fourth Edition

When the first edition of *Uprooting Racism* was published in the mid-90s, there were books about racism, but few documented how white people benefited from and participated in perpetuating it. Even fewer examined the way racism influenced the workings of our institutions. But, perhaps as a legacy of the Civil Rights movement, there was still a vigorous discussion of racism in US society and a widespread acceptance that we had work to do to make racial justice a reality.

Over 20 years later there are a massive number of studies and other forms of documentation demonstrating the workings of racism in everything from its devastating impact on the lives and opportunities of people of color to how white people think, act and talk about racism, what benefits we gain from it and how it is perpetuated in the everyday practices and policies of our organizations and institutions.[1]

Despite all of this documentation, it has taken the disruptive, bold, and creative leadership of the Movement for Black Lives, the courageous resistance of Native peoples at Standing Rock and the national prisoner's strike, coupled with the increasing visual evidence of everyday violence against people of color, to bring racism to the attention of white people in the US. And even with this leadership and visual evidence, there is a white culture of denial and minimization about the existence and centrality of racism. Despite pervasive segregation and discrimination in education, housing, health care, and the job market; despite widespread surveillance, control, and punishment of people of color through the welfare, child welfare, foster care, education, police, immigration and criminal/legal systems; despite hate crimes, police brutality, racial profiling, and everyday forms of what has been called micro-aggression against people of color, a November 2015 poll showed that while most white people believe acts of racism still occur, less than half (43%) believe racism is a major societal problem[2] and 56% said racism wasn't a problem in their community.[3]

In fact, I often hear references to a "post-racial" society, a belief the Civil Rights movement and subsequent legislation "took care of all that," and a feeling that having had a black man as president proved we have moved beyond race in the United States.

We are now in a third, major phase of racism/white supremacy in US history. The first phase included the military invasion and conquest of North America including theft of the land, genocide against Native Americans, and the mass enslavement of Africans. The second phase encompassed Jim Crow exploitation, segregation, industrialization, violence, and the assimilation of European immigrants into a system of white Christian cultural supremacy. The third and current phase is the stage of capitalism termed neoliberalism. Racism, a constantly shifting and adaptive system of white dominance, has looked different in each of these phases.

Neoliberalism is the current strategy of the ruling class (basically "the 1%") dating from the 1960s. It promotes so-called market strategies, i.e., deregulation and privatization, over public institutions and public services. These strategies eliminate public oversight, eliminate restrictions on corporate practices, and drastically reduce the size and scale of government at every level, especially the social services they provide. Attacks on unions, wages, and working conditions follow, along with attempts to divide poor, working-, and middle-class people around issues such as immigration, gay rights, reproductive rights, and Islamophobia. Claiming to be "race-neutral" (even though their policy applications and impact are intentionally racialized), neoliberal advocates use phrases such as "individual choice," "meritocracy," "standards," "efficiency," and "level playing field" to justify policies which continue to strip resources from communities of color and poor and working-class white communities while concentrating even more wealth in the white, Christian ruling class.

The evidence of pervasive, life-destroying racism throughout our society persists—not only in statistics and broad patterns of discrimination, exclusion, and marginalization, but also in the everyday experiences of people of color. Recently, for example, three of the African American women who live in the apartment next door to me described how they have been harassed by a white resident in the apartment on the other side of them. This person not only drops trash and dog shit onto their driveway and parking spots, but also calls them "n*****s" when they complain. When they call the police, the officers don't take down all the details of the situation, minimize the incident, and discourage them from pursuing the matter. On our neighborhood's NextDoor listserve, I routinely read vague racialized descriptions of the suspicious activity of my neighbors of color which I know often lead to calls to police and harassment for them. And I constantly see the displacement of entire communities of long-time residents of color from my city by young white gentrifiers who can afford higher rents, and expect cafes and upscale restaurants, better services, and "safer" streets.

Every day I hear a new story, read a new report, witness the devastating impact of racism on our community. I don't ask for these stories, but I listen carefully when I hear them. I don't take them personally or try to defend white people. I know these stories are not about me, and sometimes the white people involved have no conscious intention of hurting a person of color. These stories are about the everyday discrimination and disrespect toward people of color racism produces and people of color have to live with.

I have become even more acutely aware of how interdependent our lives are and how dependent I am on the low-paid work of people of color in the United States and in other countries. I look at the label on my jeans, shirts, and underwear; I track the work that produced my computer, TV, and cell phone; I learn more about who grows, picks, packages, and prepares the food I eat; I notice who cleans the public buildings and classrooms I use. Usually people of color perform the poorly paid, low-status jobs which allow me to enjoy the benefits of inexpensive clothes, low-priced electronic equipment, cheap food, and clean and well-maintained public spaces.

Just walking down the street to the park makes me aware of our interconnection and dependency. I meet people like Renee, an immigrant from the Philippines who maintains the flowers and trees in the park down the block from us. I see the immigrant women who are caring for white babies in the park or who arrive to clean houses in the neighborhood.

My daily life is interwoven with the lives of hundreds, if not thousands, of people of color. Yet so much of their lives, work, and culture is ridiculed, exploited, or rendered invisible by our society I often don't see or make the connections. My ignorance and subsequent inaction contribute to their exploitation, discrimination, and marginalization. I become a partner in racism, a collaborator in injustice.

A few years ago I was hopeful we were making some inroads in recognizing and addressing racism. However, watching the response to the September 11, 2001 World Trade Center and Pentagon bombings, the response to the disasters of Hurricanes Rita and Katrina, and the collapse of the stock and housing bubbles, I fear the US has suffered major setbacks. There has been an alarming increase in hate crimes against Arab Americans and Muslims. African Americans, Latinx, Native Americans, and Asian Americans are threatened by racial profiling and murder on our streets and at our borders. Mosques are being attacked across the US. The housing and financial meltdowns have disproportionately affected communities of color—transferring even more wealth to white communities.[4] And all of us face attacks on our civil liberties, increased police and military surveillance, and the further shifting of resources from education, health, and other social programs to war, surveillance, and prisons. The election of Donald Trump seemed to give permission for even more white resentment and attack, while showing once again the deep roots of racism, anti-immigrant sentiment, and misogyny in US society.

I know many white people find it hard to read about racism. I have been told stories of students who, required to read this book, would read a chapter and then throw the book across the room because they were so upset at what I was saying and what it meant for their lives. But then they would go across the room, pick up the book and read another chapter. Determination is what it takes to confront racism. We need to keep going back and picking up the task no matter how uncomfortable, angry, or frustrated we become in the process. Being an ally is like that. We keep learning, doing our best, leaving something out, making mistakes, doing it better next time. It is a practice, not an identity—and it is best done in collaboration with others.

In a world in which racism continues to be one of the bedrocks of our organizations and institutions, in which most people of color, every single day, are confronted with the repercussions of racial discrimination, harassment, and exploitation, we must ask ourselves:

- What do I stand for?
- Who do I stand with?
- Do I stand for racial justice, the end of discrimination and racial violence and a society truly based on equal opportunity?
- Do I stand with people of color and white allies in the struggle to uproot racism?

These are the challenging questions I offer you as you begin to read this book. I hope *Uprooting Racism* helps you to be clearer and more effective in answering them.

— Paul Kivel
June, 2017

A Note on Language

Language is important because it invites in or excludes people from conversation and other forms of participation in community life. I strive for respectful and inclusive language. That's why I use the gender inclusive third-person pronoun "they" instead of "he" or "she." It is also why I use the term *Latinx*, an alternative to Latino, Latina, and Latin@. Used by scholars, activists, and an increasing number of journalists, Latinx aims to move beyond gender binaries and is inclusive of the intersecting identities of Latin American descendants.[1]

A Note to Readers Outside the US

Most of the examples used in the book are from the United States, where I live and about which I have more access to information. Many reports, studies, and accounts of racism in other white majority societies—Great Britain, Canada, France, Germany, Australia, and New Zealand—show similar patterns of racism against people of color. For example, the Parekh Report, *The Future of Multi-ethnic Britain*, documented extensive institutional and cultural racism throughout Great Britain.[1] The anti-immigrant, anti-Indigenous people and racism in public policy and daily practice in Canada, Australia, and throughout Europe are quite visible. If you live in a white majority country, talk with people of color, read the studies and reports, and don't let yourself be complacent or indifferent simply because your situation is not exactly the same as that in the United States.

Introduction:
"Only Justice Can Put Out the Fire"[1]

There is fire raging across the United States—usually a series of brush fires erupting whenever conditions are right—sometimes a firestorm, always a smoldering cauldron. Whether it is major urban uprisings, intellectual debates, or everyday conflicts in our neighborhoods and schools, racism is burning us all. Some of us have third-degree burns or have died from its effects; many others live in charred wreckage. Most of us suffer first- and second-degree burns at some time in our lives. We all live with fear in the glow of the menacing and distorted light of racism's fire.

As white people we do many things to survive the heat. Some of us move to the suburbs, put bars on our windows, put locks on our hearts, and teach our children distrust for their own protection. Some of us believe the enemy is "out there"—and we can be safe "in here." When we don't talk about our fears, we are prevented from doing anything effective to put out the fire.

Poll after poll shows most white people are scared. We are scared about violence; about the economy; about the environment; we are scared about the safety, education, and future of our children.[2] Much of the time those fears are directed toward people of color whether they are long-term residents or recent immigrants. It is easy for us to focus on them, and yet doing so devastates our ability to address critical national issues of economic inequality, war, social infrastructure, family violence, and environmental devastation which affect everyone.

Since the attacks of the World Trade Center and the Pentagon in 2001, white people are even more afraid. We have been shown our vulnerability and our complicity.[3] Many of us wanted to do something, to pick up a bucket and throw water on the flames, but the size of the blaze seemed to make our individual efforts useless. Besides, many of us thought we were too far away from the cause of the fire to make a difference. Arabs and Muslims were defined as the problem; the danger was anywhere and everywhere. Unending war was declared the only solution.

In fact, there are already flames in our (all too often predominantly white) schools, churches, neighborhoods, and workplaces. Poverty, family violence, drugs, and despair are not limited to somewhere "out there" nor to "those people." Our houses are burning too, and we need to pick up our buckets and start carrying water now. But just like the volunteer fire departments in rural communities and small towns, we need to be part of a fire line where everyone realizes that when the sparks are flying, anything can begin to burn. As a community we can be alert for sparks and embers so they can be put out before a bigger blaze develops.

We don't need scare tactics. They just reinforce fear and paralysis. We don't need numbers and statistics. They produce numbness and despair. We need to talk with each other, honestly, simply, caringly. We need to learn how to talk about racism without rhetoric (which fans the flames); without attack or intimidation (which separates people from one another). We need to share firefighting suggestions, skills, and experience so we can work together to end racism.

I think it is crucial each of us speaks up about issues of violence and injustice. It is true our words would have more moral credibility if we were leading a mistake-free life and were totally consistent in what we say and do. We have to "walk the walk," not just "talk the talk."

However, issues of social justice are not fundamentally about individual actions and beliefs. This book is about racism, an institutionalized system of oppression. Although my actions can either support or confront racism, it is completely independent of me. In fact, even if most of us were completely non-racist in our attitudes and practices, there are many ways unequal wages, unequal treatment in the legal system, and segregation in jobs, housing, and education could continue.

This book is about uprooting the *system* of racism. You may need to reexamine your individual beliefs and actions in order to participate effectively in that uprooting. This book will help you look at how you have learned racism, what effects it has had on your life, what have been its costs and benefits to you, and how you have learned to pass it on. More importantly, this book will help you become a member of a network of people who are committed to racial justice. It offers you strategies and guidelines for becoming involved in the struggle.

Don't take it too personally. You did not create racism. You may have many feelings while reading this book. Confronting racism may trigger a range of emotions including guilt, defensiveness, sadness, or outrage. Acknowledge the feelings, talk with others, but don't get stuck. If our feelings immobilize us, we cannot strategically plan how to transform the system. I am reminded of the statement to white people by Maurice Mitchell, a leader in Ferguson Action and Black Lives Matter: "Your anxiety about getting it right has nothing to do with black liberation."[5]

This book is not about unlearning racism.[6] Unlearning racism makes it easier for people of color to live and work with us, but it doesn't necessarily challenge racist structures. Unlearning racism may or may not be a path toward eliminating racism. In a society where individual growth is often not only the starting place, but also the end point of discussion, strategies for unlearning racism often end in complacency and inaction.

Uprooting Racism begins with the understanding that racism exists, it is pervasive and that its effects are devastating. Because of this devastation, we need to start doing everything possible to work for racial justice. The first step is for us to talk together, as white

people. For as white Southern civil rights activist Anne Braden reminded us:

> In a sense, the battle is and always has been a battle for the
> hearts and mind of white people in this country. The fight
> against racism is not something we're called on to help people
> of color with. We need to become involved as if our lives de-
> pended on it because, in truth, they do.[7]

PART I

What Color Is White?

Let's Talk

I AM TALKING TO YOU as one white person to another. I am Jewish, and I will talk about that later in this book. You also may have an ethnic identity you are proud of. You likely have a religious background, a culture, a country of origin, and a history. Whatever your other identities, you may not be used to being addressed as white.

Other people are African American, Asian American, Pacific Islanders, Native American, Latinx, or Muslims. *Other* people have countries of origin and primary languages that are not English. White people generally assume people are white unless otherwise noted, much as humans can assume people and animals are male.

Read the following lines:

- *This new sitcom is about a middle-aged, middle-class couple and their three teenage children.*
- *They won a medal on the Special Olympics swim team.*
- *He did well in school but was just a typical all-American kid.*
- *They didn't know if they would get into the college of their choice.*
- *My grandmother lived on a farm all her life.*

Are all these people white? Read the sentences again and imagine the people referred to are Chinese Americans or Native Americans. How does that change the meanings of these sentences? If you are of Christian background, what happens when you imagine the subjects as Muslim or Jewish?

White people assume we are white without stating it because it is "obvious." Yet there is something about stating this obvious fact that makes white people feel uneasy, marked. What's the point of saying "I'm white?"

White people have been led to believe *racism* is a question of particular acts of discrimination or violence. Calling someone a name, denying someone a job, excluding someone from a neighborhood—that is racism. These certainly are acts of racial discrimination. But what about working in an organization where people of color are paid less, have more menial work or fewer opportunities for advancement? What about shopping in a store where you are treated respectfully, but people of color are followed around or treated with suspicion?

People of color know this racism intimately. They know that where they live, work, and walk; whom they talk with and how; what they read, listen to, or watch on TV—their past experiences and future possibilities are all influenced by racism.

For the next few days, carry your whiteness with you. During the day, in each new situation, remind yourself that you are white. How does it feel? Notice how rarely you see or hear the words white, Caucasian or Euro-American.

- *Where is it implied but not stated specifically?*
- *Who is around you? Are they white or people of color? What difference does it make?*
- *Write down what you notice. Discuss it with a friend.*

Particularly notice whenever you are somewhere there are only white people.

- *How did it come to be that no people of color are present?*

- *If you ask about their absence, what kinds of explanations/ rationalizations do people give?*
- *Are they really not there, or are they only invisible?*
- *Did they grow some of the food, originally own the land, build the buildings, or clean and maintain the place where you are?*

"I'm Not White"

I WAS ONCE doing a workshop on racism in which we divided the group into a caucus of people of color and a caucus of white people to elicit more in-depth discussion. Immediately some of the white people said, "But I'm not white."

I was somewhat taken aback because although these people looked white, they were clearly distressed about being labeled white. A white Christian woman stood up and said, "I'm not really white because I'm not part of the white male power structure that perpetuates racism." Next a white gay man stood up and said, "You have to be straight to have the privileges of being white." A white, straight, working-class man from a poor family then said, "I've got it just as hard as any person of color." Finally, a straight, white, middle-class man said, "I'm not white, I'm Italian."

My African American coworker turned to me and asked, "Where are all the white people who were here just a minute ago?" I replied, "Don't ask me. I'm not white, I'm Jewish!"

Those of us who are middle-class are more likely to take it for granted that we are white without having to emphasize the point, and to feel guilty when it is noticed or brought up. Those of us who are poor or working-class are more likely to have had to assert our whiteness against the effects of economic discrimination and the presence of other racial groups. Although we share benefits of being white, we don't share the economic privileges of being middle-class, and so we are more likely to feel angry and less likely to feel guilty than our middle-class counterparts.

6

In the US it has always been dangerous even to talk about racism. "N***** lover," "Indian lover," and "race traitor" are labels that have carried severe consequences for white people. You may know the names of white civil rights workers Goodman, Schwerner, and Luizzo who were killed for their actions. Many of us have been isolated from friends or family because of disagreements over racism. A lot of us have been called "racist."

I want to begin here—with this denial of our whiteness—because racism keeps people of color in the limelight and makes whiteness invisible. *Whiteness* is a concept, an ideology, which holds tremendous power over our lives and, in turn, over the lives of people of color. Our challenge as white people will be to keep whiteness center stage. Every time our attention begins to wander off toward people of color or other issues, we must learn to notice and refocus. We must not try to escape our white identity.

- *What parts of your identity does it feel like you lose when you say aloud the phrase "I'm white?"*
- *When they arrived in the North America, what did members of your family have to do to be accepted as white? What did they have to give up?*
- *Has that identification or pride ever allowed you or your family to tolerate poverty, economic exploitation, or poor living conditions because you could say, "At least we're not colored?"*

I realize there are differences between the streets of New York and Minneapolis, Vancouver, and Winnipeg, and between different neighborhoods within each city. But in US and Canadian society, there is a broad and pervasive division between those of us who are treated as white people and those of us who are treated as people of color. If, when you move down the streets of major cities, other people assume, based on skin color, dress, physical appearance, or total impression that you are white, then in US society that counts for being white.

Several studies have shown that young people between the ages of two and four notice differences of skin color, eye color, hair, dress, and speech and the significance adults give to those differences.[1] This is true even if parents are liberal or progressive. The training is too pervasive within our society for anyone to escape. Anthropology and sociology professor Annie Barnes recounts the following interview with a parent who noticed how early in their lives white children learn racism.

> I experienced it [racism] through my three-year-old daughter. One day at preschool, the students had a "show and tell." All the students had brought their toys to school. My daughter forgot her toys, so I had to go home and get them. My daughter told me specifically what to bring. She wanted her pretty black Barbie doll with the white dress. She loved this doll and thought that it was pretty and often said, "When I grow up, I want to look just like my Barbie."
>
> All the other children were white. While my daughter brought out her Barbie during show and tell, they screwed up their faces and said, "Yuck. That's not Barbie. She's ugly."... She cried for hours and never carried her doll to school again, I couldn't believe those little children's actions. That was racism by babies, so to speak.[2]

Say "I am white" to yourself a couple of times.

- *What are the "buts" that immediately come to mind?*
- *Do you try to minimize the importance of whiteness ("We're all part of the human race")?*

White people are understandably uncomfortable with the label white. Being white is an arbitrary category that overrides our individual personalities, devalues us, deprives us of the richness of our other identities, stereotypes us, and yet has no scientific basis. However, in our society being white is just as real and governs our day-to-day lives just as much as categories and labels confine people of color. To acknowledge this reality is the first step to uprooting racism.

When I'm in an all-white setting and a person of color walks in, I notice. I am slightly surprised to see a person of color, and I look again to confirm who they are and wonder to myself why they're there. I try to do this as naturally and smoothly as possible because I wouldn't want anyone to think that I was racist. Actually what I'm surprised at is not that they are there, but that they are there as an equal. All of my opening explanations for their presence will assume they are not. "They must be a server or delivery person," I might tell myself. I think most white people notice skin color all the time, but we don't notice race unless our sense of the proper racial hierarchy is upset.

Since I was taught to relate differently to people who are African American, Latinx, Asian, or Arab American, I may need more information than appearance gives me about what kind of person of color I am with. I have some standard questions to fish for more information, such as: "That's an interesting name. I've never heard it before. Where's it from?" "Your accent sounds familiar, but I can't place it." "You don't look American. Where are you from?" And the all-too-common follow-up "No, I mean where are you really from?" It took me a long time to realize that despite my benign intention, these kinds of questions, regularly asked of people of color by white people, are harsh reminders that white people see people of color as outsiders.

Sometimes I ask these questions of white Americans who have unusual names or unfamiliar accents. But I have noticed that most often I use these questions to clarify who is white and who isn't and, secondarily, what kind of person of color I am dealing with.

Occasionally I hear white people say, "I don't care whether a person is black, brown, orange, or green." Human beings don't come in orange or green. Those whose skin color is darker are treated differently in general, and white people, in particular, respond differently to them. As part of growing up white and learning racial stereotypes, most of us have been trained to stiffen up and be more cautious, fearful, and hesitant around people of color. We can notice these physiological and psychological responses in ourselves and see them in other white people.[3] These responses belie our verbal assurances that we don't notice racial differences.

There's absolutely nothing wrong with being white or with noticing the differences that color makes. You are not responsible for having white skin or for being raised in a white-dominated, racist society in which you have been trained to have particular responses to people of color. However, you are responsible for how you respond to racism (which is what this book is about), and you can only do so consciously and effectively if you begin by realizing it makes a crucial difference that you are perceived to be and treated as white.

"I'm Not Racist"

WHETHER IT IS EASY or difficult to say we're white, the phrase we often want to say next is "But I'm not racist." There are lots of ways we have learned to phrase this denial:

- *I don't belong to the Klan.*
- *I have friends who are people of color.*
- *I do anti-racism work.*

Uprooting Racism is not about whether you are racist or not, or whether all white people are racist or not. We are not conducting a moral inventory of ourselves, nor creating a moral standard to divide other white people from us. When we say things like "I don't see color," we are trying to maintain a self-image of impartiality and innocence (whiteness).

The only way to treat all people with dignity and justice is to recognize that racism has a profound negative effect upon all of our lives. Noticing skin color helps to counteract that effect. Instead of being color-neutral, we need to notice much more acutely and insightfully exactly the difference skin color makes in the way people are treated.

Of course you're not a member of the Klan or other extremist groups. Of course you watch what you say and don't make rude racial comments. But dissociating from white people who do is not helpful. You may want to dissociate yourself from their actions, but you still need to challenge their beliefs. You can't challenge them or

11

even speak to them if you have separated yourself, creating some magical line with the racists on one side and you over here. This division leads to an ineffective strategy of trying to convert as many people as possible to your (non-racist and therefore superior) side. Other white people will listen to you better, and be more influenced by your actions, when you identify with them. Then you can explore how to work your way out from the inside of whiteness together.

Since racism leads to scapegoating people of color for social and personal problems, all white people are susceptible to scapegoat in times of trouble. Notice the large number of white people who blame African Americans or immigrants of color for economic problems in the US. Visible acts of racism are, at least in part, an indication of the lack of power a white person or group has.

More powerful and well-off people can move to segregated neighborhoods or make corporate decisions harder to see and analyze as contributing to racism. Those of us who are middle-class can inadvertently scapegoat poor and working-class white people for being overtly racist. For example, in the 2016 presidential election, those who voted for Trump had a mean income of $72,000 per year and nearly half had college degrees—they were solidly middle-class. Yet many people assume Trump's supporters are uneducated working-class and poor whites who were unable to really see what he stands for.[1]

We do need to confront racist words and actions because they create an atmosphere of violence in which all of us are unsafe. We also need to understand that most white people are doing the best they can to survive. Overtly racist people are scared and may lack the information and skills to challenge racism. We need to challenge their behavior, not their moral integrity. We also need to be careful we don't end up carrying out an upper-class agenda by blaming poor and working people for being racist when people with wealth control the media, the textbooks, the housing and job markets, and the police. Staying focused on institutions and decision-makers challenges societal racism.

What Is Racism?

I DEFINE RACISM, also referred to as white supremacy, as pervasive, deep-rooted, and long-standing exploitation, control, and violence directed at people of color, Native Americans, and immigrants of color. The benefits and entitlements of racism accrue to white people, particularly to a white, Christian, male-dominated ruling class. Racism is an uneven and unfair distribution of power, privilege, land and material goods favoring white people—a system in which people of color as a group are exploited and oppressed by white people as a group.

Often white people think of racism as prejudice, ignorance, or negative stereotypes about people of color. In this thinking, the solution to racism is challenging people's misinformation about people of color or other marginalized groups or convincing white people to be more tolerant and accepting. In fact, prejudice, ignorance, and stereotypes are results of racism, not the cause. Every one of us in this society—growing up with the lies, misinformation, and stereotypes found in our media, textbooks, cultural images, and every other aspect of our lives—carries deep-seated and harmful attitudes toward many other groups. It is our responsibility, as people with integrity, to unlearn the lies and misinformation we have learned and to replace them with more truthful and complex understandings of the people and cultures around us.

Racism operates on four different levels.

Interpersonal Racism

When a white person takes their misinformation and stereotypes toward another group and performs an act of harassment, exclusion, marginalization, discrimination, hate, or violence, they are committing an act of *interpersonal racism* toward an individual or group.

When we move beyond talking about prejudice and stereotypes in our society, we generally focus on acts of interpersonal racism. These are the kinds of acts we hear about in the media—a hate crime, an act of job or housing discrimination, negative racial comments about people of color, racial profiling or violence by a police officer toward a person of color.

These acts are definitely damaging. But the system of racism is much larger than these personal acts. And racism would not be eliminated by ending them. If we limit our discussion to acts of interpersonal racism, it seems like racism is limited in its impact to specific individuals and perpetrated by the acts of individual "rotten apples." All we need to do is punish/censor/screen out these particularly racist individuals and things would be mostly pretty good.

- *What are a couple of examples of interpersonal racism you have seen personally or heard about from the media recently?*
- *What harm do these kind of acts do on a personal and collective level to people of color?*

Institutional Racism

Racism also operates within the institutions in our society. It is built into the policies, procedures, and everyday practices of the health care and education systems, the job and housing markets, the media, and the criminal/legal system to name a few. It operates both systematically and without the need for individual racist acts. People can be just following the rules and produce outcomes benefiting white people and harming people of color because the rules are set up to reproduce racism. For example, during most of the history of the US, it was illegal for white and black people to marry across racial lines, eat together in public, travel together, or shop together on an equal basis.[1] Therefore shopkeepers, bus and train conductors, public officials, and others weren't unusually racist to enforce segregation—they were just following the law, acting as law-abiding white citizens.

Similarly a white schoolteacher could be teaching their students equally, addressing the needs of each individual student and helping every single one advance to the next grade level. But if they were teaching in a school or school system where there were no teachers of color, where white students were tracked into higher-level courses than students of color, where students of color were disciplined more harshly than white students, and/or the curriculum did not reflect the contributions of people of color to our society, then the school would be racially discriminatory despite the efforts of the "color-blind" teacher.

- *What are a couple of examples of institutional racism in our society?*
- *What harm does institutional racism do to people of color?*
- *How does it benefit white people?*

Structural Racism

The cumulative impact of all of the interpersonal and institutional racism within our society creates a system of structural racism. The racism of different institutions overlaps, reinforces, and amplifies the different treatment people of color and Native Americans receive compared to that which white people receive, ensuring different life outcomes.

For example, people have described the school-to-prison pipeline in which young people of color are pushed out of our schools and into the criminal/legal system.[2] Racism within the school system, the welfare system, child protective services, the foster care system and at all levels of the criminal/legal system interact to produce a society which disproportionately limits the educational opportunities of young people of color and disproportionately disciplines them and locks them up.

In another example, lack of affordable health care and access to affordable healthy food options, coupled with higher exposure to toxic chemicals and other forms of pollution, coupled with job discrimination and housing segregation produces greater health problems, shorter life spans, lower wages, and greater levels of poverty for communities of color.[3]

- *What are examples of structural racism—the interplay between different forms of institutional racism?*

Cultural Racism

Structural racism is reinforced by the many layers of *cultural racism* in our society. Systemic and pervasive images, pictures, comments, literature, movies, advertisements, and online media consistently portray people of color, Native Americans, and immigrants of color as inferior, lazy, dangerous, sexually manipulative, infantile, and less smart than white people. These cultural stereotypes hold up white people in general as capable, honest, hard working, patriotic, safe— the heroes, leaders, and builders of our country. Cultural racism can be explicit or implicit, subtle or obvious. Every institution produces forms of cultural racism, but some, such as the media, educational systems, and religion, are particularly active in producing and maintaining a dominant white worldview that binds together the entire system of structural racism.

The anthropologist Audrey Smedley has described racism as a "world view" and as "a culturally structured, systematic way of looking at, perceiving, and interpreting various world realities...[that] actively, if not consciously, mould...the behavior of their bearers" and generates racializing meanings and associated discriminatory actions.[4] Anthropological linguist Jane Hill added that this worldview or frame "generates racialized meanings and associated discriminatory actions...[and] endows a racialized world with commonsense properties that exist below the level of consciousness. They are invisible to us, and yet constitute our world."[5]

- *What examples of cultural racism have you seen recently?*
- *What do you imagine is their cumulative impact on people of color, Native Americans, and immigrants of color?*
- *What do you see as their cumulative impact on white people— what attitudes and expectations do they produce in us?*

Anti-Jewish and Anti-Muslim Oppression

As we have witnessed many times in European and US history, the fires of racism include flames of anti-Jewish oppression and anti-Muslim oppression (Islamophobia).[6] Historically, dominant Christianity has always treated Muslims and Jews with suspicion and hostility—the external and internal enemies of Christendom. Most of the Jews in the United States are of European background.[7] Sometimes these Jews are considered white and sometimes not, just as Asian and Arab Americans have sometimes been considered white or not.

Jewish people have experienced the same kinds of violence, discrimination, and harassment most people of color have experienced; at the same time, Jews who are of white European descent are buffered from racism's worst aspects by the benefits of being white. In this book Jews of European descent will be referred to both as white *and* as targets of anti-Jewish oppression. Jews of color are always targets of racism from white people and even from white Jews of European descent. They are also vulnerable to anti-Jewish oppression.

Originally called Moors or Saracens, Muslims have been labeled the unrelenting foe of the Christian West since the first Crusade was declared in 1095 CE. A European Christian identity was first established in this period by uniting people against the Moors as a common enemy. Muslims, like Jews, were one of the many groups treated as dangerous by Christians.[8] Even though there are white Muslims in the US, they have never experienced the acceptance white Jews have received. White people who are Muslims do retain some of the benefits of being white while being vulnerable to many of the penalties for being a person who is not Christian. Muslims of color experience racism and anti-Muslim oppression.

Anti-Jewish oppression and anti-Muslim oppression are similar to, different from, and intertwined with racism. European Christian ruling classes have exploited, controlled, and violated other groups of people based on religion, race, culture, and nationality (as well as gender, class, physical and mental ability, and sexual orientation) for many centuries. There is tremendous overlap in the kinds of violence that have been directed at these groups and the justifications used to legitimize it. Racism, anti-Jewish, and anti-Muslim oppression are primary, closely related tools the powerful have used to maintain their advantage.

What Is Whiteness?

RACISM IS BASED ON the concept of whiteness—a powerful fiction enforced by power and violence. Whiteness is a constantly shifting boundary separating those who are entitled to certain benefits from those whose exploitation and vulnerability to violence is justified by their not being white.

Racism itself is a long-standing characteristic of many human societies. The beginnings of biological racism go back to the Spanish Inquisition. Trying to create a pure Christian society, the Catholic ruling class gave Jews and Muslims the choice of conversion, exile, or death. Many converted. Soon, however, trying to root out false converts but unable to reliably do so, the courts ruled that anyone with a Jewish or Muslim parent or grandparent could not be a Christian. Even this proved unreliable in their eyes, so the courts ruled that any person with any Muslim or Jewish blood was incapable of being a righteous Christian because they did not have clean blood (*limpieza de sangre*).[1]

In more recent historical times in Western Europe, those with English heritage were perceived to be pure white. The Irish, Russians, and Spanish were considered darker races, sometimes black and certainly non-white. The white category was slowly extended to include northern and middle European people, but still, less than a century ago, it definitely excluded eastern or southern European peoples such as Italians, Poles, Russians, and Greeks. In subsequent decades, although there is still prejudice against people from these geographical backgrounds, they became generally accepted as white in the United States.[2]

The important distinction in the United States has always been binary—first between those who counted as Christians and those who were pagans. As historian Winthrop Jordan has written:

> Protestant Christianity was an important element in English patriotism... Christianity was interwoven into [an English-man's] conception of his own nationality, and he was there-fore inclined to regard the Negroes' lack of true religion as part of theirs. Being a Christian was not merely a matter of subscribing to certain doctrines; it was a quality inherent in oneself and in one's society. It was interconnected with all the other attributes of normal and proper men.[3]

As Africans and Native Americans began to be converted to Christianity, such a simple distinction was no longer useful, at least as a legal and political difference. Because Europeans, Native Americans, and Africans often worked and lived together in similar circumstances of servitude, and resisted and rebelled together against the way they were treated, the landowning class began to implement policies to separate European workers from African and Native American workers. Drawing on already established popular classifications, the concept of lifelong servitude (slavery) was introduced from the West Indies and distinguished from various forms of shorter-term servitude (indenture). In response to Bacon's rebellion and other uprisings, the ruling class, especially in the populous and dominant territory of Virginia, began to establish a clear racial hierarchy in the 1660s and 70s.[4] By the 1730s racial divisions were firmly in place legally and socially. Most blacks were enslaved, and even free blacks had lost the right to vote, the right to bear arms, and the right to bear witness. Blacks were also barred from participating in many trades during this period.

Meanwhile, whites had gained the right to corn, money, a gun, clothing, and 50 acres of land at the end of indentureship; they could no longer be beaten naked and had the poll tax reduced. In other words, poor whites "gained legal, political, emotional, social, and financial status that was directly related to the concomitant degradation of Indians and Negroes."[5] Typically, although poor whites gained some benefits vis-à-vis blacks and Indians, because of the increased productivity from slavery, the gap between wealthy whites and those who were poor widened considerably.

Although racism was legally, socially, and economically long established in US society, it was only defined "scientifically" as a biological/genetic characteristic about 150 years ago with the publication of Darwin's theory of species modification. From his work, Social Darwinism, a pseudo-scientific theory emerged which attempted to classify the human population into distinct categories or races and put them on an evolutionary scale with whites on top. The original classifications consisted of 3, 5, up to as many as 63 categories, but a standard became one based on Caucasoid, Negroid, and Mongoloid races. These classifications were not based on genetic differences, but on differences Europeans and European Americans perceived to be important. They were in fact based on stereotypes of cultural differences and (mis)measures of physiological characteristics such as brain size.[6]

From the beginning, the attempt to classify people by race was fraught with contradictions. Latin Americans, Native Americans, and Jewish people did not fit easily into these categories, so the categories were variously stretched, redefined, or adapted to meet the agenda of the people in Europe and the US who were promoting them.

For example, in the 19th century Finns were doing most of the lowest-paid, unsafe mining and lumbering work in the upper Midwestern US. Although logically, having light skin, they were white, in terms of political, cultural, and economic "common sense," they were considered black because they were the poorest and least respected group in the area besides Native Americans. The courts consistently ruled they were not white, despite their skin color, because of their cultural and economic standing. In another case, the courts ruled that a Syrian was not white, even though he looked white and had the same skin color as Caucasians, because "common sense" dictated that a Syrian was not white.[7]

On the West Coast during the constitutional debates in California in 1848–49, there was discussion about the status of Mexicans and Chinese. There were still Mexicans who were wealthy landowners and business partners with whites, while the Chinese were almost exclusively heavily exploited railroad and agricultural workers. The courts eventually decided that Mexicans would be considered white and Chinese would be considered the same as blacks and Indians. This decision established which group could become citizens, own land, marry whites, and have other basic rights.[8] (Eventually the status of Mexicans was degraded to that of the Chinese and other people of color.)

Although a few scientists still try to prove the biological existence of races, most have long abandoned the use of race as a valid category to distinguish between humans. There is such tremendous genetic difference within these arbitrary groupings and such huge overlap between them that no particular racial groupings or distinctions based on skin color or other physical characteristics are useful or justified.[9] The Human Genome Project has found that all humans share 99.9% of the same genes and has confirmed there are no human "races." Of the .1% of the human genome that varies from person to person, only 3 to 10% is associated with geographic ancestry or "race" as classically defined.[10] People do have what has been labeled "ancestry groups." These are the genetic markers indicating geographic root areas or origin areas. Most individuals have mixed ancestry groups, and certainly, "knowing a person's geographical origin[s] does not give us enough information to predict his or her genotype" because the majority of genomic variation occurs within, not across, ancestry groups.[11] For example, a person perceived as or self-identified as African American in the United States would have anywhere between 1 and 90% ancestry in either Europe or Africa.[12]

Yet despite the conclusions of the Human Genome Project, some are reasserting that there are important racial differences. These assertions are driven by political and economic motivations, not scientific research. For example, the first racially marketed drug, BiDil, was about to lose its patent protection as a drug for the treatment of heart disease. Even though the drug had failed to perform better than other products in tests and works with patients of all ethnic backgrounds, the company claimed the drug was effective for African Americans and was able to extend its lucrative patent monopoly on the basis of the claim. It is now marketed extensively on that basis, which reinforces the common misperception that there are significant biological differences based on race.[13]

There is likewise no scientific (i.e., biological or genetic) basis to the concept of whiteness. All common wisdom notwithstanding, the skin color of a person tells you nothing about their culture, country of origin, character, or personal habits. Because there is nothing biological about whiteness, it ends up being defined in contrast to other labels, becoming confused with ideas of nationality, religion, and ethnicity.

For example, Jews are not a racial group. People who are Jewish share some cultural and religious beliefs and practices but come from every continent and many different cultural backgrounds. Jews range in skin color from beige to dark brown. Because race was falsely assumed to be a scientific category, being Jewish has often been falsely assumed to mean a Jew is genetically different from non-Jewish people.[14]

Of course, as long as racism exists, there are new attempts to prove to us that race can predict superiority or inferiority.[15]

- *What residual doubts do you have that there may be something genetic or biological about racial differences? ("But, what about...?")*
- *How can you respond to people who say there are specific differences between races?*

From the old phrases referring to a good deed—"That's white of you" or "That's the Christian thing to do" to the New Age practice of visualizing oneself surrounded by white light—white has signified honor, purity, cleanliness, and godliness in white western European, and mainstream US and Canadian culture. Because concepts of whiteness and race were developed in Christian Europe, references to whiteness are imbued with Christian values. We have ended up with a set of opposing qualities or attributes that are said to define people either as white or as not white.

Most of us who are white, no matter how color-blind we aspire to be, associate positive qualities with white people and negative ones with people of color. As sociologists Picca and Feagin observe, "...when given a test of unconscious stereotyping, nearly 90 percent of whites quickly and implicitly associate black faces with negative words and traits (for example, evil character or failure). They have more difficulty linking black faces to pleasant words and positive traits than they do white faces."[16] These unconscious emotional resonances, passed on to us by parents, schools, and the media, i.e., through forms of cultural racism, have been labeled implicit bias.

Implicit Bias

Implicit bias refers to the attitudes or stereotypes that affect our understanding, actions, and decisions in an unconscious manner. These biases, which encompass both favorable and unfavorable assessments, are activated involuntarily and without an individual's awareness or intentional control. Residing deep in the subconscious, these biases differ from known biases individuals may choose to conceal for the purposes of social and/or political correctness.

We harbor implicit associations in our subconscious; they cause us to have feelings and attitudes about other people based on characteristics such as race, ethnicity, age, and appearance. These associations develop over the course of a lifetime beginning at a very early age through exposure to direct and indirect messages. We are not aware they exist, yet they can have a tremendous impact on decision-making. Everyone has implicit biases, regardless of race, ethnicity, gender, or age. Consequently, the range of implicit bias implications for individuals in a wide range of professions and for all of us in our everyday interactions is very broad. For example, researchers have documented implicit biases in health care professionals, law

1.1. Non-White and White Qualities

Which words in each pair do you associate with white people? Which words on the left do you use to discount people of color's demands for fair and equal treatment ("they are too…"), or to blame them for how they are treated in our society ("They would be successful if they weren't so…")?

pagan	Christian
godless	god-fearing, wholesome
animal-like	god-like
primitive, wild, uncivilized	civilized
less than human	human
superstitious	scientific
subjective	objective, detached, neutral
immoral	moral
sinful	innocent
soulless, damned	saved
abnormal	normal
emotional, angry	calm
rude	polite
crude, brutish	refined
impulsive, irrational	thoughtful, rational
present time oriented	future oriented
low class	middle-class
manipulative	sincere
undignified	respectable
devious	straightforward
malicious	loving
prone to dishonesty	well-intentioned, honest
dirty, contaminated	clean, pure
sexual, promiscuous	chaste, committed
intellectually inferior	intelligent
weak link	strong specimen
traditional	modern
un-American, traitor	American, patriot
needing permission	authorized
colorful	bland
impatient	patient
self-righteous	righteous
rhythmic	stiff

enforcement officers, and even individuals whose careers require avowed commitments to impartiality, such as judges.[17]

We generally tend to hold implicit biases favoring our own in-group, though research has shown we can also hold implicit biases against our in-group. They can result in actions and outcomes that do not necessarily align with explicit intentions. However, because our brains are incredibly complex but are also malleable, the implicit associations we have formed can be gradually unlearned through a variety of debiasing techniques.[18]

Despite implicit bias, there have always been white people who have challenged racism and the false dichotomies upon which it is based. Labels such as "n***** lover," "race traitor," "un-American," "feminist," "liberal," "Communist," "unchristian," "Jew," "fag," "lesbian," "crazy," "illegal alien," "terrorist," and "thought police" have all been used to isolate and discredit these people, to imply they are somehow outside the territory of whiteness and therefore justifiably attacked. A powerful way to discredit any critique of whiteness or racism is to discredit the speaker by claiming they are not really white. This is a neat, circular convention that stifles serious discussion of what whiteness means and what effect it has on people.

If we bring attention to whiteness and racism, we risk being labeled not really white or a "traitor to our race." These accusations discredit our testimony and potentially lose us some of the benefits of being white such as better jobs and police protection from violence. Behind the names lies the threat of physical and sexual violence such as ostracism, firing, silencing, condemnation to hell, institutionalization, incarceration, deportation, rape, lynching, and other forms of public violence used to protect white power and privilege.

We could usefully spend some time exploring the history and meaning of any particular pair of words on the list above. I encourage you to do so. Each one reveals some vital aspect of whiteness and racism.

Next I want to point out three concepts that many of these words cluster around: Christian, American, and male.

Christian

One cluster of concepts and practices of whiteness grows out of dominant Western Christianity. Whiteness has often been equated with being a Christian in opposition to being a pagan, infidel, witch, heathen, Jew, Muslim, Native American, Buddhist, or atheist. Racial violence has been justified by a stated need to protect Christian families and homes. Pogroms, crusades, holy wars, and colonial conquests have been justified by the need to save the souls of uncivilized and godless peoples (often at the cost of their lives).

Jewish people have lived within Christian-dominated societies (when permitted to) for nearly 1,700 years, since Christianity became the official religion of the Roman Empire. There is substantial history of Christian teaching and belief that Jewish people are dangerous and evil. Because they are built into Christian religious texts and literature, these beliefs have been sustained even during periods of hundreds of years when Jews were not living near Christians.[19] To many Christians, Jews, along with Muslims, have become symbols of the infidel. This anti-Jewish oppression, originally based on religious and cultural differences, has become racialized as Christian values were combined with racial exploitation and an ideology of white superiority. It has exposed Jews to the same harsh reality of violence that pagans, Roma,[20] witches, and Muslims have experienced.

In addition, anti-Jewish and anti-Muslim hatred has been passed on to Christians of color. Religious leaders of both Eastern Orthodox and Catholic branches of Christianity, as well as most Protestant denominations, have accused the Jews of killing Jesus, using the blood of Christian children for Passover ritual, refusing to recognize the divinity of Jesus, and consorting with the devil. Muslims were accused of colonizing the Holy Land, attacking Europe, and being mortal foes of Christendom. As Christianity was spread by Western colonialism and missionary practice, these teachings were incorporated into the beliefs of many Christians of color.[21]

At the same time, there are core Christian values of love, caring, justice, and fellowship that have inspired some Christians to work against racism. For example, many white abolitionists were Christians inspired by religious teachings and values.

American

Yet another cluster of meanings centers on the concept of American.[22] In the United States, the idea of who is an American is often conflated with who is white. In fact, "all-American" is often used as a thinly disguised code word for white. A third-generation Swedish or German American child is considered an all-American kid when a third-generation Japanese or Chinese American child may not be.

In the same way, the patriotism of anyone with darker skin color is routinely questioned. During World War II, US citizens of Japanese heritage were interned in concentration camps and US citizens of Italian or German heritage were not.[23] Even when they fought in the armed services in wartime, the loyalty of Asian American, Latinx, Native American, Arab American, and African American soldiers was challenged. Today, even though some Arab Americans and Muslim Americans are US soldiers fighting in Iraq and Afghanistan and serve as fire fighters and police officers throughout the US, they and their communities are accused of being disloyal and dangerous.[24]

In the US, immigration policies and quotas consistently favored Europeans, and much of the time completely excluded people not considered white. Today, even when they have legally arrived here, non-Native American people of color are routinely asked where they came from and told to go back home. For example, even though many Spanish-speaking citizens have roots in the Southeast, Southwest, and California going back more than three centuries, native-born Latinx in these areas are often stopped by police and immigration officials and asked to show proof of citizenship. The passage of an Arizona law in April, 2010 mandating police to stop anyone who looks like they could be in the country illegally—in other words racial profiling anyone who looks Latinx—is just the most recent manifestation of racist targeting of the entire Latinx community.[25] The reluctance of many white people to fully accept people of color as patriotic Americans has meant that many feel forever foreign and vulnerable to discrimination and marginalization.

Male

Finally, whiteness strongly leans toward male virtues and male values. While terms of whiteness apply to men and women, significantly different qualities are associated with each.

White women are held to higher standards of chasteness, cleanliness, and restraint than white men. White women hold onto whiteness by the authority and protection of white men or by their willingness to adapt to male roles and exert authority in traditionally male spheres to protect their white privilege as employers, supervisors, or teachers. They can also be cast out of the circle of white male protection by being rebellious or by violating racial or gender norms. White women have both colluded with and resisted their role and the violence it has justified.[26]

People who are transgender are usually not included in discussions of racism, and therefore trans people of color are rendered both invisible and even more vulnerable to various kinds of violence.

In most discussions of masculinity, we underestimate the role racism plays. Training in white male violence against people of color starts early. White male bonding at work, at school, or in the extended family includes significant levels of racism toward men of color ranging from sitting around joking about people of color to bonding as a team against an opposing team of color, to participating in an attack upon a specific person of color, to joining an explicit white supremacist group. Not participating in such "rites of passage" makes white men vulnerable to physical and sexual aggression from their peers.

White men also bond with others and "prove" their heterosexuality by verbally and sexually assaulting women of color, Muslim, and Jewish women. The ability to have sex with, but not to be undermined or entrapped by, exotic and dangerous women is a sign of male sexual prowess and reaffirms that a man is in control, is one of the (white Christian) boys and that he knows and accepts the sexual and racial order.

When a young man is pushed by white male peers to assault or harass a person of color, a lot is riding on the line—and he knows it. It is hard for most young men to avoid responding to such pressure because the threat of violence from other white men is real and immediate. We can help young men refuse to participate in white male violence by giving them tools for resisting white male socialization, which would make our communities much safer.[27]

Racism is a many-faceted phenomenon, slowly and constantly shifting its structures, dynamics, and justifications. But at its core, it maintains a racial hierarchy and protects white power and wealth. This dominant construct has wide-ranging effects on our lives and on the lives of people of color. Our work is to understand and challenge such a destructive system.

Words and Pictures

SINCE WHITENESS has been a defining part of European and North American culture for hundreds of years, the idea that white people are good and people of color are bad and dangerous is embedded into our everyday language. Most phrases containing "black" have negative meanings, while those containing "white" have positive meanings. Looking more deeply, we can find hundreds of words that imply people of color and people of different cultures and ethnicities are dangerous, threatening, manipulative, dishonest, or immoral. In fact, anything foreign or alien (and these two words themselves) has connotations of being not white, not pure, not American, and not Christian. We reinforce racism every time we use such language.

My goal in the following exercise is not to enforce some kind of political correctness. We are trying to understand how racism becomes embedded in our culture, our language, and the way we see the world so we can develop ways of talking with each other that counter historical patterns of exploitation and domination and are respectful.

We also need to challenge racially demeaning visual images. For example, images of darkness in advertisements, movies, and TV images convey danger and provoke white fear. Disney movies provide many examples of such color-coding. Throughout *The Lion King*, lightness is associated with good, darkness with evil. Everything from the coloring of the manes of the lions, the color of different animals to the sunshine in the lions' kingdom versus the murky land of the hyenas reflects the racial and moral hierarchy in this film. This hierarchy is reinforced by the language of the characters:

the lions talk in middle-class "white" English and the hyenas in a more colloquial street dialect. Similarly in *Aladdin*, Jafar, Kazim, and the bazaar merchants all have exaggerated, stereotypical "Arab" features and speak in heavy accents while Aladdin, Jasmine, and the Sultan have "European" features and no trace of an accent.[1] These color-coded values can be found consistently in Disney movies going back to *Sleeping Beauty* and *Dumbo* (remember the crows).

1.2. Racially Charged Words

Each of the following words and phrases contains a derogatory racial meaning in its definition or derivation or puts a positive spin on whiteness, white people, or white culture. Can you list alternative, racially neutral words to use in their place? What other racially derogatory words or phrases would you add to this list?

blacklist _____

blackmail _____

black market _____

black sheep _____

white lie _____

white knight _____

black magic _____

Dark Ages _____

to gyp (from gypsy) _____

yellow peril _____

red menace _____

to scalp _____

to Jew down _____

war paint (referring to women's makeup) _____

Indian giver _____

whitewash _____

pure/white as snow _____

that's white of you _____

- *What films have you seen where the use of images of white and black, light, and dark, or the racial casting of the heroes and villains was used to reinforce white = good and dark = bad?*

the dark side _____

to be in the dark _____

to be dim-witted _____

wampum _____

gypsy blood _____

macho _____

manana _____

tribal warfare _____

natives _____

squaw _____

peace pipe _____

feather in your cap _____

on the warpath _____

banana republic _____

china doll _____

Chinese fire drill _____

far east, near east, middle east _____

dark continent _____

third world _____

red-blooded _____

wandering Jew _____

grandfather clause _____

call in the cavalry _____

Byzantine _____

blue blood _____

assassin _____

In pictures, movies, and video games, the white male body, whether upper-class or working-class, is handsome—fit, tall, with hair, blue eyes, fair skin, and strong features. It speaks with authority, dominates others, and is muscular/athletic and competitive. It stands or sits in postures of strength commanding respect and attention. It is a body under control which controls others. It is also a body that can be roused to anger and violence to protect the innocent (usually white women) and pursue the guilty.[2]

The ideal white female body is portrayed as the standard of beauty. Blond, blue-eyed, thin, sexually inviting, and even fairer than her male counterpart, this female body is portrayed in postures and roles conveying submission, availability, and seductiveness.

Whiteness represents pure, Christian goodness (although white women can also carry the stigma of original sin). White people are almost always central characters, hero or heroine, consistently juxtaposed to images of darker-skinned men and women representing, dirt, animality, danger, and moral corruption.[3] The marketing of the normalness, naturalness, and essential goodness of idealized whiteness prompts millions of women and men, both white and people of color, to spend endless amounts of time and money bleaching, dyeing, or straightening their hair; lightening their skin color, losing weight, using cosmetics, or having cosmetic surgery.

If we pay attention to the images around us, we will notice the pervasive influence racism has on our everyday lives. Racial difference and racial hierarchy, like gender hierarchy, are built into our language, our visual imagery, and our sense of who we are.

White Benefits,
Middle-Class Privilege

IT IS NOT NECESSARILY a privilege to be white, but it certainly has its benefits. That's why so many of our families gave up their unique histories, primary languages, accents, distinctive dress, family names, and cultural expressions. It seemed like a small price to pay for acceptance in the circle of whiteness. Even with these sacrifices, it wasn't easy to pass as white if we were Italian, Greek, Irish, Jewish, Spanish, Hungarian, or Polish. Sometimes it took generations before our families were fully accepted, and then it was usually because white society had an even greater fear of darker-skinned people.

Privileges are the economic extras those of us who are middle-class and wealthy gain at the expense of poor and working-class people of all races. *Benefits*, on the other hand, are the advantages all white people gain at the expense of people of color regardless of economic position.[1] Talk about racial benefits can ring false to many of us who don't have the economic privileges we see others in this society enjoying. But though we may not have substantial economic privileges, we do enjoy benefits from being white.

We can generally count on police protection rather than harassment. Depending on our financial situation, we can choose where we want to live and choose safer neighborhoods with better schools. We are given more attention, respect, and status in conversations than people of color. Nothing that we do is qualified, limited, discredited, or acclaimed simply because of our racial background. We don't have to represent our race, and nothing we do is judged as a credit to our race or as confirmation of its shortcomings or inferiority.

These benefits start early. Others will have higher expectations for us as children, both at home and at school. We will have more money spent on our education, we will be called on more in school and given more opportunity and resources to learn. We will see people like us in textbooks. If we get into trouble, adults will expect us to be able to change and improve and therefore will discipline or penalize us less harshly than young people of color.

These benefits accrue and work to the direct economic advantage of every white person in the United States. First of all, we will earn more in our lifetime than a person of color of similar qualifications. We will be paid $1.00 for every $.60 a person of color makes.[2] We will advance faster and more reliably and, on average, accumulate nearly thirteen times more wealth. A white family will, on average, accumulate $144,200 in assets, a black family $11,200.[3] The gap for single-women-headed households is even more stark—in 2007 42% of single white women had zero or negative wealth while 52% of black and 57% of Hispanic female-headed households had zero to negative wealth.[4]

There are historically derived economic benefits too. All the land in the US was taken from Native Americans. Much of the infrastructure of this country was built by enslaved labor, incredibly low-paid labor, or prison labor performed by men and women of color. Much of the housecleaning, childcare, cooking, and maintenance of our society has been done by low-wage-earning women of color. Today men, women, and young people of color still do the hardest, lowest-paid, most dangerous work throughout the US. And although there are millions of white people who are struggling financially, most white people enjoy less expensive food, clothing, and consumer goods because of the exploitation of people of color. Then these same white people are socialized to blame people of color and recent immigrants for their problems. This is the ruling class neoliberal agenda in action, and that class profits enormously: Think Walmart and the Walmart family, combined net worth $106.5 billion; Microsoft and Bill Gates, net worth $81 billion; the Koch Brothers combined net worth $84 billion, and investors in these corporations such as Warren Buffet, net worth $65.5 billion.[5]

We have been taught history through a white-tinted lens that has minimized our exploitation of people of color and extolled the hardworking, courageous qualities of white people. For example, many of our foreparents gained a foothold in the US by finding work in such trades as railroads, streetcars, construction, shipbuilding, wagon and coach driving, house painting, tailoring, longshore work, bricklaying, table waiting, working in the mills, or dressmaking. These were all occupations that blacks, who had begun entering many such skilled and unskilled jobs, were either excluded from or pushed out of in the 19th century. Exclusion and discrimination, coupled with immigrant mob violence against blacks in many northern cities (such as the anti-black draft riots of 1863), resulted in recent immigrants having economic opportunities blacks did not. These gains were consolidated by explicitly racist trade union practices and policies that kept blacks in the most unskilled labor and lowest-paid work.[6]

It is not that white people have not worked hard and built much. We have. But we did not start out from scratch. We went to segregated schools and universities built with public money. We received school loans, Veterans Administration (VA) loans, housing and auto loans unavailable to people of color. We received federal jobs, apprenticeships, and training where only whites were allowed.

Much of the rhetoric against more active policies for racial justice stems from the misconception that all people have been given equal opportunities and started from a level playing field. We often don't even see the benefits we have received from racism. We claim they are not there.

White Benefits?
A Personal Assessment

WHEN I BEGAN to take careful stock of my family's history, I began to see the numerous ways my father and I, and indirectly the women in my family, have benefited from policies that either favored white men, or explicitly excluded people of color and white women from consideration altogether. Of course, my foreparents were considered white enough to immigrate to the United States during a period most people of color could not—a monumental white benefit which provided the foundation for all the future ones.

My father had an overseas desk job in the military during World War II. When he returned to the US, he was offered many government programs specifically designed to reintegrate him into society and help him overcome the disadvantage of having given his time to defend the country.

During most of World War II, the armed services had been strictly segregated. After the war, many people of color were denied veterans' benefits because they had served in jobs not considered eligible for such benefits. Many more were deliberately not informed about the benefits, were discouraged from applying when they inquired about them, or simply had their applications for benefits denied. One study of the recipients of such benefits concluded, "Thus, not only were far fewer blacks than whites able to participate in these programs, but those blacks who could participate received fewer benefits than their white counterparts."[1]

My father was able to continue his education on the G.I. bill (attending the nearly all-white and largely male University of Southern California). He was not unique: 2.2 million men received higher education benefits from the GI Bill. In fact, by 1947 half of all college students were veterans.[2]

My father applied for a training program to become a stock-broker—just one of many lucrative professions reserved for white men. When my father completed his training and joined a firm, he was on the road to economic success with all the resources of a national financial corporation behind him. Besides the immediate income from his wages and commissions as a stockbroker, the company had a generous pension plan, a significant factor later on in our family's life. At the time it meant my parents could save money for a car and for their children's college education because they knew their retirement was secure.

My father was also able to contribute to Social Security, which had been set up primarily to benefit white male workers during the Depression. My father (and mother and, indirectly, their children) benefited from the program when he retired. Although many people with jobs were eligible to contribute to Social Security, millions more were not. US President Franklin Roosevelt knew he could not pass the Social Security bill without the votes of Southern agricultural and Western mining interests that controlled key Congressional committees. These interests were unwilling to support the bill if people of color, particularly agricultural workers, were included.[3] Their compromise was to create a system in which the benefits were specifically set up to exclude large numbers of people of color (and, incidentally, white women) by excluding job categories such as agricultural and domestic work. Many hundreds of thousands more people of color were in job occupations that qualified for Social Security, but earned too little to be able to participate.[4]

My father had secured a good job and was eligible for a housing loan because of affirmative action. Of course, he still had to find a house that could be both a shelter for his family and an investment, a white suburban neighborhood with good schools, no crime, and rising property values. Many people, however, were excluded from buying houses in precisely those areas because they were not white males.

For example, the Federal Housing Administration (FHA) specifically channeled loans away from the central city and to the suburbs, and its official handbook even provided a model restrictive covenant (an agreement not to sell to people of color or, sometimes, Jews) to prospective white homebuyers and realtors.[5] The FHA and the VA financed more than $120 billion worth of new housing between 1934 and 1962, but less than 2% of this real estate was available to non-white families.[6]

In addition, the federal home-mortgage interest tax deduction meant the government subsidized my father's purchase of a house at the direct expense of people who did not have affirmative action programs or other means to help them buy a house and therefore were renters. This provided my father additional tens of thousands of dollars of support from the government over his adult lifetime. Researchers estimate these affirmative action housing programs for white men have cost the current generation of African Americans approximately $82 billion.[7]

The results of all this affirmative action provided my family with more than just financial benefits. For me, specifically, I was able to go to a public school with many advantages. These included heavy investments in science programs, sports programs, college preparatory classes, and leadership programs. There were no students or teachers of color at my school, so these advantages were only for white people. And most of these programs were designed for the boys; girls were discouraged from participating or straightforwardly refused the opportunity.

Meanwhile the government was subsidizing suburban development, and my family enjoyed parks, sports facilities, new roads—an entire infrastructure primarily directed to the benefit of white men and their families, even though the entire population paid taxes to support it.

Of course my mother and my sister enjoyed substantial benefits as long as they stayed attached to my father. They did not receive these benefits on their own behalf or because they were felt to deserve them. Even though my father was verbally and emotionally abusive toward my mother, she did not contemplate leaving him, partly because she did not have the independent financial means to do so nor did she have access to the affirmative action programs he did.

Growing up as the son of a white male who had access to so much, I viewed these benefits as natural and inevitable. I came to believe that because I lived in a democracy where equal opportunity was the law of the land, white men must be successful because they were superior to all others. They must be smarter and work harder; my father must be a superior person. No one ever qualified his success to me by describing all the advantages he had been given or labeled him an affirmative action baby.

My father made good, sound decisions in his life. He worked hard enough and was smart enough to take advantage of the social support, encouragement, and direct financial benefits available to him. Many white women, and men and women of color, were just as smart and worked just as hard and ended up with far, far less than my father.

As a result of all of these white benefits, my father retired as a fairly wealthy and successful man at the age of 50. By then I was already enjoying my own round of affirmative action programs.

My parents could afford private college tuition, but in case they could not, my father's company offered scholarships for white males, the sons of employees. There were more specific affirmative action programs offered at many of these schools called legacy admissions: children of alumni were given special preferences. I was told that if I wanted to go to my father's alma mater, USC, I had an excellent chance of getting in regardless of my qualifications because my father had gone there.[8]

I attended Reed College in the mid 1960s, a school that had no faculty of color, only one white woman faculty member, and barely a handful of students of color until my senior year. During my college years, I was strongly encouraged in my studies and urged to go on to graduate school, which I could see was even more clearly a white male preserve.

By the late 1960s, the United States was fully engaged in the Vietnam War. The US government reinstated the draft and developed yet another affirmative action program for white males—especially white males from affluent families: the college draft deferment. Proportionately few students of color were attending college in those years, and large numbers of white males were. This deferment naturally resulted in fewer young men being eligible for the draft, so the armed forces adjusted its requirements so more men of color, who had previously been rejected, could be recruited. The results of these policies were that, in 1964, 18.8% of eligible whites were drafted, compared to 30.2% of eligible blacks. By 1967, when there was larger-scale recruitment, still only 31% of eligible whites were inducted into the military compared to 67% of eligible blacks. I was able to avoid the draft entirely because of affirmative action for white men and what Michael Eric Dyson has called the affirmative retroaction policies of the military, which targeted men of color for recruitment.[9]

When I graduated from college, I was presented with a wide variety of affirmative action options. In fact, corporate recruiters were constantly at my predominantly white college offering us job opportunities. Many of my working-class friends had to take any job they could get to support themselves or their parents or younger siblings. Since I had no one else to support, I could pursue the career or profession of my choice.

After college, when my partner (who is also white) and I wanted to buy a house, we were given preferred treatment by banks when we applied for loans in the form of less paperwork, less extensive credit checks, and the benefit of the doubt about our financial capacity to maintain a house. Our real estate agent let us know we were preferred neighbors in desirable communities and steered us away from less desirable areas (neighborhoods with higher concentrations of people of color). In addition, because of my parents' secure financial position, they could loan us money for a down payment and cosign our loan with us.[10]

Most of the government programs and institutional policies described above were not called affirmative action programs. Programs benefiting white men never are. They are seen as race and gender-neutral, even though most or all of the benefits accrue to white men. These programs were not contested as special preferences nor were the beneficiaries stigmatized as not deserving or not qualified.

Your parents probably did not own slaves. Mine did not even arrive in the US until after slavery. Nor were my parents mean bosses, exploiting workers in factories or otherwise discriminating against people of color. Nevertheless, they and I benefited directly and specifically from public and private policies—various forms of white male affirmative action at the expense of people of color. And these benefits continue to accrue to me and my family.

Think about your grandparents and parents and where they grew up and lived as adults. What work did they do? What are some of the benefits that have accrued to your family through your foreparents and to you directly because of racism?

You may be thinking at this point, "If I'm doing so well, how come I'm barely making it?" Some of the benefits listed above are money in the bank for each and every one of us. Some of us have bigger bank accounts—much bigger. According to 2013 figures, 1% of the population controls about 37% of the net household wealth of the US, and the top 20% own 89%.[12] In 2015, women generally made about 80 cents for every dollar that men made in average week of full-time work. African American women made 64½ cents and Latinas 56½ cents.[13] In studies looking at a 15-year period, women's income averaged just 35–40% of men's.[14]

As with so many economic issues, white women, experiencing sexism, are disadvantaged compared to white men, and women of color are disadvantaged more severely by experiencing the combined effects of sexism and racism. In other words, benefits from racism are amplified or diminished by relative privilege. People with disabilities, people with less formal education, and people who are lesbian, gay, bisexual, or trans face discrimination from multiple directions. All of us benefit in some ways from whiteness, but some of us have cornered the market on significant benefits to the exclusion of others.

1.3. White Benefits Checklist

Look at the following list.[11] Put a check beside any benefit you enjoy that a person of color of your age, gender, and class probably does not. Think about what effect not having that benefit would have had on your life. (If you don't know the answer to any of these questions, do research. Ask family members. Do what you can to discover the answers.)

The purpose of this checklist is not to discount what we, our families, and foreparents have achieved. But we do need to question any assumptions we retain that everyone started out with equal opportunity.

☐ My ancestors were legal immigrants to this country during a period when immigrants from Asia, South and Central America, or Africa were restricted.

☐ My ancestors came to this country of their own free will and have never had to relocate unwillingly while here.

☐ I live on land that formerly belonged to Native Americans.

☐ My family received homesteading or land staking claims from the federal government.

☐ I or my family or relatives receive or received federal farm subsidies, farm price supports, agricultural extension assistance, or other farm-related federal benefits.

☐ I lived or live in a neighborhood that people of color were discouraged or prevented from living in.

☐ I lived or live in a city where redlining prevents people of color getting housing or other loans.

☐ My parents or I went to racially segregated schools.

☐ I live in a school district or metropolitan area where more money is spent on the schools that white children go to than on those that children of color attend.

☐ I live in or went to a school district where children of color are more likely to be disciplined than white children, or are more likely to be tracked into non-academic programs.

☐ I live in or went to a school district where the textbooks and other classroom materials reflected my race as normal, heroes and builders of the United States, and there was little mention of the contributions of people of color.

☐ I was encouraged to go on to college by teachers, parents, or other advisors.

☐ I attended a publicly funded university or a heavily endowed private university or college, and/or I received student loans.

☐ I served in the military when it was still racially segregated, achieved a rank where there were few people of color, or served in a combat situation where there were large numbers of people of color in dangerous combat positions.

☐ My ancestors were immigrants who took jobs in railroads, streetcars, construction, shipbuilding, wagon and coach driving, house painting, tailoring, longshore work, bricklaying, table waiting, working in the mills, dressmaking, or any other trade or occupation where people of color were driven out or excluded.

☐ I received job training in a program where there were few or no people of color.

☐ I have received a job, job interview, job training, or internship through personal connections of family or friends.

☐ I worked or work in a job where people of color made less for doing comparable work or did more menial jobs.

☐ I have worked in a job where people of color were hired last or fired first.

☐ I work in a job, career, or profession or in an agency or organization in which there are few people of color.

☐ I received small business loans or credits, government contracts, or government assistance in my business.

☐ My parents were able to vote in any election they wanted without worrying about poll taxes, literacy requirements, or other forms of discrimination.

☐ I can always vote for candidates who reflect my race.

☐ I live in a neighborhood that has better police protection and municipal services and is safer than one where people of color live.

☐ The hospital and medical services close to me or which I use are better than those of most people of color in the region in which I live.

☐ I have never had to worry that clearly labeled public facilities, such as swimming pools, restrooms, restaurants, and nightspots, were in fact not open to me because of my skin color.

☐ I see people who look like me in a wide variety of roles on television and in movies.

☐ My skin color needn't be a factor in where I choose to live.

☐ A substantial percentage of the clothes I wear are made by poorly paid women and young people of color in the US and abroad.

☐ Most of the food I eat is grown, harvested, processed, and/or cooked by poorly paid people of color in this country and abroad.

☐ The house, office building, school, hotels and motels, or other buildings and grounds I use are often cleaned or maintained by people of color.

☐ Many of the electronic goods I use, such as TVs, cell phones and computers, are made by people of color in the US and abroad.

☐ People of color have cared for me, other family members, friends, or colleagues of mine either at home or at a medical or convalescent facility.

☐ I don't need to think about race and racism every day. I can choose when and where I want to respond to racism.

☐ What feelings come up for you when you think about the benefits white people gain from racism? Do you feel angry or resentful? Guilty or uncomfortable? Do you want to say "Yes, but…?"

The Economic Pyramid

As the economic pyramid shows, wealth is tremendously concentrated in the US.[1] People of color are preponderantly on the bottom and in the middle of the pyramid. The top of the pyramid is primarily white. There are also large numbers of white people in the

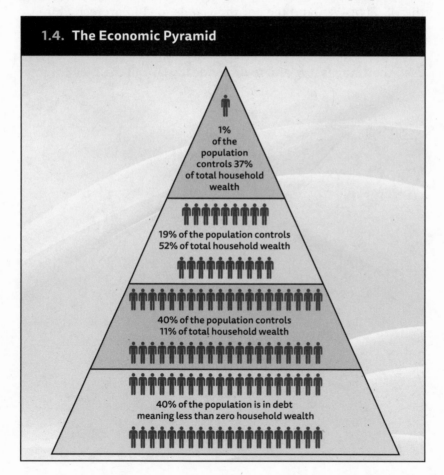

1.4. The Economic Pyramid

1%
of the
population
controls 37%
of total household
wealth

19% of the population controls
52% of total household wealth

40% of the population controls
11% of total household wealth

40% of the population is in debt
meaning less than zero household wealth

middle and on the bottom. With wealth so concentrated at the top, most white people have much to gain from working with people of color to redistribute wealth and opportunity. However, racism often keeps poor, working, and middle-class white people from identifying their common struggles with people of color. Feelings of intraracial solidarity keep many white people focused on our racial connections with people at the top rather than acknowledging economic connections with others lower down. The small amount of benefit we receive from being white can distract us from recognizing the large amount of exploitation we experience at the hands of those economically on top. For example, many poor and working-class southern white men fought in alliance with landowning whites in the US Civil War, and tens of thousands died to protect white supremacy. However, the landowning class of the South used the slave-based economy to ensure poor whites remained disenfranchised, to keep their wages low, and to dramatically curtail their civil rights.[2]

The Costs of Racism
to People of Color

THE OPPOSITE of a benefit is a *disadvantage*. People of color face distinct disadvantages. If we were to talk about running a race for achievement and success in the US and white people and people of color lined up side by side, every white benefit would put white runners steps ahead of the starting line and every disadvantage would move people of color steps back from the starting line before the race even began.[1]

The disadvantages of being a person of color in the United States today include personal insults, harassment, discrimination, economic and cultural exploitation, stereotypes, and invisibility, as well as threats, intimidation, and violence. Not every person of color has experienced all these disadvantages, but they each have experienced some of them, and they each experience the vulnerability to violence that being a person of color entails.

Institutional racism is discussed in detail in Parts IV, V, and VI, but personal acts of harassment and discrimination committed directly by individual white people can also take a devastating toll.[2] People of color never know when they will be called names, be ridiculed, or have jokes and comments made to them or about them by white people. They don't know when they might hear that they should leave the country or go back to where they came from. Often these comments are made in situations where it isn't safe to confront the person who made the remark.

People of color also have to be ready to respond to teachers, employers, or supervisors who have stereotypes, prejudices, or lowered expectations about them. Many have been discouraged or prevented from pursuing academic or work goals or have been placed in lower vocational levels because of their racial identity. They have to be prepared to receive less respect, attention, or response from a doctor, police officer, court official, city official, or other professional. They are likely to be mistrusted, accused of stealing, cheating or lying, or stopped (and possibly arrested or killed) by police because of their racial identity. They are also likely to have experienced employment or housing discrimination or know someone who has.

There are cultural costs as well. People of color see themselves portrayed in degrading, stereotypical, and fear-inducing ways in the media. They may have important religious or cultural holidays that are not recognized where they work or go to school. They have seen their religious practices, music, art, mannerisms, dress, and other customs distorted, "borrowed," ridiculed, exploited, used as mascots, or otherwise degraded.

If they protest, they may be verbally attacked by whites for being too sensitive, too emotional, or too angry. Or they may be told they are different from other people of their racial group. Much of what people of color do or say, or how they act in racially mixed company, is judged as representative of their race.

On top of all this, they have to live with the threat of physical violence from police and vigilante groups. Some are survivors of racial violence or have close friends or family who are. Perhaps even more disheartening, they have to teach their children at a young age how to respond to this as well.

Although all people of color have experienced some of the disadvantages mentioned above, other factors make a difference in how vulnerable a person of color is to the effects of racism. Economic resources help buffer some more egregious effects. Depending upon where one lives, people with different racial identities are treated differently. Discrimination varies in form and ranges from mild to severe depending on one's skin color, ethnicity, level of education, location, gender, sexual orientation, physical ability, age, and how white people and white-run institutions respond to these factors.

- *Is it hard for you to accept that this kind of pervasive discrimination still occurs? Which of the above statements is particularly hard to accept?*
- *What does it mean for you to live in a community where these kinds of things are common experiences for people of color— and that you and other white people don't name and challenge them?*

Most of us would like to think that today we have turned the tide and people of color can run the race equally with white people. The US has had an African American president, and some people of color who are wealthy or in positions of power. But, if we honestly add up the benefits of whiteness and the disadvantages of being a person of color, we can see there is not equal opportunity or a level playing field. Racism is still prevalent in all aspects of our society.

There is a 2015 YouTube clip of anti-racist educator Jane Elliot addressing a room full of white people. She asks members of the audience to stand if they would be happy to be treated the same way black people are treated in our society. She repeats the question three different times, and yet nobody in the audience stands. She then says, "Nobody is standing here. That says very plainly that you know what's happening and you don't want it to happen to you. I want to know why you are so willing to accept it or allow it to happen to others."[3]

There are no biological, physiological, or psychological attributes making people of color different from white people. They don't bring housing, educational and employment discrimination, hate crimes, or racial profiling on themselves. These disadvantages are perpetrated by white people (like you and me) and by white-run institutions.

The Culture of Power

WHY DON'T WHITE PEOPLE see white benefits? Whenever one group of people has benefits at the expense of another group, people in the in-group are accepted as the norm; if you are in that group, it can be very hard to see the benefits you receive.

Since I'm male and I live in a culture in which men have more social, political, and economic power than women, I often don't notice that women are treated differently than I am. I'm inside a male culture of power. I expect to be treated with respect, to be listened to and to have my opinions valued. I expect to find books and newspapers written by people like me, reflecting my perspective and showing me in central roles. I don't necessarily notice that the women around me are treated less respectfully, ignored, or silenced; they are not visible in positions of authority nor welcomed in certain spaces, and they are not always safe in situations where I feel perfectly comfortable.

Remember when you were a young person entering a space that reflected an adult culture of power such as a classroom, store, or office? What let you know you were on adult turf?

Some of the things I remember are that adults were in control. They made the decisions. They might be considerate enough to ask me what I thought, but they did not have to take my concerns into account. I could look around and see what was on the walls, what music was being played, what topics were being discussed, and most importantly, who made decisions.

I felt I was under scrutiny. I had to change my behavior—how I dressed, how I spoke, even my posture ("Sit up, don't slouch")—so

I would be accepted and heard. I couldn't be as smart as I was, or I'd be considered a smart aleck. Sometimes I had to cover up my family background and religion in order to be less at risk from adult disapproval. And if there was any disagreement or problem between an adult and myself, I had little credibility. The adult's word was almost always believed over mine.

The effects on young people of an adult culture of power are similar to the effects on people of color of a white culture of power. As an adult, I rarely notice I am surrounded by an adult culture of power. Similarly, as a white person, when I'm driving on the freeway, I am unlikely to notice people of color being pulled over based on skin color. Or when I am in a store, I am unlikely to notice people of color are being followed, not being served as well, or being charged more for the same items. In a society that proclaims equal opportunity, I may not even believe other people are being paid less than I am for the same work, or being turned away from jobs and housing because of their surname, the color of their skin, or their accent. Most of the time I am so much inside the white culture of power it is invisible to me, and I have to rely on people of color to point out to me what it looks like, what it feels like, and what impact it has on them.

We can learn to notice any culture of power around us. I was giving a talk at a large university and was shown to my room in the hotel run by the university's hotel management department. When I had put my suitcase down and hung up my clothes, I looked around the room. There were two pictures on the wall. One was of a university baseball team—22 white men wearing their team uniforms. The other picture was of a science lab class—14 students (13 white men and 1 white woman)—dressed in lab coats and working at lab benches. In total I had 35 white men and 1 white woman on the walls of my room. "This clearly tells me who's in charge at this university," I said to myself, and it would probably send a message to many people of color and white women who stayed in the room that they could expect to be excluded from the culture of power in this institution. I lodged a complaint about the composition of the pictures to the hotel management and referred to it again in my talk the next day.

The pictures themselves, of course, were only symbolic. But as I walked around the campus, talked with various officials, and heard about the racial issues being dealt with, I could see that these symbols were part of the construction of a culture of power which excluded people of color and women. I have learned that noticing how the culture of power works in any situation provides a lot of information about who has power and privilege and who is vulnerable to discrimination and exclusion, and this university was no exception.

Our white male culture of power reflects a worldview built on the last thousand years of white Christian male ruling-class dominance in Western societies. Developed by Western Christian elites, elaborated upon and extended by science, capitalism, and "Enlightenment" thinkers, certain core concepts have coalesced into a dominant worldview affecting all of our thinking. This worldview has been enforced through Crusades, inquisitions, witch burnings, invasion, conquest, slavery, genocide, and assimilation.[1]

The problem with a white culture of power is that it reinforces racial hierarchy. As white people, many of us expect to have things our way, the way we are most comfortable with. We may go through life complacent in our monoculturalism, not even aware of the limits of our perspectives, the gaps in our knowledge, the inadequacy of our understanding. Of course a white culture of power also dramatically limits the ability of people of color to participate in any event, situation, or organization. They are only able to participate on our terms, at our discretion, and this puts them at an immediate disadvantage. They often have to give up or hide much of who they are to be accepted. Before they even show up, they've been described in the culture of power as not normal, a problem, possibly even dangerous. If there are any problems, it becomes too easy to identify people of color as the source of those problems and blame or attack them rather than the problem itself.

It is important we learn to recognize the white culture of power so we can challenge the confinement of people of color to the margins of our society. Use the previous paragraphs and the questions to guide you in thinking about the white culture of power around you.

1.5. The Culture of Power

1. Is there a white culture of power, and, if so, what does it look like:
   a. In your office or other workplace?
   b. In your school or classroom?
   c. In your living room or living space?
   d. In your congregation?
   e. Where you go out to eat?
   f. Where you shop for clothes?
   g. In agencies whose services you use?
2. Some questions you might ask yourself to identify the culture of power and its appearance include:
   a. Who is in authority?
   b. How is the space designed?
   c. What is on the walls?
   d. What languages are used? Which are acceptable?
   e. What music and food is available?
   f. Who is treated with full respect?
   g. Whose experience is valued?
   h. Who decides?
   i. Who is viewed with suspicion or as an outsider?

(These questions may be used to identify cultures of power based on gender, class, sexual orientation, religion, age, or physical ability as well as race.)

In your workplace, insofar as you have control over it, what changes can you make to diminish the impact of the white culture of power on people of color?

It is probably inevitable that, when faced with the reality of the unequal distribution of benefits and harm of racism, we will have strong feelings. Recognize and accept your feelings and any resistance you have to the information presented above. We can support each other through the feelings. We need a safe place to talk about how it feels to be white and know about racism. Turn to other white people for this support.

- *Who are white people you can talk with about racism?*
- *When people say, "We all have it hard," or "Everyone has an equal opportunity," or "People of color just want special privileges," how can you use the information in this book to respond? What might be difficult about doing so?*
- *What additional information or resources will you need to be able to do this with confidence? How might you find those resources?*

You will find more information about racism in the Bibliography and Other Resources section at the end of this book. Later chapters offer more advice about how to be a strong anti-racist ally to people of color.

Entitlement

HAVING BENEFITS and being part of the culture of power encourages a person to develop a sense of entitlement to special treatment. _Entitlement_ is the sense you are owed certain rights, privileges, services, or material goods because of who you are. In Western countries a person's race, class, and gender strongly influence what they feel entitled to.

Of course, there are some entitlements we might all agree are legally or morally good. A right to a decent job, to food and housing, to free speech, to be able to vote—we might call these basic rights.

But I use entitlement here in a different way. When you don't expect to have to wait your turn or wait in line or take a number, when you do have to do these things and you see other people being served ahead of you, you may feel angry at these people who, even though they arrived earlier than you, you perceive as being given preference. In fact, it is simply your sense of entitlement being challenged.

When I was younger, there were times when I would walk past a receptionist and into my office without saying anything to her. There were times when I did not acknowledge or talk with the people maintaining the building in which I went to school, or the people who cleaned my dorm room in college or my motel room when I traveled. When this behavior was pointed out to me and I began to notice it in myself, I realized I felt entitled to other people's services and assumed they existed to take care of my needs. At first I thought that to correct this I had to become friends with people who provided services for me. However, I soon realized what was required from me was not friendship, but acknowledgement of and respect for people who were contributing to my well-being and the well-being of the community. I needed to see them differently, as full human beings, rather than as support staff for my life and activities.

How does entitlement show itself? I have noticed it in the following ways. (I have put the word *white* in parentheses because although I think that it is usually white people exhibiting these behaviors, this is not always the case. There are certainly people of color, especially those with economic means, who do these things as well.)

(White) People cutting in line in front of others because they think their needs have a priority.

(White) Drivers cutting in front of other cars because they are in a hurry.

(White) People walking by or ignoring people like receptionists, maintenance staff, or cleaning staff.

(White) People feeling OK about paying childcare workers, *au pairs*, gardeners, in-home attendants, and other workers less than a living wage.

(White) People who become impatient when they don't receive the prompt service or the attention they feel entitled to and direct abusive comments at the staff who are dealing with them.

(White) People who leave a paltry tip or no tip at all when they can well afford to tip generously.

(White) People quickly judging the motives and behavior of people they don't know and holding their own group up for comparison.

(White) People taking up more time and attention than their fair share in conversations, classrooms, meetings, and public events.

(White) People speaking for others, about others, or using phrases like "we," "they," or "that group" rather than "I think," "I feel," "In my opinion."

(White) People using possessive adjectives in such phrases as "They are taking our jobs, invading our country, destroying our neighborhood, or disrupting our workplace."

I know I have often acted from a sense of entitlement, but because I grew up believing in equal opportunity and equal rights, I had to develop a rationale for my behavior. I had to explain to myself why I deserved better treatment, quicker access, prompter service, and more airtime in meetings. As a result I have consciously or unconsciously told myself that I deserve preferential treatment because:

I am better educated
I have more experience
I am more rational
My time is more valuable
I worked hard to get to where I am
They probably don't need as much to live on
I don't actually have direct contact with them so I am not responsible
I need to get there on time

I have only just begun to see the sense of entitlement these excuses mask and the degree to which they are rationalizations for inequality and racism.

Besides lessening our own sense of entitlement, we can also challenge the behavior of those around us. In a public place, we can ask

1.6. Entitlement

1. Look over the list of entitlements above and note the ones that you have felt at times.
2. What others would you add to the list?
3. Which rationalizations have you used to explain the preference you felt you deserved?
4. Has your sense of entitlement ever led you to ignore the needs or rights of others?
5. What impact does it have on others and on the community when you act out of a sense of personal entitlement?
6. How can you better notice the impact of entitlement on your family, work, and school environments?

people to wait their turn. In a meeting, we can ask those who have spoken a lot not to speak again until everyone has had a turn. We can ask people to use "I" statements and not make generalizations about others. And we can challenge people's rationalizations for unequal and inadequate wages, benefits, tips, and other forms of monetary compensation. In public discussions, we can challenge people about their sense of entitlement to jobs, education, or housing when past policies of discrimination have given preference to white people or restricted access to people of color.

Cultural Appropriation

THE SENSE OF ENTITLEMENT white people are socialized to have leads directly to *cultural appropriation*: taking traditional knowledge, cultural expressions, or artifacts from someone else's culture without permission. This can include unauthorized use of another people's dance, dress, music, language, folklore, cuisine, traditional medicine, or religious symbols. It's most likely to be harmful when the source community is a group that has been oppressed or exploited in other ways or when the object of appropriation is particularly sensitive, e.g., sacred objects.[1]

Cultural appropriation is often an extension of genocide, enslavement, forced removals, and land theft, as settlers take what does not belong to them. It can be the final step in a genocidal process that continues long after a nation or culture has been physically defeated. Memorialization, respect for, and acknowledgement of the cultural contributions of the defeated can even be used to demonstrate the "benevolence" of the conquering culture.

Cultural appropriation is based on unequal power relationships. People with less power cannot protect their cultures nor dictate the terms of exchange between themselves and others. They have been opened up and made vulnerable by the colonization process and a neoliberal economic market system in which everything can be commodified (made into an object and assigned a value or price) and then bought and sold, stolen, or traded. Others are then free to come along and appropriate, distort, stereotype, and exploit whichever parts of the culture they want to.

Those of us in the US (and in other overdeveloped countries) are used to "discovering" or taking (stealing) things we like with little thought, understanding, or consequence. For white people, this sense of entitlement can be all encompassing. After all, the original concept of Doctrine of Discovery sanctified by Papal Bulls in the 15th century gave Christians authority not only to "invade, search out, capture, vanquish, and subdue" all people who were not Christian, but also to take their "dominions, possessions, and all movable and immovable goods." This included the land, the people themselves (slavery was encouraged), and all physical and cultural possessions.[2]

Cultural appropriation can take many forms such as:

- Unauthorized use or misuse of sacred objects, prayers, and rituals
- Native American mascots
- The use of other people's names, images, icons, and ritual objects out of context, modifying them, or turning them into products bought and sold in the marketplace
- The use of other people's names, images, icons, and ritual objects solely for personal gain
- The use of other people's sayings, music, literature, art, food, genes, or knowledge without permission, credit or as a commodity or for monetary gain
- Camp Fire Girls, Cub Scout, and Brownie/Boy and Girl Scout activities and many other Indian named and themed camps, party themes, covering songs and other music, and the adoption of cultural objects and rituals
- Halloween costumes
- Mock Spanish or disrespectful use of African American idioms or other forms of language
- Taking, exploiting, and misunderstanding history and symbols meaningful to people of other cultures
- Neglecting to recognize and acknowledge the origins of what one is using
- Speaking as an expert on a culture or set of practices as an

academic/researcher, writer, teacher, or guide without initiation or authorization

As with all forms of white privilege, rather than examining the roots of our privilege in the harm done to others, we resort to rationalizations to justify our cultural appropriation. Justifications that I and other white people give for these kinds of appropriation include:

- We are actually memorializing, respecting, or honoring the culture
- We don't intend to be disrespectful
- We were told by somebody that it was OK
- We were taught by someone from that culture
- This practice is universal or is universally useful
- We gain so much personally from this practice
- There is always cultural exchange going on; cultures borrow and adapt from each other
- We don't see the harm in what we're doing

Jarune Uwujaren writes that "Using someone else's culture to satisfy a personal need for self-expression is an exercise in privilege and entitlement regardless of the intentions of the one who appropriates. There needs to be some element of mutual understanding, equality, and respect for there to be true exchange."[3] Otherwise we who take are contributing to the further exploitation and marginalization of another people. We have a responsibility to listen to people of marginalized cultures, understand as much as possible the blatant and subtle ways in which their cultures have been appropriated and exploited, and educate ourselves enough to make informed choices when it comes to engaging with them. "*Cultural exchange* is engaging with a culture as a respectful and humble guest, invitation only."[4]

Encouraging this awareness is not about telling people what they can wear or do. We live and act within a social and historical context, and without understanding the implications of that context and the historical harm white people have done and continue to do to people of color, we cannot avoid feeling entitled to take things that don't belong to us. The racial double standard could not be clearer when people of color are prohibited or prevented from practicing their cultures while white people are allowed to and even rewarded for appropriating them.

There are no legitimate claims of ignorance or innocence for cultural appropriation, and the intentions of the inadvertent appropriator are irrelevant in this context. Therefore, as Jarune Uwujaren said so succinctly, "educate yourself, listen, and be open to reexamining the symbols you use without thinking, the cultures you engage with without understanding, and the historical and social climate we all need to be seeing."[5]

The Costs of Racism to White People

WE TEND TO THINK of racism as a problem for people of color and something we should be concerned about for their sake. It is true racism is devastating to them, and if we believe in equity and justice for all, we should work for racial justice. However, as we've seen in previous chapters, although racism produces material benefits for white people, there are significant costs we've been trained to ignore, deny, or rationalize away.

For example, one of the conditions of assimilating into white mainstream culture—to be accepted as white—people are asked to leave behind the languages, foods, music, games, rituals, and expressions their parents and/or foreparents used. We lose our own families' cultures and histories. Sometimes this loss can lead us to romanticize other cultures.

White people have a distorted and inaccurate picture of history and politics because the truths about colonialism, racism, and US military aggression have been excluded; the contributions of people of color left out, and the roles of white people cleaned up and highlighted. We also lose the presence and contributions of people of color to our neighborhoods, schools, and relationships. Our experiences will be distorted and limited the more they are exclusively or predominantly white.

Racism affects our interpersonal relationships in many ways. We may have had to silence our voice and ignore or deny racism in order to remain accepted by family, friends, and coworkers. This betrayal of trust can damage our sense of our own integrity as well as that of people around us.[1] We may have lost important relationships with those close to us due to disagreements, fights, and tension over racism. At the same time, we may have lost relationships with people of color because the tensions of racism can make those relationships difficult to sustain.

These interpersonal costs lead to white fear, anxiety, and apprehension in situations where racism is visible or unavoidable. This fear in turn leads to lower racial awareness, pretense, and lack of authenticity toward people of color, fewer interracial friendships, less openness to diversity, and other negative features. It also leads to lower empathy and sensitivity toward people of color.

Racism distorts our sense of danger and safety. We are taught to live in fear of people of color. We are exploited economically by the ruling class and unable to resist or even see this exploitation because we are taught to scapegoat people of color. On a more personal level, many of us have been brutalized by family violence and sexual assault. We are less able to resist it effectively because we have been taught people of color are the real danger, never the white men we live with.

There are also spiritual costs. Many of us have lost a connection to our own spiritual traditions, and consequently have come to romanticize (and appropriate) those of other cultures, such as Native American, Buddhist, or Hindu rituals and practices.

Our moral integrity is deeply damaged as we witness situations of discrimination and harassment and do not intervene. We become callous and cold toward our fellow human beings, able to ignore or even support and rationalize aggression, torture, rape, hate, terrorism, expulsion, and war toward others. Our feelings of guilt, shame, embarrassment, or inadequacy about racism and about our responses to it lower our self-esteem. Because racism makes a mockery of our ideals of democracy, justice, and equality, it leads us to be cynical and pessimistic about human integrity and about our future, producing apathy, blame, despair, self-destructive behavior, and acts of violence.[2]

It can be hard for us to be honest with ourselves about the costs of racism in our own lives. The following is a checklist[3] you can use to evaluate the costs of racism to white people. Check each of the items that apply to you.

1.7. Costs of Racism to White People Checklist

☐ I don't know exactly what my European American heritage is, what my great-grandparents' names were, or what regions or cities my ancestors were from.

☐ I grew up, lived, or live in a neighborhood, or went to school or a camp, which, as far as I knew, was exclusively white.

☐ I grew up with people of color who were servants, maids, gardeners, or babysitters in my house.

☐ I did not meet people of color in person, or socially, before I was well into my teens.

☐ I grew up in a household where I heard derogatory racial terms or racial jokes.

☐ As a young person, I heard that people of color or recent immigrants were dangerous and were to blame for violence, lack of jobs, or other problems.

☐ The US history I was taught in school and by the media was biased, distorted, or misleading.

☐ I have seen or heard images, in magazines, on TV or radio, on CDs, or in movies of (check all that apply):

☐ Mexicans depicted as drunk, lazy, or illiterate
☐ Asians depicted as exotic, cruel, or mysterious
☐ South Asians depicted as excitable or "silly"
☐ Arabs depicted as swarthy, ravishing, or "crazed"
☐ African Americans depicted as violent or criminal
☐ Pacific Islanders depicted as fun-loving or lazy
☐ American Indians depicted as drunk, savage, or "noble"

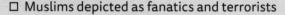

☐ Muslims depicted as fanatics and terrorists

☐ Women of color portrayed as exotic, erotic, or dangerous

☐ Any character roles from non-white cultures depicted by white actors

☐ I was told not to play with children of particular other ethnicities when I was a child.

☐ As a young person, I tried to question or challenge racism and was shut down by parents, teachers, or others.

☐ I have sometimes felt "white" culture was bland—empty and boring—or that another racial group had more rhythm or more athletic ability, was better at math and technology, or had more musical or artistic creativity than mine.

☐ I have felt that people of another racial group were more spiritual than white people.

☐ I have been nervous and fearful or found myself stiffening up when encountering people of color in a neutral public situation (for example, in an elevator, on the street).

☐ I have been sexually attracted to a person from another racial group because it seemed exotic, exciting, or a challenge.

☐ I was in a close friendship or relationship with a person of color, where the relationship was affected, stressed, or endangered by racism between us or from others.

☐ I am not in a close significant relationship with any people of color in my life right now.

☐ I have been in a close friendship or relationship with another white person where the relationship was damaged or lost because of a disagreement about racism.

☐ I have felt embarrassed by, separate from, superior to, or more tolerant than other white people.

☐ I have worked in a place where people of color held more menial jobs, were paid less, or were otherwise harassed or discriminated against, and I did nothing about it.

☐ I have been paid less or have been more vulnerable to exploitation at work because corporate leaders have pitted white workers against workers of color and immigrant workers.

☐ I have participated in an organization, work group, meeting, or event which people of color protested as racist or which I knew to be racist and did nothing about it.

☐ I have had degrading jokes, comments, or put-downs about people of color made in my presence and did not protest or challenge them.

☐ I have felt racial tension or noticed racism in a situation and was afraid to say or do anything about it.

☐ I have seen a person of color being attacked verbally or physically and did not intervene.

☐ I am concerned there is not enough attention paid to family violence and sexual assault in my community because of the focus of police and criminal/legal resources on communities of color.

☐ I am concerned drug abuse in my white community is not taken seriously enough because disproportionate attention is on drug use in communities of color.

☐ I experience a heightened and intrusive state of surveillance and security in my neighborhood, where I shop, in my school, when I cross borders, or when I use airports because of social fears about the dangers of people of color.

☐ I have had to accept unnecessary limits on my basic civil liberties because of social fears that people of color are dangerous.

☐ I have felt angry, frustrated, tired, or weary about dealing with racism and hearing about racial affairs.

☐ I live in a community where, for whatever reason, few people of color are present, so some of these questions don't apply.

When I use this list in an exercise with a white group and every person answers "yes" to a substantial number of the questions, I can see we have all paid some of the costs of racism. Realizing what those costs are can easily make us angry. If we are not careful, we can turn our anger toward people of color, blaming them for the problems of white racism. Sometimes we say things like "If they weren't here we would not have these problems." But racism is caused by white people, by our attitudes, behaviors, and institutions. How is it that white people can justify retaining the benefits of being white without taking responsibility for perpetuating racism?

Retaining Benefits, Avoiding Responsibility

DURING THE FIRST YEARS I worked with men who are violent, I was continually perplexed by their inability to see the effects of their actions and their ability to deny the violence they had perpetrated. I only slowly became aware of the complex set of tactics men use to make their violence invisible and to avoid taking responsibility for their actions. These tactics are listed below in the rough order men employ them.

These tactics are part of a cycle which can justify anger leading to further violence. As I began to understand the interconnection between the systems of gender, race, class, and sexual orientation,

1.8. List of Tactics to Avoid Responsibility

Tactic	Typical Statement
Denial	"I didn't hit her."
Minimization	"It was only a slap."
Blame	"She asked for it."
Redefinition	"It was mutual combat."
Unintentionality	"Things got out of hand."
It's over now	"I'll never do it again."
It's only a few men	"Most men wouldn't hurt a woman."
Counterattack	"She controls everything."
Competing victimization	"Everybody is against men."

I came to see how these tactics are used, consciously and unconsciously, by those in power to cover over their violence and retain their power and privileges.

Although these tactics follow a logical progression from outright denial to competing victimization, they are often used in combinations that make them confusing to confront. They may appear to be based on logical reasoning, but they are part of a strategy for explaining or justifying already existing injustice and violence.

We can learn to recognize and counter these tactics. I am going to use the history of the relationship between white Europeans and Native Americans to illustrate how these tactics have been (and still are) used to cover up the violence white people commit toward people of color. There is more detailed information about that history in Part IV.

Denial

Denial is usually the first tactic employed and works very simply. The batterer says, "I didn't hit her."

White people say Columbus was just looking for a trade route, the Pilgrims found a vast wilderness, and the early colonists befriended the Indians and exchanged presents with them. At this level there is absolute denial that violence occurred and therefore of any responsibility for it.

Today we are using the tactic of denial when we say, despite all evidence to the contrary, "It's a level playing field," "Discrimination is a thing of the past," or "This is a land of equal opportunity." White people can also deny the existence of racism by claiming that class or some other factor is really the issue.

Minimization

If the denial doesn't hold up because of the evidence—for instance, she has a broken arm—then the violence is minimized. The batterer says, "I didn't hit her. Well, it was only a slap."

White people killed Native Americans and took their land. In response, we say, "A few Indians died because they didn't have immunity to European diseases." We try to minimize the presence of

"Pioneers"

the 12 to 15 million Native Americans in North America prior to 1492 and to minimize the land theft and genocide we committed against them.

Today we continue to minimize racism by saying, "Personal achievement mostly depends on personal ability," "Racism isn't prevalent anymore," or (about slavery) "There were a lot of kind slave owners."

Blame

If the minimization doesn't hold up because the victim is in the hospital, then the batterer's effort shifts to a combination of justifying the violence and blaming the victim: "She asked for it" or "She should have known not to say that to me." If the discussion is more general, then men might make statements like "Women are too emotional/manipulative/backstabbing."

Similarly, we know that millions of Native Americans died, not only from intentional transmission of diseases, but also because white people shot, tortured, and enslaved them. Since the blame has to fall on entire societies, we make statements like "Indians were primitive." "They had not developed the technology to compete." "They were not physically able to resist the diseases, hold up under slavery." "They were naive, simple heathens."

Historically there have been continual attempts to blame white violence against people of color as the inevitable result of genetic/biological, physiological, or psychological differences. These differences often do not exist. Where they do, they are seldom related to real differences in behavior. In any case, differences never justify injustice and violence.

When we describe the agency of people with power, explanations become clearer: He hit her. He broke her arm. He put her in the hospital. Columbus invaded, killed, and enslaved the Taino/Arawak peoples. The US Army at Fort Clark deliberately distributed smallpox-infected blankets to the Mandan in order to kill them.[1]

Today we blame people of color for racism by saying, "Look at the way they act," "If they weren't so angry...," "They have different cultural values," or "They are immoral, lazy, dumb, or unambitious."

Redefinition

We want to hold adults responsible for what they do. Therefore we must carefully and accurately investigate what happened so we can stop violence. If we don't look at the overall context and take differentials of power into account, we can be susceptible to the tactic of redefinition. For example, the batterer says, "It was mutual combat." "She hit me first." "It takes two to fight."

If we can no longer claim Columbus innocently discovered America, we try to redefine the event. The 1992 quincentennial museum exhibit in New York was called "Encounter," a word implying some level of mutuality, equality, and neutrality. In the same vein, we say, "The settlers had to protect themselves from Indian attacks."

Today we redefine racism as a mutual problem by saying, "This country is just a big melting pot," "Anybody can be prejudiced," or "People of color attack white people too." The popular movie *Crash* was an example of redefinition of the "anybody can be prejudiced" variety. In the film all the characters—white and people of color— act with prejudice. The filmmakers make racism appear to be just a problem of prejudiced people not treating each other with respect.[2]

It Was Unintentional

At this point, the group or individual with more power, who has clearly done something that resulted in some kind of devastation, might claim the damage was unintentional and therefore their responsibility was minimal. The batterer says, "I didn't intend to hit her." "I didn't mean to hit her so hard." "Things got out of hand."

First of all, claims of innocence by someone who has hurt you are always suspect. Adults are responsible for their actions and for the results of those actions. "I didn't mean to" is not an acceptable legal or moral excuse for being violent toward another person. Secondly, actual intent is often discernible from the pattern of action. When a man systematically tries to control a woman and then says, "I didn't mean to hit her," he is saying that he hoped to control her by non-physical means. When all else failed, he resorted to hitting. The issue is power and control. Intent is clearly evident in the entire pattern of behavior.

White people have claimed the near-eradication of Native Americans and their food supplies, hunting areas, and natural resources was the unintended result of European immigration. We now know that the complete elimination of Native Americans from the United States was government policy as well as part of the general, everyday discourse of white Americans (see Part IV for details).

Today we continue to claim racism is unintentional by saying, "Discrimination may happen, but most people are well intentioned." "They probably didn't mean it like that." "It was only a joke." Judge abuse by impact, not intention.

It's All Over Now

Another way to defuse responsibility is by claiming the violence happened in the past and is no longer an issue. The batterer may finally claim responsibility (often indirectly), but he asserts that things have changed. He says, "It's over with" or "I'll never do it again." Part of his claim is that the trauma, pain, and vulnerability should just be forgotten. This claim discounts the seriousness of the violence, blames the survivor for not being able to let go of it and move on, and focuses on the perpetrator's words, not his actions. Ignoring real injury, all he offers is a promise it won't happen again.

White people often claim genocide, land grabbing, and exploitation are things of the past. Most of our images of Indians reinforce that belief by focusing on Native Americans who lived 100 to 300 years ago. The reality is that effects of colonial violence are still readily apparent today: the small number of remaining Native Americans, their poor economic conditions, the alcoholism, the shattered traditions, and devastated communities are the direct result of 500 years of systematic oppression.

Furthermore, the same policies exist today as they did hundreds of years ago. Across the US and Canada, land is still being taken; treaties broken; Native culture, religion, and artifacts stolen and/or exploited. Native American nations are still denied sovereignty—their land, including their sacred sites, are still exploited and laid waste on a massive scale. Some of the violence takes different forms than it did 100 years ago. It is important we not use those differences to claim we are not responsible for the violence occurring today. When we are dealing with structural violence, the proof of change is structural change, not claims of innocence.

Today we claim racism is all over by saying, "Slavery was over a long time ago." "The days of land grabbing are long gone." "That was before the Civil Rights era." "There aren't any Indians left."

It's Only a Few People

If we are unable to maintain the violence was all in the past, we may switch to another tactic to make a current situation seem isolated. We might say it's really only a few people who are like that—racism is not systemic or institutionalized. In the case of domestic violence, we contend that only a few men are batterers; most men treat women well. However, if 31% of all women experience at least one incident of intimate partner abuse from a man over their lifetime— 4.8 million such incidents a year—then we are clearly talking about a social issue, not the isolated anger of a few men.[3]

Similarly, it wasn't just officers like Custer disobeying orders, or cruel, greedy men like Columbus, or a few cowboys who killed Native Americans. Slavery, genocide, and racism were built into the structure of all the institutions of our society and were everyday occurrences. We have inherited, perpetuated, and benefited from these actions. As long as these injustices continue, all of us are implicated.

Today we continue to use this tactic when we say, "Housing and job discrimination are the result of a few bigoted people." "The Far Right is behind the scapegoating of immigrants." "It's only neo-Nazis and Skinheads who do that sort of thing," or "Some people may be prejudiced but...."

Counterattack and Competing Victimization

When all else fails and responsibility for the violence is inexorably falling on the shoulders of those who committed the acts themselves, there is a counterattack, an attempt to claim a reversal of the power relationships. This approach is usually combined with the final tactic, competing victimization. An individual batterer might say, "She really has all the power in our family." "If I didn't hit her she would run all over me." On a national level, there are claims that women batter men too, women win child custody and men don't when divorce occurs, and there is too much male-bashing.

To counter this tactic, we must go back to what happened, who has power and what violence is being done. Who ended up in the hospital, and who remained in control of the family resources? In the claims above, we find that in more than 90% of intimate partner abuse involving systematic, persistent, and injurious violence, women are the victims.[4]

Some people claim people of color and women have so much power US society itself is threatened. We are told that Muslims, recent immigrants, and other people of color are dangerous and a threat to our national unity and way of life. White people are filing lawsuits against affirmative action, claiming to be the victims of racism.

We need to ask ourselves who was killed and who ended up with the land base of this country? Today, who has the jobs, who gets into the universities, who is paid more, and who gets more media attention for their concerns—white people or people of color?

Some white people are counterattacking by saying, "Political correctness rules the universities." "We just want our rights too." "They want special status." "They're taking away our jobs." Some of the things we say when we claim to be victims include: "White males have rights too." "I have it just as bad as anybody." "White people are under attack."

Even though all of these statements are demonstrably untrue, those with power have a lot at stake in maintaining the *status quo*. They will employ the tactics described above to defend their interests. We must be aware of these tactics and able to counter them.

White Fragility
and White Power

Robin diAngelo, in her insightful article on white fragility, writes, "White Fragility is a state in which even a minimum amount of racial stress becomes intolerable, triggering a range of defensive moves. These moves include the outward display of emotions such as anger, fear, and guilt, and behaviors such as argumentation, silence, and leaving the stress-inducing situation. These behaviors, in turn, function to reinstate white racial equilibrium."[1]

Think about the responses to racism you've noticed in yourself and in other white people.

- *What forms of white fragility, such as those diAngelo mentions, have you used to avoid dealing with racism?*
- *How have those responses impacted people of color?*
- *What have they cost you?*

White vulnerability can turn into aggression to attack the person (whether white or a person of color) bringing up racism, to recenter whiteness, and to end the conversation. Because the white person is tacitly calling on both a long history of silencing and abuse of people of color, and multiple levels of interpersonal, institutional, and cultural support to back them up, they are escalating the situation not just to extricate themselves from complicity, but to exert control. White response to racism may be triggered by feelings of emotional fragility and defensiveness, but white people under pressure usually end up using their white privilege to assert and strengthen white power.

Our strongest tools against white backlash and fragility are a critical analysis of who has power and an understanding of the patterns and consequences of present actions and policies. Parts IV, V, and VI of *Uprooting Racism* will help sharpen your analysis and increase your understanding of how racism plays out in current institutional and interpersonal practices.

"Thank You for Being Angry"

A PERSON OF COLOR angry about discrimination or harassment is doing us a service by pointing out something wrong, something contradicting the ideals of equality set forth in the US Constitution and Bill of Rights. They are bringing our attention to a problem that needs solving, a wrong that needs righting. We could convey our appreciation by saying, "Thank you, your anger has helped me see what's not right here." What keeps us from responding in this way?

Anger is a scary emotion in our society. In mainstream, white, middle-class, Christian culture, we are taught to be polite, never raise our voices, be reasonable and calm. People who are demonstrative of their feelings are discounted and ridiculed. We are told by parents to obey "because I said so." We are told by bosses, religious leaders, and other authorities not to challenge what they say, "or else" (you'll be fired, go to hell, be treated as mentally ill). When we have seen someone expressing anger, it has often been a person with power who was abusing us or someone else physically, verbally, or emotionally. We were hurt, scared, or possibly confused. Most of us can remember a time from our youth when a parent, teacher, or coach was yelling at us abusively. It may have made us afraid when those around us became angry. It may have made us afraid of our own anger.

Relationships between people of color and whites often begin as friendly and polite. We may be pleased we know and like a person from another cultural group, pleased they like us. We are encouraged because, despite our fears, it seems possible for people from different cultures to get along together. The friendship may confirm our feeling we are different from other white people.

But then the person of color becomes angry. Perhaps they are angry about something we said or did, or about a comment or action by someone else or about racism in general. We may take it personally and back off in response, fearing the relationship is falling apart. We fear we aren't liked anymore or have been found out to be racist.

For a person of color, this may be a time of hope the relationship can become more honest. The anger may be an attempt to test the depths and possibilities of the friendship. The person may be open about their feelings to see how safe we are, hoping we will not desert them. Or the anger may be a more assertive attempt to break through our complacency to address some core beliefs or actions.

Many white people have been taught to see anger and conflict as signs of personal failure. But anger and conflict may instead be signs we're becoming more honest, dealing with the real differences and problems in our lives. If it is not safe enough to disagree, express anger, and struggle with each other, what kind of relationship can we have?

We could say, "Thank you for pointing out the racism because I want to know whenever it is occurring," or "I appreciate your honesty. Let's see what we can do about this situation." Too often white people get scared and disappear or become defensive and counterattack—forms of white fragility described earlier. In any case, when we don't focus on the root of the problem, racism continues unimpeded.

When people of color are angry about racism, it is legitimate anger. It is not their oversensitivity but our lack of sensitivity that causes a communication gap. People of color are vulnerable to the abuse of racism everyday. They are experts on it. Most of us rarely notice it. In fact, white people consistently deny the existence of racism. Even before the civil rights gains of the mid-1960s, polls showed white people did not consider racism a problem and believed African Americans had opportunities equal to whites in the United States.[1] Recent polls confirm high levels of denial among white people of the impact of racism. Even with all the high-profile cases of unarmed black people being killed by police and persistent racism is all aspects of our society, a November, 2015 CNN/Kaiser Family Foundation poll found 57% of whites don't think racism is a big problem in the US.[2]

The anger and actions of people of color may call our attention to the injustice of racism. It is tremendously draining, costly, and personally devastating for people of color to have to rage about racism. They often end up losing their friends, their livelihoods, even their lives. Rather than attacking them for their anger, we need to examine the layers of complacency, ignorance, and privilege we have put into place that require so much outrage to get our attention.

The 1965 riots in Watts, California, as never before, brought attention to the ravages of racism on the African American population living there. In 1968 a national report by the Kerner Commission warned of the dangers of not addressing racial problems. Yet in 1992, when there were new uprisings in Los Angeles, white Americans focused again on the anger of African Americans, on containing that anger, protecting property, and controlling the community rather than on solving the problems that cause poverty, unemployment, crime, and high dropout rates. African Americans, Latinx, immigrants, other people of color, and their allies are frequently out in the streets protesting police brutality, cutbacks in human services, racial profiling, attacks on immigrants, and other forms of racism. The only way to break this cycle of rage is for white people to join in seriously addressing the sources of the anger, the causes of the problems. And in order to do that, we need to talk about racism directly with one another.

It's Good to Talk about Racism

RACISM HAS GREAT POWER partly because we don't talk about it. Talking about racism lessens its power and breaks our awful, uncomfortable silence. Talking about it makes it less scary.

Talking about racism is an opportunity to learn about people of color and to reclaim our lives and true histories. We can ask questions, learn, and grow in exciting ways previously denied us.

Talking about racism helps make our society safer for people of color and safer for us as well. Talking about it keeps us from passing racism on to our children. Talking about it allows us to do something about it.

We actually talk about race all the time, but we do it in code. Much in our discussions about economics, military issues, neighborhood affairs, public safety and welfare, education, sports, and movies is about race—but using code words. These words allow white people to speak about race or about people of color without the risk of being accused of racism. We can count on the connotations and implications of our words to convey meaning, and therefore we don't have to worry about being accountable for what we say.

I want to look briefly at eight words and phrases to decipher the meanings they contain, including the ways class perceptions are intertwined with racial ones. This analysis should help us challenge other white people when they use racial code words.

Underclass

Underclass generally stands for African Americans who are poor. It suggests they are a separate group from other poor people, a class by

themselves below the rest of us. It connotes hopelessness, desperation, and violence, implies that this group lives by values different
from ours and they have no ability to change their economic circumstances.

This word operates, like most racially coded words, by labeling a
particular group and then creating or exaggerating its characteristics so we feel completely separate from the group's members. The
negative qualities attributed to this group then become justifications for our treatment of "them."

African Americans have no monopoly on poverty in the US.
There are almost twice as many poor whites as poor blacks or Latinx.[1]
Nor is there a special "culture of poverty" (another racially coded
phrase). There are certainly significant negative effects of poverty,
but well-paying jobs, access to decent housing, and schooling have
been shown to mitigate most of these effects very quickly.

Welfare Mothers

This is another phrase that seems to have a clear definition but actually has several layers of racial meaning. For most white people, our
image is of an African American woman with several children who
lives rather well for long periods of time on welfare to avoid working
for a living. In turn, the expense of providing for welfare mothers
is said to be draining our country financially, contributing to the
national deficit, and providing a disincentive for African American
teens to work. The reality is quite different. Welfare recipients are
primarily women who have, on the average, two children and stay
on welfare for less than two years. Government assistance does not
provide more than poverty-level support. The average payment in
2014 for a family of three was $900 per month, or $10,800 per year.[2]
If you had two children, would you give up a job for this amount of
money? Would you be able to survive on it?

Inner City

Both of the terms examined above come together in this phrase. For
most white people, *inner city* means anywhere there are large con-

centrations of people of color, regardless of their economic status. The central sections of most large metropolitan areas in the US are highly diverse economically and racially. In many cities there are now neighborhoods of upper-income whites in gentrified houses and condos. Poor people in general, and women on government assistance in particular, can be found throughout the country, not just in urban areas. For example, in small towns, the suburbs, or in poor white Appalachian communities.

Illegal Alien

The use of the word *illegal* in this context is racist. No one is intrinsically illegal, and white people would never be described this way. When someone robs a bank or commits a murder, we do not say they are illegal; we say that they have committed an illegal act. In addition, the word *alien* sounds like immigrants are from another planet.

Which immigrants are legal or illegal at any particular time has always been a function of white-determined immigration policies. Today, discussion about undocumented residents or immigrants without papers focuses on Mexicans, Central and South Americans, and Asians but not on Canadians or Europeans. This racial bias justifies extending discriminatory policies such as racial profiling to legal residents and long-standing US citizens who are Spanish-speaking, while claiming that profiling is a legal not a racial issue.

Terrorist

Terrorist has become a code word for Arabs and Muslims. When using it, we can mask Islamophobic and anti-Arab statements and policies while ignoring the terrorist acts of white people and the US government, such as the bombings of civilian areas in Bosnia, Afghanistan, Pakistan, and Iraq. Domestically, according to the Center for Research on Globalization, over 90% of all so-called terrorist attacks carried out in the United States were by non-Muslims, overwhelmingly by white Christian men.[3]

Politically Correct

People of color and white allies have long been challenging disrespectful and abusive language as well as discriminatory policies and practices. People opposed to racial progress use *politically correct* to divert attention from racism by counterattacking the people who are challenging it. The people who use these words claim to be concerned about freedom of speech but avoid addressing issues of discrimination and harassment.

Invasion

Why don't we ever say Europeans invaded North America? Didn't the US invade Afghanistan and Iraq? Most of the time, we use the word *invasion* to set ourselves up as victims, describing how we—white Americans—are being invaded by Japanese investment, Chinese imports, people of color moving into "our" neighborhood, or Haitian refugees. We avoid the word when it might accurately focus attention on our country's role attacking others.

Model Minority

White people use this phrase the way we refer to well-behaved children. Implicit in the statement is a comparison to badly behaved children. Groups labeled *model minority*, often Asian Americans, are judged by white people to behave well by white standards and are contrasted with groups judged unruly, ungrateful, or unsuccessful. This label, while seemingly positive, is still a stereotype applied indiscriminately to an entire community. It overlooks the complexity of Asian American communities, judges the entire group by white standards of obedience, docility, and accommodation and is used to berate, by implication, African Americans or Latinx for not behaving in these ways.

- *Crime, gentrification, busing, taxes, quotas, state's rights, reverse racism, hard working, all-American, zero tolerance, pioneer, frontier, discover, and thug are other code words and phrases. How would you decipher them to another white person? What are other code words have you heard white people use to talk about people of color, avoiding overt racial references?*

We can only develop effective strategies for uprooting racism with language that reflects reality. The use of racially coded words allows white people to build white racial solidarity and blame people of color for racism while strengthening the racial hierarchy.

Who Is a Victim?

SOME OF US BELIEVE being a victim has a certain glamour. We may think victims get more attention, more respect or simply have some inherently virtuous quality. We may even believe some people prefer to be victims and take active steps to achieve victim status. And sometimes, those of us with more power or privilege or less vulnerability to violence may think the way to redirect attention, resources, or virtue back to ourselves is to claim that we are victims too.

Men do this in custody cases, counter-harassment and discrimination suits, and in charges of reverse discrimination. White people do this routinely when they protest affirmative action and reparative programs for people of color.

There is nothing, absolutely nothing, good about being a victim. Being a victim means you were not powerful enough to protect yourself from someone else's abuse. Those who have been raped, robbed, battered, harassed, or discriminated against know how painful and long-lasting the effects of abuse can be. Nor is it necessarily safe to step forward and describe one's victimization. Survivors of abuse are routinely blamed, not believed, and thus revictimized.

Claiming to be victimized is not the same as being victimized. In order to understand clearly who was victimized, we must ask the questions "Who has the power?" and "Who did what to whom?"

Actual reverse discrimination is rare, and many claims lack merit. Charges of reverse racism are usually a white strategy to deny white racism and attack attempts to promote racial justice. We know discrimination against people of color is extensive and pervasive in our society. Every year there are thousands of discrimination cases brought forward, many of them class action suits involving tens of thousands of plaintiffs. A study from the National Bureau of Economic Research showed that discrimination plays a large part in the job market. But it's not discrimination against white people: for every 15 resumes someone with an African American-sounding name sends out, they will receive one callback while an individual with a white-sounding name sending out the exact same resume will receive one callback for every ten they send out.[1]

What is going on when white people claim reverse racism or claim to be victimized by people of color? Often we are being victimized, but not by people of color. We may be economically exploited by white-owned corporations that move jobs overseas, leaving our communities stranded and some of us unemployed. Deceived about the true cause of our exploitation, we are incited to blame people of color and recent immigrants.

An individual white person can be abused by a person of color. This is unfair and needs to be addressed. Any person can decide to hurt other people. However, in the chapters on white benefits and the costs of racism, we have seen that whites are not victims of people of color in any way similar to how people of color are hurt by racism everyday, in every aspect of their lives.

PART II

The Dynamics of Racism

The Enemy Within

ONE OF THE PURPOSES of racism and religious-based oppression is to keep people of color, Muslims, Jews, and others at the center of attention while keeping white people in general, and white male Christians in particular, at the center of power and at the top of the economic pyramid. The majority of people in the US have been abused, economically exploited, and discriminated against. We experience tremendous physical, economic, and emotional loss from social inequity and personal abuse. Like the proverbial thief who points off in the distance to get you to look away and then deftly picks your pocket, systems of oppression divert our attention from those who have the real power to rob and hurt us. In our pain and anger, we often turn against traditional scapegoats and blame people who are less powerful than we are.

People of color, immigrants, and people who are not Christian have long been portrayed as economic threats to white Americans. We have heard and perhaps used phrases like "They take away our jobs." "They are a drain on our economic system, eating up benefits." "They drive wages down." Or, about Jewish people in particular, "They control everything." "They rob us blind."

In fact, these targeted groups of people are not the ones who make the economic decisions that affect our communities. Corporate leaders lower wages, inflate prices, and sell us shoddy and dangerous products with impunity. In the US, there has been an enormous redistribution of income toward the rich in the last 40 years, while the standards of living for the rest of us have decreased.[1] Simultaneously, our national infrastructure has deteriorated, living wage jobs and affordable housing are beyond the reach of millions, and our schools are falling apart. We hurt ourselves and make it impossible to solve our social problems when we don't understand the economic basis of racism. Meanwhile, the rich keep getting richer.

In order to address racism effectively, we need to become better at analyzing where real power lies. Which groups are making important political and economic decisions and which are being blamed

2.1. Where Does Economic Power Lie?

1. In your community, which corporations are the largest employers?
2. What decisions has this group made in the last few years that have affected employment levels and wages (e.g., opening or closing offices or plants, downsizing or moving production abroad)?
3. Which companies were taken over or bought out? Who took over and what happened to jobs, wages, and working conditions after the take-over?
4. How would you describe the people who own these companies? Are they mostly or exclusively white? Are they primarily Christian? Are they men? (The fact that those who gain most are well-off Christian white men does not mean that most Christian white men benefit from their actions.)
5. Which particular racial groups are being blamed for economic and social problems in your local area? In your state?
6. How much money have businesses put into promoting this scapegoating through political contributions, lobbying, political ads, or public campaigns?
7. How do you benefit and what do you lose from these actions?

or scapegoated? The seven questions can guide you in making such an analysis.

The relationship between these issues is complex, and I have only sketched the briefest outline here.[2] Even so, it should be clear that effective action against racism makes the white community stronger and safer, and allows us to join in multiracial alliance with people of color in the struggle for economic justice. Most white people have as much to gain as people of color from the struggle to redistribute wealth to poor, working-, and middle-class communities. Rather than letting racism divide us, let's work together.

Fear and Danger

MANY OF US in the United States today are afraid. We worry about crime, drugs, our children's future, and our own security. Our fear, a result of many social and personal factors, is also linked to violence and messages of danger in the media. Racism helps produce a fear-based society in which no one feels safe. However, *being afraid is not the same as being in danger*.

For example, white people often fear people of color, and most people of color fear white people. White people are not usually in danger from people of color, whereas people of color are in danger of individual acts of discrimination, hate crimes, and police brutality at the hands of white people, as well as of institutional practices that kill people due to lack of health care and affordable housing and lack of police protection. White people are rarely killed, harassed, or discriminated against by people of color.

- *Have you ever been in your car when a person of color drove past? Did you reach over to lock your car door?*
- *When a man of color walks by, do you touch your wallet or purse or hold it tighter?*
- *Have you ever watched suspiciously, closed a window, pulled a blind, locked a door, or called the police when you saw a person of color in your neighborhood?*
- *Have you ever had an adult or young person of color in your house and wondered, ever so briefly, if valuables were out?*

- *Have you ever seen a person of color with quality clothes, an expensive car, or other valuable items and wondered how they got the money to buy them?*

I have done all of these things because I was taught to fear people of color. Growing up in Los Angeles in the 1950s and early 1960s, I heard repeated stories about the "masses of Mexican and Central-American people pushing against our borders, pressing to get in and overwhelm us." I remember a discussion with my parents in which I said I didn't think I wanted to have children because there were already so many people in the world. My parents tried to convince me it was important I have children because I was smart and educated and we needed "more of our kind." I understood "our kind" to be white. I was getting the message that white people had to defend ourselves, reproduce ourselves, and protect what was ours because we were under attack.

The patterns I learned have a long history. Over the course of 240 years of slavery, white people feared enslaved Africans even though they were so thoroughly dominated and publicly and routinely brutalized as to offer little threat to whites. Individual white settlers who took Native American land feared retaliation. But many white people lived in cities and were not worried about Indian attack. White settlers, in conjunction with the US government which wanted to "open up" Native American land, had to convince the public Native Americans were dangerous and needed to be exterminated. A campaign, using books, pictures, and the media, created images of Indians as primitive, cruel savages who wanted to kill white men and rape white women. There was even a special genre of story called *captivity narratives* (accounts of white women allegedly abducted, raped, and tortured by Indians) which built anti-Indian sentiment in white people.[1] This campaign made it easier to justify the appropriation of Native American lands and the killing or removal of Native Americans themselves. In the process, generations of us learned to fear Indians. Many young people growing up today still do, even though there are only about 5.2 million Native Americans in the United States—about 2% of the population.[2]

Constant reinforcement of white fear continues today. We still see selected news coverage presenting men of color, particularly African American, Latino, Native American, and Arab American men, as the embodiment of danger, making it difficult for any white person not to have an immediate feeling of fear in their presence. This fear, in turn, has justified massive and continuous control of communities of color through the schools, police, legal system, jails, prisons, and immigration system. This control starts in preschool or elementary school. It limits educational opportunities, jobs, skills, and access to health care. It is enforced by police brutality and various forms of discrimination. These conditions in turn produce stress, despair, and desperation for young men of color, leading to their killing each other and themselves at high rates, living several years less than white men on average.[3] White violence leads to white fear of retaliation, which is used to justify further white violence. Communities of color, not white people, are the victims of this cycle of violence.

On the one hand, Arab Americans and Muslims are victims of discrimination, stereotyping, and hate crimes and are portrayed as fanatical terrorists who will stop at nothing to kill us. On the other hand, the US government continues to use military force to disrupt the lives of Iraqis, Afghanis, and Pakistanis, resulting in the deaths of hundreds of thousands. While Arab Americans and Muslims are under attack in the US and elsewhere, white Americans are in comparatively little danger. The misrepresentation and demonization is so extreme I cannot remember the last time I saw a positive image of an Arab or Arab American in the mainstream US media.

Jewish people have likewise been portrayed as dangerous—economically dangerous. Stereotypes of crafty, unscrupulous Jews who own the banks and control Hollywood contribute to such anti-Jewish fears. In fact, Christians own most banks and other major corporations (including media conglomerates), and it is Christian wealth and power that determines political, economic, and cultural deci-sions.[4] Christian fear works, like all racial fear, to divert people from the source of danger—people inside the mainstream who wield power. Jews are blamed for economic problems for which they are not responsible, and they become the targets of further anti-Jewish violence.

Jewish people in the United States have been subject to verbal and physical attack, bombings, desecration of cemeteries, intimida-tion, and murder by white Christians. Jews have not attacked Chris-tians for being Christian. Again we can see that although the fear is mutual, Jewish people are in some danger from Christians whereas Christians are in no danger of being attacked by Jews.

Jews who are white are taught to fear people of color. Many white Jewish concerns about violence focus on danger from African Ameri-cans, even though most anti-Jewish violence is committed by white Christians.

Many times we use stories to justify the fear we feel toward peo-ple of color. We might introduce them by such phrases as "I was attacked once by...," "I don't want to sound prejudiced, but I know someone who had a bad experience with...," or "It's unfortunate, but my one negative experience was...." We then use these single examples to reinforce a stereotype about a whole category of peo-ple and to prove our fear is legitimate. Even if true (and many are not), anecdotes don't counter the fact that people of color are many times more likely to experience violence from white people than the reverse.

- *Is there a story you use to justify your fears of people of color?*
- *What stories have you heard other white people use?*

Sharing such stories can strengthen white solidarity against others, implying we share a common danger. Scary anecdotes reinforce our desire to be with white people and to avoid people of color. They also raise the stakes if we challenge racism, because to do so seems to threaten our own security. How can we challenge other whites when we may need them in case of an attack?

Sometimes, when I realize the extent of the stereotypes I have learned and act from, I want to disavow fear altogether and convince myself there is nothing to be afraid of. Or, to counter the stereotype, I try to assume all men of color are safe and all white men are dangerous. Yet I know I am foolish if I simply reverse stereotypes. In a society in which some people are dangerous and violence is a threat, we need to evaluate the danger from each person we're with. Any preconceived notion of danger or safety based on skin color is dysfunctional—it can actually increase our danger and make us less able to protect ourselves. For example, even as white women have moved to the suburbs, put locks on their doors and windows, and avoided urban streets at night, they have remained vulnerable to much more common physical and sexual assault from white male friends, lovers, neighbors, and coworkers.

Approximately 80% of sexual violence is committed within the same racial group by heterosexual men who know their victim.[5] If we and our children are beaten or sexually assaulted, it is most likely to be by known heterosexual white men. We justify public policies that disproportionately lock up men of color, but these changes do not make life safer for us. To use James Baldwin's phrase, on many levels racism creates an "illusion of safety" for white people.

- *Was there ever a time when you heard about violence a white man committed and said to yourself, "I never would have imagined that so-and-so could have done something like that"?*

We are often awarded a presumption of innocence if we are white; other white people assume we are safe until proven dangerous. This works to our benefit when we are stopped by the police, shopping in a store, walking down the street, or renting equipment such as cars, tools, or movies.

- *Have you ever been surprised that a Latino or African American man could commit a particular act of violence?*

We carry a presumption of guilt for men of color, expecting them to be dangerous. For example, when Susan Smith killed her two children, she claimed an African American man had kidnapped them. When Charles Stuart killed his pregnant wife in Boston, he stabbed himself and claimed an African American man had attacked them. In September, 2010, a 15-year-old San Diego girl told her parents and police she'd been kidnapped and raped by three Latino men. Before she admitted the entire story was fabricated, the police had conducted an intense manhunt in the community.[6] When the federal building in Oklahoma City was bombed, most people immediately suspected Arab men as the culprits. In each situation, the search for the guilty white man was temporarily diverted toward men of color.

Our personal vigilance is often increased when people of color are present and relaxed when only white people are around. These expectations translate into feeling uneasy whenever we are with significant numbers of people of color. This tendency to fear people of color also leads white people to exaggerate wildly how many there actually are in our society. According to a Gallup Poll, the average US American thinks 21% of the population are Hispanic, when the real number is 17.6; that 32% are black, when the real figure is 12.3; and that a large percentage are Jewish, when the actual figure is 2.2%. Not even counting Asian Americans, Arab Americans, and Native Americans, many people in the US think people of color constitute a large majority, when the combined non-white population is a little more than ⅓ of the total population.[7]

All of us who are white need to recognize just how deeply we have been trained to fear and distrust people of color, Jews, and Muslims. This fear guides our behavior because fear is easily manipulated by politicians, the media, and corporate leaders. For example, since the beginning of the Civil Rights movement, Malcolm X, Huey Newton, Eldridge Cleaver, Martin Luther King, Jr., Angela Davis, "Willie"

Horton, Mumia Abu-Jamal, Jesse Jackson, many African American rappers, and even President Obama have all been used to symbolize danger and to manipulate white people's fears. As our fears of people of color increase, we are more easily deceived by white leaders who give themselves an aura of trustworthiness simply because they are, by contrast, white.

As white people, we can start by acknowledging the violence we have done to people of color throughout our history. Our fear of violence to ourselves is related to the violence we have done and continue to do to others. We must understand how we have demonized others to justify that violence. Therefore, one way to lower our fear is to acknowledge and reduce white violence.

The Geography of Fear

THERE IS ALSO FEAR of being in certain places and certain kinds of spaces. For example, we are all taught to fear violence in the *inner city* (code words for where African Americans and Latinx live).

There is certainly more street crime in low-income neighborhoods. There are not necessarily more family violence, drugs, or economic crime. In any case, most of the crime and violence in low-income areas is not racially motivated: people of color are the most common targets of crime by people of color, and white people are the most common targets of crime by white people.[1] We tend to think we are particularly vulnerable in low-income neighborhoods because of the racism of people of color, but I have found no evidence that this is so.

There are many areas in which straight white males feel fairly safe. They can roam the countryside and the suburbs and can be alone in the woods, at the beach, or in the hills and not worry about being assaulted. White women alone are much less safe than white men alone, but white women with other women or with a man are not usually attacked. White lesbians, gay men, and bisexuals are less safe than heterosexual white people.

- *In what areas do you routinely feel safe? Why? How safe do you think people of color feel in those areas you feel safest in?*

Except in neighborhoods predominantly populated by people of a single ethnic group—where people are still vulnerable to higher

103

levels of street crime and the threat of police harassment, false arrest, and police brutality—people of color are not safe alone or in groups, neither on the streets or in their houses. In other areas they are verbally attacked; harassed by police; "mistaken" for gardeners, servants, or delivery people; and shunned or followed by shopkeepers. They are mistrusted, and their legitimacy is routinely questioned by whites.

The case of Dr. Henry Louis Gates, Jr., a prominent, internationally known professor at Harvard, shows that even educational and class privilege do not protect people of color from white intrusion. Upon returning to his home a couple of blocks from Harvard, Gates' attempt to enter his own home through his front door, which had a poorly working lock, was reported to the police by a neighbor. The police arrived, and within a few minutes, Gates was arrested in his own house and taken to the police station even though he had a Harvard ID and a driver's license, both showing his picture and the license showing his address.[2]

To sum up, there is nowhere men and women of color are safe from crime, violence, or white racism. Whites, on the other hand, are seldom vulnerable to violence from people of color and can generally avoid high-crime areas unless forced by economic circumstances to live or work in one. As white people, we have been trained to see danger in the very presence of people of color. This will not change until we alter the negative images and portrayals of people of color in our society and learn to welcome and value positively their presence and participation.

Exotic and Erotic

- *Have you ever imagined it would be exotic, erotic, or exciting to have sexual relations with a person of color, a Muslim, or Jewish person? Have you ever been in a dating or longer-term relationship with someone from one of these groups where these feelings were present?*

Racism, anti-Muslim, and anti-Jewish oppression overlap in the *eroticization of difference*.[1] White people's images of people of color, Muslim and Jewish people make them seem not only dangerous, but also exotic and erotic. Men of color, including Irish men and men from southern and eastern Europe (at times when they were not considered to be white), as well as Muslim and Jewish men have been portrayed as wild, bestial, aggressive sexual beings with little or no restraint and insatiable appetites for white (Christian) women. White men have been trained to see these men as sexual rivals and to protect white women from them.

Similarly, our dominant culture portrays women of color, Muslim and Jewish women as more passionate and sensual than white Christian women. Through economic systems of exploitation, women of color have been available to white men as slaves, domestic help, factory workers, childcare workers, and sex industry workers. White men have been able to sexually exploit these women and then justify their abuse by citing the sexual nature of their victims. In fact, sexual exploitation of women who are vulnerable says more about the sexual predation of white men than of anyone else.

White people have eroticized African Americans more than any other group. African American slaves were seen as sexual commodities, particularly after the slave trade was declared illegal. The ability of African American women to reproduce and increase the slave owner's "capital" (workforce) was nearly as important as their ability to work.

After the Civil War, when African Americans were no longer protected or valued as slaves, lynching became one form of repression against the African American community. Before that time, there were almost no reports of African American men raping white women. During the first years that lynching was prevalent, rape was not a frequent justification.

After the Reconstruction period, African Americans were no longer a credible threat to white people because of the dismantling of post-Civil War rights and the beginning of Jim Crow segregation. Lynching began to be justified by appeals to white people's fear of sexual aggression by African American men. Even then, rape of white women was only alleged in about ⅓ of the situations where men were lynched. It was only after many more years that lynching became primarily justified by claims of African American men's sexual aggression toward white women.[2] Lynching was a method to control an ex-slave population feared to be unruly and potentially dangerous—a way to terrorize them into not using their newly won freedom. Ironically, lynchings themselves became forms of eroticized violence as white men castrated and mutilated African American men.

Disproportionate criminalization and punishment of African American men for violence against women continues today in media images of African American men as sexual predators and in the disproportionate arrest, sentencing, and incarceration of African American men for sexual offences.

White women are taught that men of color are highly sexual beings whose very gaze will assault them.[3] They are told they "need" strong, aggressive, and armed white men to protect them from this menace.

White women are also taught to regard women of color as competitors—temptresses and seducers of white men. This training adds to the general images of danger associated with people of color and makes it difficult for white women to regard women of color as allies. The solidarity between women needed in the struggle against sexism is undermined by racial violence and by white women's fear and mistrust.

At times, white women's groups have supported attacks against the African American community in the name of women's safety. In the late 19th century, the US National American Woman's Suffrage Association (NAWSA) refused to take a stand against lynching and mob violence and asked Frederick Douglass, a black man and a staunch supporter of suffrage, not to come to meetings in the South because they did not want to jeopardize white southern support. The association did not support the organizing of chapters by black women for the same reason. Eventually arguments within the organization became more explicitly racist. White women argued that if they could vote, it would buttress the supremacy of the white race against the demands of black people, Indians, and newly colonized Spanish-speaking people.[4]

More recently in the 1970s, 80s, and 90s, the rape prevention and domestic violence prevention movements have called for stronger police and criminal/legal response to violence against women. At times these calls have inadvertently contributed to the targeting of African American men because they have not taken into account racial profiling, racial bias in the legal system, and the use of rape and assault charges to physically control men of color.[5] Women of color-led organizations report that this strategy makes it more difficult for women of color because calling the police for assistance can put them and their families in danger.[6]

At other times, white women's groups have been strong, if belated, allies to African American women and men in the fight against lynching, mob violence, and false accusations of rape. The Association of Southern Women for the Prevention of Lynching did important and effective work through petition drives, letters, and demonstrations. It was formed in 1930, after decades of pioneering work by black women organizers such as Ida B. Wells, Mary Church Terrell, and Mary Talbert.[7]

Similarly, there have always been some strong and vocal white women in the rape prevention and domestic violence prevention movements, supporting women of color in leadership positions, re-examining police and criminal/legal responses to violence against women, and developing an analysis that includes an understanding of race and class.[8]

Race and gender intersect in African American women's lives. This crucial perspective has given them the ability to challenge the limited focus of much political work in the US. African American women have long challenged men and white women in political leadership to sort out the myths and the realities of race- and gender-based violence. Sojourner Truth, Ida B. Wells, Josephine St. Pierre Ruffin, Mary Church Terrell, Lucy Parsons, Claudia Jones, and Frances E.W. Harper were some of the African American women leaders in the abolition, anti-lynching, and women's suffrage movements who understood the connections between gender and racial violence and provided constant challenges to the exclusive focus of each of these movements.

Today some of the most nuanced analyses of the intersections of race, gender, and class issues are in the writings of women of color and women who are Muslim, Hindu, or Jewish. Not only African American women such as Angela Davis, Paula Giddings, Patricia Hill Collins, Beth Richie, Joy James, Alisa Garza, and bell hooks but also women from differing cultural backgrounds—Cherrie Moraga, Gloria Anzaldua, Andrea Dworkin, Janice Mirikitani, Beth Brant, Chrystos, Trinh T. Minh-ha, Paula Gunn Allen, Melanie Kaye-Kantrowitz, Pat Mora, Winona LaDuke, M. Annette Jaimes and Haunani-Kay Trask—provide insightful analysis.

The previous chapter on fear and danger and this chapter on sexuality are even more intertwined than I have indicated. The merging of sex and violence with racism in our society makes people of color, who are seen as dangerous, also seem erotic. Conversely, because of Christian-based prohibitions about sexual expression, erotic projections onto people of color make them seem more dangerous. For young white people, taboos against interracial or interfaith sexual relationships, coupled with the eroticized stereotyping of people of color and others, make having relationships with these people a gesture of rebellion against white Christian norms. A sexual relationship with a person outside the norm becomes attractive—both arousing and dangerous. Given the stereotypes and the symbolism involved, any person of color—male, female, or transgender, lesbian, gay, or heterosexual—will provide some risk and therefore some excitement and attraction.

Projections, stereotypes, and symbolic values are part of all white people's conceptual baggage and affect our actual relationships with people of color. While some white people have used people of color to make their sexual lives more erotic or thrilling or to defy white (and parental) standards, there are residues of these erotic elements in our relationships with people of color even when we are not sexually involved with them. These residues interfere with our ability to treat them as valued and respected people.

This sense of the erotic and dangerous nature of people of color gets attached not only to their bodies, but also to their music, art, and other elements of their culture. Music like rock and roll and rap has been sources of intergenerational conflict in white families. National discussions about gender and family issues such as rape, domestic violence, teenage sexuality, sexual harassment, marital infidelity, interracial dating, and miscegenation often have explicit and implicit racial references.

The sexuality we project onto people of color tells us a great deal about white concepts of virtue and immorality, little about white practice, and nothing at all about people of color. If we don't examine the sexual ideology of (Christian) whiteness, we will continue to be directed by our sexual fears and fantasies, leading us to commit injustice even as we claim to uphold virtue.

The Myth of the Happy Family

IN ADDITION TO our understanding of sexuality, white people have certain understandings of what a family is and what family relationships should be like. These too are affected by racism.

- *What did you learn as a child about what a family was?*
- *What did your parents convey?*
- *What did you learn from TV and movies?*

The word *family* conveys good feelings. It is perhaps easier today than in the past to acknowledge the existence of incest, domestic violence, alcoholism, other drug abuse, and neglect, but it remains hard to see that many families function because they provide caring, support, and nurturing for some members at the expense of others.

Because of violence and unequal power, we are not equally privileged or equally safe within our families. Those of us who are safe, cared for, and thriving—or at least not vulnerable to physical or sexual violence—might have a sense of being part of a happy family, even while some members of the family are abusing others.

We believe that if everyone plays their part in a family, then the whole unit works. Each person has a role, with a set of responsibilities and privileges within the family. For most of us, this means a hierarchy where some people—such as parents, men, or elders—have more power and authority than others, such as women and younger people. The title of an old TV show, *Father Knows Best*, captured this notion: people don't know best for themselves, so they should defer to father/authority.

The majority may label people who say they are unhappy in a family or who reject its hierarchy as homewreckers who break up the family, create divisions, and disrupt the smooth functioning of the group. Those suffering in family groups are called names like rabble-rouser, complainer, whiner, rebel, or teenager; they are described as too angry, loud, and aggressive. In the 1970s and 1980s, men used these same terms to silence or discount women who were challenging incest, domestic violence, and inequality in the family. The presumption was everything was OK until women started to complain.

Racial relations in the US are often described as if people were all a big family.[1] If people of color point out racism in our neighborhoods, workplaces, or schools, white people generally react with one of two responses. The first is to defend "the family" and cast out the troublemaking person of color. "Things were just fine before you got here and made it into a problem. You can just go back to where you came from if you don't like it." (This response also makes it seem like those who are dissatisfied have no right to be present.)

The second response is to reassert white people's role as the benevolent parents who know what's best for the family. People of color are seen as rebellious or ungrateful children. The white perspective is the "overview," the apparently dispassionate consideration of everyone's interests. If the children weren't so angry and rebellious and would just leave decisions to us, we would work it out and take care of their needs too.

Just as child abuse, domestic violence, and marital rape are denied and covered over by the myth of the happy nuclear family, so too racism, poverty, and discrimination are covered over by the myth of the happy social community. Our families and family-like groups will always look happy to those with more power and privilege and will always be dangerous for those with less.

- *Have you ever been in a situation formerly all-white and subsequently integrated? Did the person (or people) of color raise issues of racism? How did others respond?*
- *Did the racism they identified exist before they arrived?*

I worked at a small nonprofit community agency at a time when all the staff was white. After some discussions about racism, we decided the next person we hired would be a person of color. We subsequently hired a Latina (I'll call her Sylvia) to join our staff. We felt very satisfied with what we had done. After all, our racism led us to believe we were taking a risk in order to do the right thing.

After working with us for a while, Sylvia began to bring to our attention various ways we were discounting her experience and excluding her from decision-making. In addition, she pointed out how we were not serving Latinx clients well.

Some of us became very upset and felt attacked and discounted. It seemed like we had *more* racism now that Sylvia was on staff. It was easier before she came because we didn't have to watch what we said or did. She was labeled a troublemaker by some and called ungrateful by others. But neither she nor the problems would go away. We were eventually forced to take Sylvia's complaints seriously and decide what to do about them. Even then, we did not include her or other Latinx in the process.

All of our responses had elements of the happy family syndrome in them. The racism Sylvia identified existed before she arrived, but we blamed her. Paternalistically, we felt she was unappreciative of all we had done for her. When we acknowledged racial problems, we still felt that we, the white people, should decide how best to fix things. We were the parents and she was the child, and the parents knew what was best.

Sylvia didn't stay long with this organization. However, the group did learn some lessons about how our expectations regarding her and our roles prevented us from acting effectively to identify and solve racial problems.

- *Many of us will be in all-white situations that become racially integrated.*
- *What can you do to support people of color if they are attacked for pointing out racism?*

Beyond Black and White

WHEN I BECAME an adult and looked back on my childhood, I thought racism referred to black-white relations. When I began to read about racism, I came across books about the civil rights struggle, slavery, and the black power movement.

When I looked more closely at my childhood, I began to notice *other* people of color in my life who were less visible but still present. I watched Westerns and played cowboys and Indians with my friends; my food was grown by Latinx farmworkers; the parks I played in were maintained by Japanese American gardeners; the high school I went to employed Latinx custodians and used a Native American mascot (the Birmingham Braves); and when my parents sold our house in West Los Angeles to a Japanese American family, they received hate calls because of it.

There are important reasons why the African American struggle for justice and equality is at the forefront of US consciousness. The existence of slavery and Jim Crow segregation and the struggles for justice led by African Americans have been defining historical forces in our development as a nation. African Americans have powerfully and unrelentingly challenged the myths of US democracy and economic opportunity.

However, US society is not just black and white. Many people in this society are bicultural. Many people of color and white people are of racially mixed heritage. Some people of color are so light that they can pass as white.

A black-white division makes it seem as if white people are

homogeneous. On the contrary, what counts as white has been contested throughout US history. For example, people from the Middle
East have been primarily considered white in our courts and people
of color on our streets. There is tremendous complexity, intermingling, struggle for inclusion, and resistance to incorporation within
European heritages and histories alone.

Nor has African American culture been homogeneous. Some
African Americans have been free for hundreds of years; others remained virtually enslaved until just a generation ago. African Americans came from complex and very different African cultures and
retained some of those differences for long periods in this country.
African Americans have intermarried with Native Americans and
with members of other ethnic groups. Ethnic, regional, and class
differences make most generalizations about African Americans
tenuous at best.

The division of racial discussion into black and white is misleading in other ways.

1. It obscures the long and devastating struggle of *Native Americans* for survival, cultural autonomy, and sovereignty. Their
   struggle is largely misunderstood because it is so different from
   the African American struggle.
2. The struggle of *Spanish-speaking peoples*, which is heavily
   intertwined with Native American struggles since both include
   resistance to colonization, is ignored and trivialized.
3. In a similar way, the presence, diversity, and achievements
   of the many different *Asian, Pacific Islander, and Asian and South
   Asian American* communities are lumped together as one and
   oversimplified. Asian and South Asian Americans are invisible
   in much of white culture and are usually excluded from political representation and social power.

Black-white thinking renders us unable to understand and develop
truly multicultural environments. Racism is an issue not only for
large cities. Most communities in the United States are multiracial.

There are often Native Americans, Latinx, Asian Americans, and Arab Americans in communities where no African Americans are present.

- Which communities of color are routinely ignored or not seen by white people you know?
- What groups are habitually left out in your thinking?

Conversely, we may believe we have integrated an event, neighborhood, or workplace if there are African Americans present, even though other groups are absent. This belief can foster opportunism. On the one hand, white people can claim that if we are addressing African American concerns we are speaking about the concerns of all people of color. On the other hand, we can avoid dealing with the harsh effects of racism on the African American community by pointing to examples of the integration or progress of other non-white groups such as Asian Americans.

We must delve into *complexity*: we cannot be satisfied with what has been achieved. We have to keep asking the questions "Who is still excluded?" "Who remains unseen?" "Who is still being exploited?" When new groups of immigrants arrive from Africa, South Asia, or South America, we cannot conveniently forget that long-established communities of color still face racism everyday.

Nor can we say we should put our attention on groups with more members. Racist actions and policies in the past have determined the numbers of people in particular communities of color living today in the United States. The breeding of slaves, the killing of Native Americans, and restrictions on Asian immigration have all helped to determine how many people of color from different cultures are currently in this country. More importantly, human dignity and opportunity are not measured in quantities. Relatively small population groups such as Native Americans deserve large amounts of reparations.

Complexity also exists within the categories we use. "People of color," "Asian American," "South Asian," or even "Korean American" as categories may confuse and mislead us more than they help. We need to be talking about inclusion within categories. If we are talking about the Korean American community or the Lakota community or the Salvadoran community, we need to ask, "Are the women of that community included? Are the young people? Are the elders? Are the poor, those who are queer and trans, and the physically challenged included?"

Democracy means the inclusion of *all people* in the process of making the decisions affecting their lives. Our society is undemocratic to the extent anyone is excluded from decision-making processes. Fighting racism means extending democracy to include all people of color and moving beyond a black-white—or even a simple white–people of color focus.

What's in a Name?

THE WORDS WE USE to describe groups of people have developed historically within the system of racism. These words have changed and continue to change, partly in response to the struggle to end racism, and partly in the resistance to and backlash against that struggle. All of our vocabulary is inadequate and frustrating. However, there is much to learn from attempts to use accurate and respectful language. It is important we pay attention to the words we use because language itself is used to maintain racism.

The phrase "people of color," which I use in this book, is one such problematic term. Every human being is a person of color. The word "white" (which has been used to describe European Americans) does not reflect anyone's skin color so much as a concept of racial purity that has never existed. I use the phrases "people of color" and "communities of color" to suggest the multitude of peoples and cultures exploited by European American society for the last 500 years. However, if we are not careful, this term will allow whiteness to stay unmarked at the center of power, while all other groups are "colorful" and marked as different. Even the phrase "European American" as a substitute for white is a problem because there have been communities of different skin colors, origins, and cultures in Europe for centuries. Used as a racial descriptor, the phrase denies non-white Europeans their history and presence.

Other troublesome words used to refer to people of color include:
- *minority*—People of color are a majority of the world's population and a majority in some of our communities.
- *third world*—This implies people come from somewhere else

and don't belong in our communities; third also implies less worth than first or second.

- *non-white*—This term equates white as the norm or standard and everything else as different or "non," i.e., negative.

The phrase "people of color" itself covers over so much complexity and diversity it's sometimes more useful to state explicitly the group of people being referred to. However, African American, Asian American, Arab American, Native American, or Latinx—each of these terms are also abstractions, engulfing the particular lives of millions of people.

More specific referents like Japanese American, Hopi, or Puerto Rican are still generalizations hiding significant differences; they can give a false appearance of inclusiveness. The male bias of our society also gives most racial terms a male identification. I keep the gender-neutral form *Latinx* precisely to remind us that women, men, and people who are transgender are included in this category.

- *Who else is excluded from these racially defined categories?*
- *Does African American connote "poor" to white people?*
- *Does Latino mean heterosexual?*
- *Does Asian American assume able-bodied?*

Racial referents can be coded for specific meanings relating to class, sexual orientation, and physical ability, reflecting broad patterns of inequality within our society.

Language is important not because it should or can be *correct*, but because it should convey respect for and dignity to the people referred to. Everyone should have the choice to name themselves. Many Native Americans, African Americans, and immigrants from around the world had their names taken from them and were re-named by missionaries, immigration officials, slave owners, military officers, teachers, and representatives of government agencies.[1] Re-claiming lost names, rejecting demeaning names, renaming oneself, or reclaiming geographic names is a powerful step for an individual or group to take because it challenges the history of subordination in which others have dictated your name.

Sometimes there is not agreement within a community about what people want to be called, often because there is really no coherent community in the first place. Nonetheless, there is always a clear difference between respectful terms and disrespectful ones.

Within the African American community, there are differences over whether to retain use of the word black, or to use *African American*. Neither term is without problems, although both terms are respectful. Similarly, in the Native American community, there is disagreement over whether *Native American* or *American Indian* is the better term. These discussions reflect concerns about cultural pride, historical roots, the meaning of multiculturalism, and strategies for resisting racism. We can learn a lot about the concerns of people of color by listening to their discussions of the issues raised by different terms of self-identity. It is more important we support those concerns than we use what we judge as "the most correct" words.

- *How have different communities of color renamed or redefined themselves during your lifetime?*

It can be hard for white people to accept new terms because they challenge long-standing social relationships. Different words call forth different behavior. We may take advantage of changing terminology to try to discredit people of color with comments such as "Why can't they make up their minds about what they want to be called?" or "Their names are too difficult to pronounce." Focusing on language is a way to divert attention from the underlying challenge to white power and control that the changing vocabulary represents. We may feel less secure we know the racial rules—what to say and how to act. This alone can cause anxiety for many middle-class people, for whom knowing and following the rules is important.

In the United States, upper-class and successful middle-class people have long prided themselves on using correct language and being well-behaved and respectful. The use of correct racial terminology has been a signifier of class or breeding and has been used to disparage poor and working-class people. In the South, respectable whites, deriving great advantage from segregation, referred to African Americans as *Negroes* and looked down on people who used words like "n*****."[2] Of course, being overtly polite or respectful in language or personal encounters made these whites no less complicit in systemic racism.

Some of us wonder why people of color want to be called African American, Chinese American, or Mexican American. Why can't they just be *Americans*? Are they holding something back? Do they owe allegiance to another country or continent? Many people from particular ethnic groups want simply to be *American*. However, because white people regularly perceive them to be Latinx or Asian and therefore not completely 100%-loyal Americans, the force of racism makes it nearly impossible for them to be "just" American. Sometimes people of color use two-part names to assert that they, too, are Americans.

At other times, people use two-part names to indicate cultural and social connections that they feel to the countries or continents from which their foreparents emigrated. These names can indicate feelings of connection to distinct cultural communities, especially in response to the strong pressure in the US to give up one's culture in order to be accepted. Such naming can also be a call to a collective political identity. None of these practices has anything to do with one's loyalty to the United States.

We have adopted the word *American* for people who are citizens of the United States. However, there is no single national culture defining what it means to be an American, however much some of us wish there were. Literally, any of the one billion people in the 37 sovereign nations in North, Central, and South America and the Caribbean is an American.[3] The United States encompasses thousands of distinct cultures, languages, and communities: being a resident of the US doesn't mean denying one's own culture or fitting into someone else's.

Some of our foreparents resisted assimilation and carried on strong and proud Italian, Greek, Irish, Swedish, German, Russian, or Portuguese traditions. The traditions of others were lost over time, and most of us grew to believe the US was a land of newness, separated from the old tired traditions of European countries. Today many of us can hardly identify with any specific ethnic identity or culture. Our assimilation and cultural losses make it difficult to acknowledge the strengths and contributions of people from various cultures, particularly non-European ones, to the US mix.

There is no reason we can't be proud of being from the United States and of the positive achievements of our fellow citizens. And we can be proud of being New Yorkers or Texans or from the Northwest. We can take pride in our cultural, religious, ethnic, and other identities. However, when we use *American* or *All-American* as code words for who we, white people, consider good, rich, smart, or successful enough to be part of *our* country, we are maintaining racism in disguise. When we blame our problems on immigrants without papers, Japanese and Chinese capitalists, South American drug cartels, or Islamic terrorists, we are refusing to look at our own complicity in political and economic situations and failing to take responsibility for our own problems. It then becomes easy for our leaders to stir up fear and anger against *foreigners*, which can fuel militarism and racial violence.

Nationalism can be used to reinforce racism: if we claim we have all assimilated into one large melting pot so completely that differences of culture, tradition, and community no longer exist, we can maintain white norms and white racism. Saying "We're all just Americans and therefore nobody should claim to be Asian American" can deny the inequality and injustice that still operate in the US. We can use nationalism to reinforce white dominance.

People will always make choices about what traditions to keep or discard and what to name themselves. They deserve respect for the choices they make. Many people in the US have cultural or social ties to other countries—some Irish to Ireland, some Vietnamese to Vietnam, some Iranians to Iran, and some African Americans to Ghana or Nigeria. We each live within complex webs of international culture and communication, and no US border limits these kinds of cultural connections. Connecting to traditions and cultures that reach beyond US borders is a source of strength, inspiration, and support for many. We need to encourage those connections, not use them to persecute people for having "divided loyalties."

At a different level, Asian and South Asian Americans, Arab Americans, Latinx, and Native Americans have formed broad coalitions to strengthen their political bargaining power for the distribution of resources, services, and political representation. In earlier historical periods, for example, there were no Asian Americans: there were only Japanese Americans, Chinese Americans, and Korean Americans. Now these groups sometimes work together, downplaying their differences for strategic reasons, to claim resources and representation against white or African American claims or to counter exclusion and stereotyping.

At the same time as they work in coalition as Asian Americans, however, particular ethnic and national groups are reasserting the uniqueness of their experiences and the importance of their needs for resources—as Korean Americans, Filipino/as, or South Asians. This is a strategic response because white culture denies the importance of cultural identity on the one hand and, on the other hand, tends to see all people of color as simply *other*, without recognizing their specificity.

There is nothing essential about any named form of identity. Resistance to white racism might appear to white people to create clearly delineated, separable groups and thus be racist itself. The terms "people of color," "African American," "Korean American," "Latinx"—all self-chosen labels in reaction to white racism—reflect real, but not necessarily stable or long-term, cultural or political groupings. They are not biological or genetic labels: They are important, serious, and significant in the struggle to end racism. They will not go away when racism is eliminated, although they might look very different then.

White people cannot forget that communities of color are trying to survive in a white-controlled society. They have constantly to redefine their strategies for survival and resistance. Many of their words are co-opted, commercialized, or lose their meaning over time. For example, the slogan "Black is beautiful," originally coined to strengthen pride and self-esteem in the African American community, is now being used by advertisers to market cosmetics, alcohol, and clothes.

Individual responses to the fluctuating dynamics of resistance are varied. There is much debate within communities of color about tactics of resistance, including naming practices. Finally, to add one last complicating but crucial factor: race/ethnicity is only one of the factors that make up our identities. At times other factors, such as geographical origin, gender, sexual orientation, parental or work role, may supersede ethnicity as a primary focus. It is important to respect the choices individual people of color make about when and how much to identify with their racial identity, knowing that our society gives a distorted and overemphasized meaning to it.

Separatism

MANY WHITE PEOPLE become upset when people of color get together without us. In our workshops, my colleagues and I sometimes separate people into racial caucuses. There are always white people who protest by saying, "I want to know what they have to say." "How can we deal with racism without people of color?" "How come they get their own group?" "I think their group will be more interesting."

Racism is divisive. Each of these responses reflects some of the pain and confusion of that divisiveness. Although being white—with all its benefits, costs, and opportunities—has heavily influenced our lives, it can be difficult to look around and identify with other white people and to recognize we are in this together. We need to learn how to challenge and support each other.

It is particularly hypocritical for white people to complain about people of color being separatist. For the last 500 years, it is white people who have excluded people of color from "our" homes, "our" schools, "our" workplaces, "our" neighborhoods, and from "our" country. There have been literally thousands of sundown towns throughout the country—cities, towns, and neighborhoods in which people of color were prohibited from staying even one night.[1] These ordinances and covenants were usually enforced with violence. Even today people of color are routinely excluded, harassed, or told to leave and "go home" by white people—constantly treated as outsiders.

Physical and emotional safety is a crucial concern. Women know they aren't necessarily safe with men just because they say "I'm liberated" or "I'm a feminist." For the same reasons, people of color know they aren't necessarily safe when white people make similar declarations. At least in terms of racial abuse, it is generally safer for people of color when white people are not around. It is also safer for them to talk about difficult issues, to be vulnerable, and to acknowledge conflicts and disagreements within their community without the danger white people will use these things against them.

Congregating in a group without white people is also less distracting for people of color. Rarely do we whites sit back and listen to people of color without interrupting, without being defensive, without trying to redirect attention to ourselves, without criticizing or judging. People of color cannot interact with each other with the same amount of attention and respect when white people are present.

Most people of color spend a tremendous amount of time and energy taking care of white people. This has been true historically as people of various ethnic groups cared for our children, took care of our homes, cooked our food, and made our clothes. It has also been true emotionally. People of color have often counseled us, nurtured us in our old age, been our nannies or teachers, assuaged our guilt about racism, covered over their pain and anger to protect us, assured us that we were OK even though we were white, and out of economic necessity, put aside the needs of their families and communities to take care of ours. One of the assumptions of whiteness, particularly for people of middle-class economic status or higher, is that people of color will put our needs before theirs.

There are many reasons people congregate. Safety, shared interests, and mutual support are primary ones. These are the same reasons white people congregate. If you looked around a school cafeteria, you might see white students, Latinx students, and Asian American students sitting in separate groups. If you looked closer and knew more about the groups, you might discover that most of the social groupings of white students were based on shared concerns. Yet many of us who are white might say the people of color are cliquish or separatist, and we might feel offended. We probably would not question why white students sit together. Nor would we necessarily notice the many ways the white students might be discouraging the presence of people of color at their tables.[2]

Since so many public spaces in our society are white in tone, structure, and atmosphere, people of different ethnic groups need space to enjoy their own cultural uniqueness, strengths, and styles. They are not necessarily rejecting individual white people, plotting revenge or revolution.

Our fear, however, can lead us to ignore our responsibility for most of the separation. People of color do not choose to live in barrios, ghettos, and reservations any more than white people do. White-controlled institutions and individual discrimination have created their lack of choice. But when a group voluntarily congregates, we are quick to oppose its right to do so.

It is to our advantage when people of color congregate voluntarily without whites because when people of color come together for discussion and support, they become more able to point out and challenge racism.

At the same time, in an all-white group, we have a chance to explore our questions, concerns, and fears about racism. Since intervening with other white people is an important way to act as allies to people of color, this can be seized as an opportunity to learn ourselves and to gently challenge other white people. Let's take advantage of it!

- *How could you bring together white people you know to think about some of the issues raised in this book?*
- *Who are some white people who can help you do this?*

PART III

Being Allies

Mutual Interest

IT SHOULD BE CLEAR from the last sections that racism has devastating costs to people of color *and* to white people. Those costs are not the same. People of color face immediate survival level threats to their health and well-being that most white people don't experience.

If we only act from an understanding of the costs of racism to people of color, then our involvement in racial justice work is based on "helping them." The work becomes a form of charity and confirms people of color as needy and white people as having it together, knowing the answers, and being righteous. This approach reinforces white superiority and obscures the fact that white-run institutions produce the conditions harming people of color. If we only act from an understanding of the costs of racism to us, then we are acting from self-interest not out a sense of compassion, moral integrity, and an understanding of everyone's true interconnectedness. I believe racial justice work must be based on our understanding of mutual interest—we all have a tremendous stake in building a society based on inclusion, equity, caring, and justice. This is an understanding leading to long-term, sustainable multiracial alliances for justice.

Mutual interest is a core value of Showing Up for Racial Justice (SURJ). On their website, they state, "We use the term mutual interest to help us move from the idea of helping others, or just thinking about what is good for us, to understanding that our own liberation as white people, our own humanity, is inextricably linked to racial justice.... It means our own freedom is bound up in the freedom of people of color."[1]

The daily benefits I enjoy are directly related to the exploitation and violence directed at people of color both in my neighborhood and in other countries. The ruling-class neoliberal agenda tells us that through hard work, personal responsibility, individualism, competition, and choice, we can succeed even if most others can't. However, we are all in the same boat, and racism is a huge hole in our aspiration to create a democratic, multicultural ship. I may have the benefit of being on a higher deck. People of color may literally drown before me. But ultimately, we will all go down together.[2] I will return to this metaphor later in the book.

What Does an Ally Do?

ACTING AS AN ALLY to people of color is one of the most important things white people can do. *Ally* is not an identity, *it is a practice*. An ally is someone who not only shows up, but one who stays around for the long term. Acting as an ally means recognizing we are interdependent and have mutual interest in building a healthy and caring society that provides for people's needs and is environmentally sustainable.

I use the word *ally* because it has been very useful in the social justice work I do. But it is not a perfect term. Some people use the concept of *solidarity*, others of *accompanying*, others the concept of being an *accomplice*. Each word has its strengths and limits. The practice of acting as an ally is based on the idea of mutual interest, our interdependence, and the need for common struggle. But it also recognizes we are not all located in the same place in the struggle. In the work to end racism, for example, people of color, Native Americans, and immigrants of color are on the front lines. They take the most risks and pay the most severe costs—everyday their lives are at stake. They are most knowledgeable about racist oppression and how it works, and therefore they should be in leadership. White allies should look to the leadership of people of color-led organizations and be accountable to it.

The Oakland Men's Project originally adopted the concept of acting as an ally in the early 1980s while doing work to educate and mobilize men to end sexism and male violence. Some women were saying men were the problem, and many men concluded that if they were the problem, they couldn't play a role in addressing these "women's issues." Then and now, acting as an ally invites/challenges those who are disengaged to step up and work alongside—but to be accountable to the leadership of those most impacted. Just as many men are against violence against women but don't see ways to be involved, many white people believe in racial justice as an abstract ideal. It's powerful to call them in, to give them a role to play.

However, there is no simple formula, no one correct way to act as an ally because each of us is different and we have different relationships to social organizations, political processes, and economic structures. Acting as an ally to people of color is an ongoing strategic process in which we look at our personal and social resources, evaluate the environment we are in, and in collaboration with people of color and other white allies, pursue justice.

Uprooting Racism is filled with things to do and ways to get involved. These suggestions are not prioritized because they cannot be. What is a priority today may not be tomorrow. What is effective or strategic right now may not be next year. How do we put our attention, energy, and money toward strategic priorities within a long-term vision?

This task includes listening to people of color so we can support the actions they take, the risks they bear in defending their lives and challenging white hegemony. We don't need to believe or accept as true everything people of color say. There is no one voice in any community, much less in the complex and diverse communities of color spanning the US. We do need to listen carefully to many voices—particularly those on the front lines of the struggle—so we understand and give credence to their knowledge and experience. We can then evaluate the content of what others are saying by what we know about how racism works and by our own critical thinking and progressive political analysis.

- *People of color will always be on the front lines fighting racism because their lives are at stake. How do we act and support them effectively, both when they are in the room with us and when they are not?*

Showing Up as
a Strong White Ally

PEOPLE OF COLOR I have talked with over the years have been remarkably consistent in describing the kinds of support they need from white allies. The following list is compiled from their statements. The focus here is on personal qualities and interpersonal relationships. More active interventions are discussed in the next part of the book.

3.1. What People of Color Want from White Allies

Respect us	Take risks
Listen to us	Make mistakes
Find out about us	Don't take it personally
Don't take over	Honesty
Stand by my side	Talk to other white people
Provide information	Teach your children
Don't assume you know what's best for me	Interrupt jokes and comments about racism
Financial support	Don't ask me to speak for my people
Check your privilege	
Don't try to save or rescue us	Don't be scared by my anger
Interrupt white silence	Your body on the line

An Ally Is Not
a Hero or Savior

IF WE ARE WORKING from an understanding of mutual interest and responding to what people of color say they need from white people, it should be clear the struggle for racial justice is not about white people saving, rescuing, or "helping" people of color.

We've been taught white men built, produced, discovered, or created everything of importance in the world. We've been taught people of color have been lazy and unambitious. We've seen or read about all the great white male saviors from Jesus to Medieval knights; from Columbus to the Founding Fathers; from Western gunslingers to contemporary comic book, movie, and video game superheroes. It is always white men and Western civilization who protect the family/town/nation/women/children/Western civilization from dangerous others. This constantly reiterated cosmology of saviors bringing salvation can make it hard for individual white people not to assume we are the current leading edge of the salvation effort bringing democracy, "free" markets, humanitarian aid, equality, justice, safety, etc. to "those in need." In fact, a lot of the violence initiated by white people and by the US globally is in the name of self-righteous efforts to help people.

Other people don't need to be rescued. Allies aren't heroes. They are members of the community who understand injustice when they see it and do what they can to work with others to redress it.

Basic Tactics

ALTHOUGH EVERY situation is different, taking the previous statements into account, I have compiled some general guidelines.

1. *Assume racism is everywhere, everyday.* Racism affects whatever is going on. We assume this because it's true and because one of the privileges of being white is not having to see or deal with racism all the time. We have to learn to see the effect racism has. Notice who speaks, what is said, how things are done and described. Notice who is not present. Notice code words for race and the implications of the policies, patterns, and comments being expressed. You already notice the skin color of everyone you meet and interact with—now notice what difference it makes.

2. *Notice who is the center of attention and who is the center of power.* Racism works by directing violence and blame toward people of color and consolidating power and privilege for white people.

3. *Notice how racism is denied, minimized, and justified.*

4. *Assume our whiteness is also a factor.* We should look for ways we are acting from assumptions of white power or privilege. This will allow us to see our tendency to defend ourselves or to assume we should be in control.

5. *Understand and learn from the history of whiteness and racism.* Notice how racism has changed over time and how it has subverted or resisted challenges. Study the tactics that have worked effectively against it.

6. *Understand the connections between racism, economic issues, sexism, and other forms of injustice.*

7. *Take a stand against injustice*. Take risks. It is scary, difficult and may bring up feelings of inadequacy, lack of self-confidence, indecision, or fear of making mistakes—but ultimately it is the only healthy and moral human thing to do. Intervene in situations where racism is being enacted.

8. *Be strategic*. Decide what is important to challenge and what's not. Think about strategy in particular situations. Confront the source of power.

9. *Don't confuse a particular struggle with larger issues*. Behind particular incidents and interactions are larger patterns. Racism is flexible and adaptable. There will be gains and losses in the struggle for justice and equality.

10. *Don't call names or be personally abusive*. We usually end up abusing people who have less power than we do because it is less dangerous. Attacking people doesn't address the systemic nature of racism and inequality.

11. *Support the leadership of people of color and POC-led organizations*.

12. *Learn something about the history of white people who have worked for racial justice*. This is a long history. Their stories can inspire and sustain you.

13. *Don't do it alone*. You will not end racism by yourself. We can do it if we work together. Build support, establish networks, and work with already established groups.

14. *Talk with your children and other young people about racism*.

Getting Involved

IT CAN BE DIFFICULT for those of us who are white to know how to respond when discrimination occurs. In the following interaction, imagine Roberto is a young Latino student just coming out of a job interview with a white recruiter from a computer company. Roberto is angry, not sure what to do next. He walks down the hall and meets a white teacher who wants to help.[1]

Teacher: Hey, Roberto, how's it going?

Roberto: That son of a bitch! He wasn't going to give me a job. That was really messed up.

Teacher: Hold on there, don't be so angry. It was probably a mistake or something.

Roberto: There was no mistake. The racist bastard! He wants to keep me from getting a good job. Rather have us all on welfare or doing maintenance work.

Teacher: Calm down now or you'll get yourself in more trouble. Don't go digging a hole for yourself. Maybe I could help you if you weren't so angry.

Roberto: That's easy for you to say. This man was discriminating against me. White folks are all the same. They talk about equal opportunity, but it's the same old shit.

Teacher: Wait a minute. I didn't have anything to do with this. Don't blame me, I'm not responsible. If you wouldn't be so angry, maybe I could help you. You probably took what he said the wrong way. Maybe you were too sensitive.

Roberto: I could tell. He was racist. That's all. (He storms off.)

The teacher is concerned and is trying to help, but his intervention is not very effective. The teacher is clearly uncomfortable with Roberto's anger. He begins to defend himself, the job recruiter, and white people. The teacher ends up feeling attacked for being white. Rather than talking about what happened, he focuses on Roberto's anger and his generalizations about white people. He threatens to get Roberto in trouble himself if Roberto doesn't calm down. As the teacher walks away, he may be thinking "It's no wonder Roberto didn't get hired for the job" or "I tried to help but he was too angry." The teacher leaves having withdrawn his compassion, reaffirmed his own innocence and good intentions, and blaming Roberto for his own ineffectiveness as an ally.

You probably recognize some of the teacher's tactics from descriptions in Part I. The teacher denied or minimized the likelihood of racism, blamed Roberto, and eventually counterattacked, claiming to be a victim of Roberto's anger and racial generalizations.

This interaction illustrates some of the common feelings that can make it difficult for white people to intervene effectively where discrimination is occurring:

1. The feeling we are being personally attacked. It is difficult to hear the phrases "all white people" or "you white people." We want to defend ourselves and other whites. We don't want to believe white people could intentionally hurt others. Or we may want to say, "Not me, I'm different."

   If you feel attacked, remember Roberto has experienced *injustice*. You need to focus on what happened and what you can do about it, not on your feelings.

2. Someone who has been the victim of injustice is legitimately angry and may or may not express that anger in ways we like. Criticizing the way people express their anger deflects attention and action away from addressing the issue. Often, because white people are complacent about injustice that doesn't affect us directly, it takes a lot of anger and aggressive action to bring attention to a problem. If we were more proactive about identifying and intervening in situations of injustice, people would not have to be so "loud" to get our attention in the first place.

3. Just as sexism forces women to mistrust all men, part of the harm of racism is it forces people of color to be wary and mistrustful of all white people. People of color face racism everyday, often from unexpected quarters. They never know when a white friend, coworker, teacher, police officer, doctor, or passerby may discriminate, act hostile, or say something offensive.[2] They may make statements about all white people based on hurtful previous experiences. We should remind ourselves that, although we want to be trusted, *trust* is not the issue. We are not fighting racism so people of color will trust us. Trust builds over time through our visible efforts to act as allies in fighting racism.

When people are discriminated against, they may feel unseen, stereotyped, attacked—as if a door has been slammed in their face. They may feel frustrated, helpless, or angry. They are probably reminded of other similar experiences. They may want to hurt someone in return, to hide their pain or simply forget about the whole experience. Whatever their response, the experience of racism is deeply wounding and painful. It is an act of emotional violence.

It's also an act of economic violence to be denied access to a job, housing, educational program, pay raise, or promotion one deserves. It is a practice that keeps economic resources in the hands of one group and denies them to another.

When a person is discriminated against, it is a serious event, and we all need to treat it seriously. It is also a common event. We know that during their lifetime, every person of color will probably have to face many such discriminatory experiences in school, work, housing, and community settings.

People of color do not protest discrimination lightly. They know that when they do, white people routinely deny or minimize it, blame them for causing trouble, and then counterattack. (This is the "happy family" syndrome described in Part I.)

How could the teacher in the above scenario be a better ally to Roberto? We can go back to the guidelines suggested earlier for help. First, he needs to listen more carefully to what Roberto is saying. He should assume Roberto is intelligent, and if he says there was racism involved, then there probably was. The teacher should be aware of his own power and position, his tendency to be defensive, and his desire to defend other white people or presume their innocence. It would also be worthwhile for him to consider that such occurrences are usually not isolated instances, but a pattern within an organization or institution.

Let's see how these suggestions might operate in a replay of the scene:

Teacher: Hey, Roberto, what's happening?

Roberto: That son of a bitch! He wasn't going to give me a job. He was messin' with me.

Teacher: You're really upset. Tell me what happened.

Roberto: He was discriminating against me. Wasn't going to hire me cause I'm Latino. White folks are all alike. Always playing games.

Teacher: This is serious. Why don't you come into my office and tell me exactly what happened.

Roberto: OK. This company is advertising for computer programmers, and I'm qualified for the job. But this man tells me there aren't any computer jobs, and then he tries to steer me toward a janitor job. He was a racist bastard.

Teacher: That's tough. I know you would be good in that job. This sounds like a case of job discrimination. Let's write down exactly what happened, and then you can decide what you want to do about it.

Roberto: I want to get that job.

Teacher: If you want to challenge it, I'll help you. Maybe there's something we can do.

This time the teacher was being a strong, supportive ally to Roberto. He did not deny or minimize what happened or defend white people. He did not try to take over, protect, or save Roberto. Instead he believed him and offered his support in trying to figure out what to do about the situation.

Allies Leverage
Their Resources

WHITE PEOPLE GENERALLY have a lot more resources to bring to the struggle for racial justice than we take credit for. See the following page for some of the resources you may be able to draw on.

3.2. You Have Resources to Leverage for Racial Justice!

Money: direct donations, hosting house parties

Time: support work, administration, research, filing

Skills: fundraising, web-based activity, outreach, childcare, writing, music, art, carpentry

Connections: to journalists, politicians, decision-makers, funders

Space: in your house, office building, religious or community organization for meetings, living room gatherings, workshops, or art builds

Organizational leverage: working for organizational change where you work, where you go to school, where your children go to school, at your religious or community center.

Information to share: about racism and other issues of social justice, about how systems work, about organizing, fundraising

Access to and credibility with white people: family members, friends, neighbors, coworkers, classmates

Access to young people: as parents, teachers, youth workers, aunts, uncles, grandparents

Your body on the line: showing up for rallies, vigils, protests, city council meetings, school board meetings

Witnessing, recording, interrupting, and reporting: incidents of police harassment and brutality, incidents of discrimination and marginalization, overheard personal comments, organizational practices and policies, or on online sites

Amplifying information, analysis, needs, and calls for action from People of Color and Indigenous-led struggles: through personal networks, Facebook, twitter, letters to the editor, public signs, t-shirts, yard signs

Please educate yourself in the issues, work with others, be accountable to the Movement for Black Lives, Indigenous nations, and other people of color in your community, and use your resources to support them.

An Ally Educates, Mobilizes, and Organizes Other White People

THERE IS MUCH a single white person can accomplish, but large-scale social change is a collective effort. From the Civil Rights period's Student Non-Violence Coordinating Committee (SNCC) and the Black Panthers to today's Black Lives Matter movement and Indigenous struggles, the primary request to whites has consistently been to break white silence, show up in solidarity, and *educate and organize other white people so they participate in multiracial alliances for justice*. It is important I show up in the struggle, but if I show up with 2, 5, or 25 family, friends, and other educated and prepared white people, my impact is amplified.

After Barack Obama was elected President of the US in 2008, African Americans came to some of us who were white and said that, in a period of rising militia activity and racist backlash to Obama's victory, they needed more white voices challenging racism. Under the leadership of Pam McMichael at the Highlander Center and Carla Wallace at the Fairness Campaign of Kentucky a number of us began to organize a national network of organizations and individuals whose mission is to "organize White people for racial justice.... We work to connect people across the country while supporting and collaborating with local and national racial justice organizing efforts. SURJ provides a space to build relationships, skills and political analysis to act for change. This mission is in service to our vision,...a society where we struggle together with love, for justice, human dignity and a sustainable world.... That work cannot be done in isolation from or disconnected from the powerful leadership of communities of color. It is one part of a multiracial, cross-class movement centering people of color leadership.

Therefore, SURJ believes in resourcing organizing led by people of color, and maintaining strong accountability relationships with organizers and communities of color."[1]

There are now over 200 SURJ chapters and affiliates across the US moving this work forward. Whether it is with SURJ, another group, or people you bring together yourself, I encourage you to think about the work of an ally not only as a daily personal practice but something much larger, becoming part of our collective struggle for liberation.[2]

An Ally Makes
a Commitment

NOBODY NEEDS fly-by-night allies. Being an ally takes commitment and perseverance. The struggle to end racism and other forms of injustice is lifelong. People of color know this well because they have been struggling for generations for recognition of their rights and the opportunity to participate fully in society. The formal struggle to abolish slavery took over 80 years. Women organized for over 60 years to win the right to vote. I was reminded about the long haul recently when my sister sent me a news clipping about my old school in Los Angeles, Birmingham High.

The article was about the 17-year struggle to change the "Birmingham Braves" name and caricatured image of an "Indian" used by the school's sports teams. I was encouraged to hear that the name and mascot were now being changed, but was upset to read that even still there was an alumni group resisting the change and filing a lawsuit to preserve the old name.

Soon after receiving the article, I had the good fortune to talk with a white woman who had been involved with the struggle over the mascot. The challenge had originated with a group of Native Americans in the San Fernando Valley, part of a national effort by Native Americans and their allies to get sports teams and clubs to relinquish offensive names and mascots. This woman decided to join the group; she was the only white person to do so. She started attending meetings. For the first two or three years, all she did was listen, and the group hardly spoke to her. After a time, members of the group began to acknowledge her presence, talk with her, and include her in their activities. During the 15 years she was involved with this group, this woman learned a tremendous amount about herself, local Native cultures, and the nature of white resistance. The group tried many different strategies, and eventually, because they met with so much intransigence at the high school, they went to the Los Angeles school board.

When the school board finally made its decision to eliminate Native American names and logos in school programs, it affected every school in the Los Angeles area. Subsequently the decision became a model for the Dallas school district's policy and has been adopted by other school districts across the US. This was a long struggle, but much public education was accomplished in the process.[1]

If the woman I talked with had been discouraged or offended because nobody welcomed her or paid her special attention during those first meetings, or if she felt that after a year or two nothing was going to be accomplished, or if she had not listened and learned enough to be able to work with and take leadership from the Native American community, she would have gone home and possibly talked about how she had tried but it hadn't worked. She would not have been transformed by the struggle; she would not have contributed to and been able to celebrate the victory for Native American dignity and respect. Her work as an ally reminded me of what commitment as an ally really means.

I Would Be a Perfect Ally if...

WHITE PEOPLE LEARN many excuses and justifications for racism in this society. Our training makes it easy to find reasons not to act as allies to people of color. In order to maintain our commitment, we must reject the constant temptation to find excuses for inaction.

- *What reasons have you used for not taking a stronger stand against racism or for backing away from supporting people of color?*

Following are some of the reasons I've heard white people use. I call them "if only" statements because that's the phrase they usually begin with. We are saying "if only" people of color do this or that, then we will do our part. "If only" lets us blame people of color for our not being reliable allies.

I would be a committed and effective ally:
- If only people of color weren't so angry, impatient, or demanding.
- If only people of color realized I am different from other white people. I treat everyone the same.
- If only people of color would realize that we have it hard too.
- If only people of color didn't use phrases like "all white people."
- If only people of color didn't expect the government to do everything for them and wouldn't ask for special treatment.

Another way we justify our withdrawal is to find a person of color who represents, in our minds, the reason why people of color don't really deserve our support. Often these examples have to do with people of color not spending money or time the way we think they should. "I know a person who spends all their money on..."

Such justifications set standards for conduct that we haven't previously applied to white people in the same position: "Look what happened when so-and-so got into office." In most instances, we are criticizing a person of color for not being perfect (by our standards), and then using one person to exemplify an entire group.

People of color are not perfect. Within each community of color, people are as diverse as white people, with a full range of human strengths and failings. The issue is *justice* for everyone. No one should have to earn justice. We don't talk about taking away rights or opportunities from all white people because we don't like some of them or because we know some white people who don't make the decisions we think they should. Even when white people break the law, are obviously incompetent for the position they hold, are mean, cruel or inept, it is often difficult to hold them accountable for their actions. US laws call for equal treatment of everyone. We should apply the same standards and treatments to people of color as we do to white people.

People of color are not representatives of their race. Yet how many times have we said:

- But I know a person of color who...
- A person of color told me that...
- So and so is a credit to their race...
- (Turning to an individual) What do people of color think about that....?
- Let's ask so and so—they're a person of color.

We would never say a white person was representative of their race, even if the person were Babe Ruth, Mother Teresa, Hitler, John Lennon, or Margaret Thatcher, much less the only white person who happened to be in the room.

- *Imagine yourself in a room of 50 people where you are the only white person.*

  At one point in the middle of a discussion about a major issue, the facilitator turns to you and says, "Could you please tell us what white people think about this issue?" How would you feel? What would you say?

  Would it make any difference if the facilitator said, "I know you can't speak for other white people, but could you tell us what the white perspective is on this issue?" What support would you want from other people around you in the room?

In that situation, would you want a person of color to be your ally by interrupting the racial dynamic and pointing out there isn't just one white perspective and you couldn't represent white people? Would you want someone to challenge the other people present and stand up for you? Being a white ally to people of color calls for the same kind of intervention—stepping up when we see any kind of racism being played out.

It's Not Just a Joke

"DID YOU HEAR the one about the Chinaman who...?" What do you do when someone starts to tell a joke you think is likely to be a racial put-down? What do you do if the racial nature of the joke is only apparent at the punch line? How do you respond to a comment containing a racial stereotype?

Interrupting racist comments can feel scary because we risk an attack or anger toward us. We are sometimes accused of dampening the mood, being too serious or too sensitive. We may be ridiculed for being friends of the group being attacked. People may think we're arrogant or trying to be politically correct. They may try to get back at us for embarrassing them. If you're in an environment where any of this could happen, remember, no matter how unsafe it is for you, it is even more unsafe for people of color.

People tell jokes and make comments sometimes out of ignorance, but usually knowing at some level that the comment puts down some group of people and creates collusion between the speaker and the listener. Whether there are people of color present or not, racist joke telling is a form of linguistic assault and white racial performance. The joke teller is claiming "we" are normal, intelligent, and sane, and others are not. The effect is to exclude someone or some group of people from the group, to make it a little (or a lot) more unsafe for others to be there. Furthermore, by objectifying a group, the so-called joke makes it easier for the next person to tell a joke, make a comment, or take stronger action against any member of the objectified group.

The reverse is also true. Interrupting such behavior makes it less safe to harass or discriminate and more safe for the intended targets of the abuse. Doing nothing is tacit approval and collusion with abuse. There is no neutral stance. If someone is being attacked, even by a joke, comment, or teasing, there are no innocent bystanders.

As a white person, you can play a powerful role in such a situation. You, as a white person interrupting verbal abuse, may be listened to and heeded because it breaks the collusion from other white people the abuser expected. If a person of color speaks up first, then you can support the person by stating why you think it is right to challenge the comments. In either case, your intervention as a white person challenging racist comments is important and often effective.

Most white people know that making explicitly racist comments in mixed-racial settings since the Civil Rights period is considered impolite and frowned upon. However, studies show such inhibitions are much lower in all-white settings.[1] If you pay attention, you will probably notice many negative racial jokes, comments, put-downs, and stereotypes made in your presence when it appears only white people are present. People of color, Jews and Muslims who can pass as white often report witnessing such occurrences. In small and intimate family and social networks, a shared white culture is established, maintained, and passed on, and the racial order is affirmed. In these situations, white bonding, boundary setting, and justification for discrimination and abuse is occurring, and it is important for white allies to interrupt these events.

What can you actually say in the presence of derogatory comments? There are no right or wrong answers. The more you do it, the better you get. Even if it doesn't come off as you intended, you will influence others to be more sensitive, and you will model the courage and integrity to interrupt verbal abuse. Following are suggestions for where to start.

If you can tell at the beginning that a joke is likely to be offensive or involves stereotypes and put-downs, you can say something like: "I don't want to hear a joke or story that reinforces stereotypes or puts down a group of people," or "Please stop right there. It sounds like your story is going to make fun of a group of people, and I don't want to hear about it," or "I don't like humor that makes it unsafe for people here," or "I don't want to hear a joke that asks us to laugh at someone else's expense." There are many ways to say something appropriate without attacking or being offensive yourself.

Using "I" statements should be an important part of your strategy. Rather than attacking the speaker, it is stronger to state how you feel, what you want. Other people may still become defensive, but there is more opportunity for them to hear what you have to say if you word it as an "I" statement.

Often you don't know the story is offensive until the punch line. Or you just are not sure what you're hearing, but it makes you uncomfortable. It is appropriate to say afterwards that "the joke was inappropriate because...," or "the story was offensive because...," or "it made me feel uncomfortable because...." Trust your feelings about it!

In any of these interactions, you may need to explain further why stories based on stereotypes reinforce abuse, and why jokes and comments that put people down are offensive. Rather than calling someone racist or writing them off, interrupting abuse is a form of public education. It is a way to put your knowledge about racial stereotypes and abuse into action.

Often people telling racial jokes are defensive about being called out; they may argue or defend themselves. You don't have to prove anything, although a good discussion of the issues is a great way to do more education. It's now up to the other person to think about your comments and to decide what to do. Everyone nearby will have heard you make a clear, direct statement challenging verbal abuse. Calling people's attention to something they assumed was innocent makes them more sensitive in the future and encourages them to stop and think about the impact of what they say.

Some of the other kinds of reactions you can expect, and your potential responses, include the following:

- *It's only a joke.* "It may 'only' be a joke, but it is at someone's expense. It creates an environment less safe for the person or group being joked about. Abuse is not a joke."

- *I didn't mean any harm.* "I'm sure you didn't. But you should understand the harm that results even if you didn't mean it, and change what you say."
- *Is this some kind of thought patrol?* "No, people can think whatever they want to. But we are responsible for what we say in public. A verbal attack is like any other kind of attack; it hurts the person attacked. Unless you intentionally want to hurt someone, you should not tell jokes or stories like this."

Unfortunately, a claim of innocence or virtue by a white person often trumps a claim of injury by a person of color. Many white people believe if a person says something racist, they are racist and racists are bad or marginal people. Since they are certainly not a bad or marginal person, if they've said something that sounds racist, it is not actually racist and you must be mistaken or you didn't understand that what they said was a joke (and you lack a sense of humor and are oversensitive to boot). [2] It's important to keep the focus on the impact of the comment and not on the virtue or moral state of the speaker.

In our society, the importance of one's moral worth is reinforced by centuries of Christian persecution against those who don't measure up. Anxiety about one's salvation combined with terror of damnation enforces compliance.[3] Because purity of intent is believed to absolve an individual from the consequences of their actions, when someone is confronted with a simple mistake, an uncharitable act, or any questioning of their integrity, often the speaker's first response is to defend their innocence.

- I didn't do it.
- I didn't mean it.
- I didn't know about it.
- It wasn't my fault.
- I didn't intend it.
- It was only a joke.

Behind such statements is the justification, "I am really a good person regardless of what happened." In a culture based on a God who judges sinful individuals, an immediate claim of good intention can seem a defense against personal complicity in a situation where something is not right. This dynamic makes it even more important to keep the focus on the impact of the comment and not on the virtue or moral state of the speaker.

Sometimes the speaker will try to isolate you by saying everyone else liked the story, everyone else laughed at the joke. At that point, you might want to turn to the others and ask them if they like hearing jokes that are derogatory, do they like stories that attack people?

Sometimes the joke or derogatory comment will be made by a member of the racial group the comment is about. They may believe negative stereotypes about their racial group, they may want to separate themselves from others like themselves, or they may have accepted the racial norms of white peers in order to be accepted. In this situation, it is more appropriate and probably more effective to talk to the person separately and express your concerns about how such comments reinforce stereotypes and make the environment unsafe.

Speaking out makes a difference. Even a defensive speaker (and who of us isn't defensive when challenged on our behavior?) will think about what you said and probably speak more carefully in the future. I have found when I respond to jokes or comments, other people come up to me afterward and say they are glad I said something because the comments bothered them too but they didn't know what to say. Many of us stand around, uneasy but hesitant to intervene. By speaking out, white allies model effective intervention and encourage other people to do the same. We set a tone for being active rather than passive, challenging racism rather than colluding with it.

The response to your intervention also lets you know whether the abusive comments are intentional or unintentional, malicious or not. It will give you information about whether the speaker is willing to take responsibility for the impact their words have on others. We all have a lot to learn about how racism hurts people. We need to move on from our mistakes, wiser from the process. No one need be trashed.

If the speaker persists in making racially abusive jokes or comments, then further challenge will only result in arguments and fights. People around them need to take the steps necessary to protect themselves from abuse. You may need to think of other tactics to create a safe and respectful environment, including talking with peers to develop a plan for dealing with this person, or talking with a supervisor.

If you are in a climate where people are being put down, teased, or made the butt of jokes based on their race, gender, sexual orientation, age, or any other factor, you should investigate whether other forms of abuse such as sexual harassment or racial discrimination are occurring as well. Jokes and verbal abuse are obviously not the most important forms racism takes. However, we all have the right to live, work, and socialize in environments free of verbal and emotional harassment. In order to create contexts where white people and people of color can work together to challenge more fundamental forms of racism, we need to be able to talk with each other about the ways we talk to each other.

Talking and Working with White People

ONE OF THE responsibilities of a white ally is to work with other white people. But what does this mean? If we look at Western history, we see that exploited groups have rarely gained by converting more and more members of the group in power to their side.[1] Groups in power don't generally make concessions to disenfranchised groups just because they come to understand that it is right, moral, or just. Social change comes when people organize to challenge the practices and policies of organizations and governing bodies with non-violent or violent direct action, mass mobilization, electoral campaigns, or other strategies. Popular opinion is important at certain times in efforts to create change, but I believe it is unrealistic to think most white people will become active participants in the struggle for racial justice in the near future. We could spend all of our time talking with other white people, trying to convince them racism is a serious problem they should do something about, but I don't think this is an effective or strategic use of our time or energy.

Training, workshops, talks, and other forms of popular education are important. I do a lot of each of these things. But to what end? In many of the workshops, I find there are a few white people—often young or adult males—who resist even acknowledging racism exists. Sometimes loud and vociferous, sometimes soft-spoken, they demand lots of time and attention from the group. They assume they and their concerns deserve center stage. I have noticed that when white people express such common responses to discussions of white behavior as "White people are under attack," "What I said was misunderstood or misinterpreted," or "I didn't intend to hurt

158

anyone," I want to take care of them by giving them time and attention. It can be difficult for me to set limits, to ask them to stop responding and just listen for a bit, to acknowledge their feelings but to juxtapose their perceptions to the greater reality in the room. There are a lot of things I could say:

- I recognize you don't feel safe, but this is not about safety. Many of us don't feel safe, but we have to keep addressing the structures that put us at risk, which may mean operating out of our comfort level.
- Although it is, of course, personal, it is not personal. The problem under discussion is institutional racism, not your personal behavior, although you do have a responsibility for your personal behavior and for addressing racism.
- Rather than defending yourself, I encourage you to just take in what was said, understand the spirit in which it was offered, and take some time to reflect upon it before responding.

I have never found it useful to get into a long discussion with someone who is defensive. It just increases their defensiveness and my frustration. I get caught up in attempting to win them over to the anti-racist side, converting them by the power of my arguments and reasoning.

I've decided I don't want to be an anti-racist missionary trying to convert white people to a belief in racial justice. (Besides, many white people believe in racial justice, they just aren't doing anything to make it happen.) This decision has increased my effectiveness as a facilitator because it means I don't get locked into a passionate debate with participants as often, and I no longer try to meet their every defense with a response. I can listen to them and move on to working with other participants and, more importantly, with the group itself.

Make no mistake; my goal is partly to motivate white people to take a stand against racism. But there are plenty of well-intentioned white people who want to move forward in this work. I find it more useful to help them find the understanding and tools to make their work more effective than to spend large quantities of time trying to convert the unconvertible.

I also try to be clear with myself that I am not invested in how many white people I win over. My role as a facilitator is to provide the environment, information, and tools that allow people to understand their role and responsibility in working for racial justice. I have no control over what they do with the opportunity. As much as I would like to have magic dust to turn everyone I spoke with into racial justice activists, I know each person makes their own moral choices. When I work with people, I am trying to send them out the door more connected to each other as part of a community, more aware of injustice in their midst, and committed and better equipped to take some specific actions to challenge racism.

When the goal of a group is organizing against racism, we are not talking about winning people over. We are trying to achieve some concrete changes in the institutional practices we confront which requires a combination of social, economic, and political pressure. We are not trying to change the minds of government officials, judges, and corporate executives; we are trying to change public policy, judicial practice, and corporate behavior. Being persuasive by itself is rarely an effective tactic in achieving organizational or institutional change.

There were large numbers of African Americans involved at all levels of the Civil Rights movement, but perhaps not even a majority of African Americans were active participants. There were a substantial number of white allies in the struggle, but certainly they were far from a majority of whites. But those active were so effective in confronting white power, the US could not continue to operate without attending to some of the most glaring aspects of racism at the time.

There are ongoing struggles today to end racism. The question I hope to leave white people with is "Which side are you on? The side of resistance and backlash that protects white interests and colludes with injustice? Or the side fighting to end racial discrimination, racial violence, and racial exploitation?" I can challenge others with the question, but I can only answer it for myself.

Organizing with other white people to canvass in predominantly white neighborhoods is another useful activity SURJ and other organizations have employed to talk with white people. We need to get better at breaking the silence in white communities about racism and specific issues like police brutality, militarization of the local police force, the prison/industrial complex, attacks on the public school system, and local Indigenous struggles. Canvassing works best when it is tied to local issues, recommending current actions people can take. You can also have materials to offer or sell like window and yard signs ("Black Lives Matter," "I Stand with Standing Rock," or "I Love My Muslim Neighbors").

3.3. Working with White People

1. Which white people in your personal network of family and friends do you think it makes sense to talk with? Which white people would it not be useful or productive?
2. What long-term anti-racist goals are you trying to achieve in your organization, institution, or community?
3. Which white people do you need to work with, influence, and organize to achieve those goals?
4. What kind of education will raise white people's awareness and understanding to build an environment that will support those goals?
5. Which people of color will you talk with to help you answer the previous questions?
6. Which individuals or groups of white people do people of color around you want you to talk or work with?

What about Friends and Family Members?

WE MAY HAVE a lot more at stake personally when confronted with friends or family members who are outspokenly racist. Our ability to continue the relationship or to spend time with them may be at issue. Here again, unfortunately, there is no magic dust to help you change their minds. In such situations, I have had to decide whether to challenge their opinions, set limits to what they can say around me, end the relationship, or agree to disagree. Obviously your decision depends partly on how close to the person and/or how important the relationship is to you. Even in those rare times when I have decided to end a relationship, I have tried to make it clear it is because of my values and because of my commitment to my friends and colleagues of color that I could not continue to spend time with their attitude, comments, and behavior. I want them to know it is specifically because of their racism that I can't be around them, not because of personality differences or different interests.

However, in most relationships, there are grounds for engagement. All of us who are white have work to do on racism, all of us who are men on sexism, all of us who are straight on heterosexism. Rather than feeling superior or righteous because "I'm not racist," we can gently but seriously challenge each other. I try to engage people in open discussion with questions like:

- Why did you say that?
- Why do you say such stereotyped and negative things about people of color?
- I've known you a long time, and I know you're not as mean-spirited as that comment makes you sound.

162

- I love you a lot, but I can't let these things you do around people of color go unchallenged.
- You may know a great deal about.... But when it comes to talking about this issue, you're wrong/misinformed/inaccurate/ not looking at the whole picture.
- I've been told by Asian Americans the word you used is very offensive. Did you know that? Are you trying to hurt people?

I find I can quickly tell if someone is well-intentioned but unaware of the effects of their words, or if they are resistant and unlikely to change their behavior.

When relating to friends and family, I speak up because I can no longer remain silent. I refuse to bond or collude with other white people in maintaining racism. I hope my actions make it easier for people of color to be around these particular white people.

But I am also clear that my efforts at this level, as necessary as they are for me, are not going to end racism. This realization keeps me from spending all my time in discussions with Uncle Max and Aunt Jane about how they talk about people of color.

I think it is crucial that we work with other white people. But not every white person, not all of the time, perhaps not even most of the time.

Tips for Talking with White People about Racism[1]

IF WE'RE GOING to make significant change in our country, we have to break one of the taboos we have developed as white people to maintain racism—"Don't talk about race explicitly with other white people." As people in the Movement for Black Lives have emphasized, *silence = complicity*. To interrupt this silence and keeping in mind the ideas on strategic conversations discussed above, we can initiate courageous and loving conversations about racial justice and other difficult issues. All white folks need to talk about racial justice, including those of us who see ourselves as progressive. These conversations are opportunities to discuss what we can do to address racism in ourselves and our communities, and to challenge the scapegoating of "other" white people—especially poor and working-class white people and/or white people living in rural or rust belt towns.

Before You Start

- Ask yourself, "Am I coming from a place of respect, caring, and compassion?"
- Remind yourself that conversations aren't about proving yourself right, they are about changing hearts and minds.
- Drop shaming, blaming, and stereotypes. Call people in to encourage new thinking about the issues.
- Conversations about race can stir up strong emotions. Check in with yourself before you begin a conversation, and remember to be gentle with yourself and with the people you are talking to.
- Model vulnerability and validate people's fears.

- Many people will not be reached with a framework of "white privilege" or "systems of oppression," particularly rural, poor, and working-class people because they are not economically privileged. Use language and references people relate to.
- Most folks will shut down if they feel like they are being attacked. Try thinking about what you know about this person. Are they a parent? Do they volunteer in their community? What are their values? Approach from this place, not from one of disagreement but from curiosity.
- If the conversation is online, it can only progress so far. Once things get tense, take the conversation off Facebook, email, or text message. Meet in person or talk on the phone.
- Find a stopping point. You are not likely to change someone's worldview in one sitting. End when the conversation is in a place of agreement, and revisit it again later.

Ways to Get Started

- When someone asks about how you are doing, say, "I am feeling really [sad/scared/upset] about what's going on in our country."
- "I feel nervous to bring this up, but I think we really need to have a conversation about what is happening in communities of color."
- "What are you thinking about Black Lives Matter/the attacks on immigrants/something else of current interest?"
- "Are you concerned about how afraid people are feeling, particularly people of color?"
- "What would you do if you were an immigrant or Muslim person in our country right now? What would you want to happen?"
- "What are your hopes for our economy?"
- "Many people are very upset about the state of things in our country and about how their communities are suffering from racism and violence. How do you think they should express these views?"
- "People should have access to basic human rights, like the ability to feel safe and have access to healthy living-wage job,

quality education, and health care. What do you think you and
I can do to make a difference?"

If it feels safe, consider sharing your personal story. Often times, personal connection between people is what creates the possibility of
transformation.

If people are defensive and say "I'm not a racist," "I'm against
racism," "I think people should be treated equally," respond with
something supportive such as "I'm really happy to hear you say you
are against racism. So am I, and I'm worried because of how people
of color are being treated in our country. Have you thought about
ways to show up for people of color during this period?"

General Suggestions

Listen: Start by asking questions like those above. Empathize with
and affirm their hopes and fears, without agreeing with the ways
they see the problems or the solutions. Keep listening, especially
when you don't agree. Be sure you aren't just waiting to respond.

Frame issues using shared values: If they care about concepts such
as equality, human rights, justice, and international law, use that
language. If they care about strong and vibrant communities, go
from there. Give them a way to take a step closer and without feeling
like they have to give up membership in their community.

Share a personal story: "I've realized that even though I work hard
to be against racism, I have work to do too, for example, one time,
I did _____ and I learned/realized _____ . Have you had
similar experiences? How do we help each other grow and live up
to our values?"

Focus: Discern what you can agree on and then steer the conversation in the direction you want to explore.

Reframe the problem: Ask them what they think racism is really
about. Talk about what you think racism is really about.

Use historical examples: People resonate with stories already familiar to them. You can talk about black demands for full equality, dignity, and freedom from institutionalized discrimination through the lens of the American Civil Rights movement of the 1960s. You can make the analogy between current public policies to the system of institutionalized segregation and oppression that constituted apartheid policy in South Africa. You can draw on the history of boycotts to demand political change, such as the Montgomery Bus Boycott, or the 1970s farmworkers' Grape Boycott.

Don't make it a competition or a history lesson.

Avoid triggering the framework they are using: Start by describing your vision for change with a positive framing.

Show don't tell: Speak in language they can hear; don't use jargon or academic language. If you choose to use buzzwords like segregation, or colonialism, or police violence, give concrete examples.

Ask them what they know: Often people know less than they think they do. By simply asking calm questions and sharing facts, you can help them realize that they may be missing pieces of the story.

Be confident and don't worry about making mistakes: You don't have to be an expert to have an opinion about human rights issues. Start with what you know, and then learn together.

Take care of yourself: These encounters can be painful. Hang in there. Give yourself and the people you are talking with lots of appreciation for having difficult conversations.

Allies, Collaborators, and Agents

AS WE HAVE SEEN, an *ally* takes an active, strategic role in confronting racism. A *collaborator*, on the other hand, is someone who follows the rules (which are set up to benefit white people). Collaborators don't have to be overtly racist (although some are) because the organizations or institutions around them maintain racism without their active contribution. They simply collude with the *status quo* rather than challenging it. A collaborator says, "I'm just doing my job, just getting by, just raising my family. Racism doesn't affect me." But they continue enjoying the benefits of being white and ignore the costs of racism.

In reality, most of us are *agents*—more actively complicit in perpetuating racism than collaborators. Many of us find ourselves in situations in which, because of our whiteness, we have more status, seniority, experience, or inside connections than people of color. This may be in the PTA, in a civic group, in a congregation, in a recreational program, on the job, at school, or in a neighborhood. As an ally, we can be welcoming and share information, resources, and support. Or as an agent, we can be unwelcoming and not share all of the information or resources we have. We might set limits on the participation of people of color by failing to provide culturally appropriate outreach and opportunities. We may favor other white people with our warmth, information, or support. We may give people of color the message they are not as welcome, not as legitimate, not as acceptable as friends, neighbors, shoppers, or classmates. In this way, most of us, perhaps not consciously or intentionally, act as agents to maintain a white culture of power.

There is an even stronger sense in which I use the word *agent*—to refer to the way many of us have become agents of the ruling class in maintaining racism through the roles we play through our paid or volunteer work.

People in the ruling class—those who are at the top of the economic pyramid—have never wanted to deal directly with people on the bottom of the pyramid, but have wanted to prevent them from organizing for power. Therefore they have created a space that protects them from the rest of the population. I call this space the *buffer zone*. The buffer zone consists of all the jobs that carry out the agenda of the ruling class without ruling-class presence. The buffer zone has three primary purposes.

The first function is to take care of people on the bottom of the pyramid. If there were a literal free-for-all for the 6% of the financial wealth that 80% of us have to fight over, there would be chaos and many more people would be dying in the streets (instead of dying invisibly in homes, hospitals, prisons, rest homes, and homeless shelters). So there are many occupations to sort out which people get how much of the 6%, and take care of those who aren't really making it. Social welfare workers, nurses, teachers, counselors, caseworkers and caregivers of various sorts, advocates for various groups—all these workers (who are mostly women) take care of people at the bottom of the pyramid.

The second function of jobs in the buffer zone is to keep hope alive, to keep alive the myth that anyone can make it in this society, there is a level playing field, and racism and other forms of discrimination are just minor inconveniences to be overcome. These jobs, sometimes the same as the caring jobs, determine which people will be the lucky ones to receive jobs and job training, a college education, food, shelter, or health care. The people in these jobs convince people that if they just work hard, follow the rules, and don't make waves, they too can get ahead and gain a few benefits from the system. Sometimes getting ahead in this context means getting a job in the buffer zone and becoming one of the people who hands out the benefits.

Before the Civil Rights movement, there was no need to keep hope alive because most white people did not see racial apartheid as contrary to US ideals. They simply believed people of color received what they deserved and were naturally inferior. Since racial discrimination is no longer legal, a different system of explanation for racial apartheid is necessary. When a few people of color are allowed to succeed, they can be held of as examples of the end of racism, and all other people of color can be condemned for not being able to take advantage of the wonderful opportunities they supposedly have to be successful. Institutionalized racism can then be ignored.

For example, Bill Cosby, Oprah Winfrey, Michael Jordan, and most recently President Barack Obama become proof to white people that there are no barriers left. We may say, "What more could they possibly want?" or "Why are they still complaining?" We can pretend to be color-blind and simply ignore persistent discrimination, criminalization, marginalization, and the everyday racism people of color experience by keeping our attention on the exceptions.

To some extent, keeping hope alive works to keep some people of color believing they too can make it. But more importantly, it misleads white people into thinking the system works, and those for whom it doesn't have only themselves to blame.[1]

The final function of jobs in the buffer zone is to maintain the system by controlling those who want to make changes. Because people at the bottom keep fighting for change, people at the top need occupations to keep people in their place in our families, schools and neighborhoods, and even overseas in other countries. Police, security guards, prison wardens, soldiers, deans and administrators, immigration officials, and fathers in their role as "the discipline in the family"—these are all primarily male buffer zone roles designed to maintain the *status quo*.

Some of us are in more powerful positions, where we supervise people of color or allocate benefits to them such as jobs, housing, public benefits, or educational opportunities. Others of us are in jobs where we monitor or control people of color as police, immigration officials, deans, or soldiers. We are paid agents of the ruling class, instructed to use racism to insure that although a few people of color may advance individually to keep hope alive, people of color as a group don't advance and the racial hierarchy does not change.

A Web of Control

EACH SPHERE OF the buffer zone contributes to an overall web of control that is devastating to communities of color and serves to keep them out of mainstream institutions. Schoolteachers, counselors, and administrators often monitor youth of color closely, isolating them in "special needs" classes, writing them up as behavior and discipline problems, readily suspending them, and then blaming their families for not caring and their communities for being dysfunctional.

Social workers monitor and intervene in families of color much more often than they do in white families. Because of system-wide white assumptions that people of color are more likely to scam programs for unneeded benefits and because of limited program funding requiring staff to deny benefits to as many as possible to save money, people of color often face more scrutiny, more paperwork, harsher personal treatment, and greater levels of rejection than comparable white people. Limited language proficiency, inadequate educational background, lack of access to public transportation, childcare, and other resources prevent many people of low income from needed access to services. Low-income people of color are more likely to face a host of these barriers, and in addition, to be treated as undeserving and suspect.

Social service providers are also more likely to intervene quickly in the affairs of families of color by calling the police, child welfare, and protective services. Young people of color are far more likely to be removed from their families by child welfare and protective service workers, and are quicker to be placed into residential programs and foster care.[1]

Police, sheriffs, and immigration officials monitor communities of color with great intensity leading to racial profiling, illegal deportations, police brutality, disproportionate citations and arrest rates for petty crimes such as traffic violations, alcohol and marijuana use, prostitution, loitering, and being a public nuisance.

Apartment owners, real estate agents, bank loan officers, security guards, Bureau of Indian Affairs staff, youth recreation program staff, public and state parks staff, small business owners, store clerks—there are literally tens of thousands of white people whose jobs include monitoring people of color and limiting where they can be and what they can do.

Studies show that many of these people exhibit unintentional and unconscious discriminatory behavior (implicit bias). Of course there are many apartment owners, real estate agents, and bank loan officers who try to be fair and unbiased in their practices. Even so, the National Fair Housing Alliance estimates there are over a million race-based acts of discrimination a year just in the rental market alone. Overall, these professions and the system of housing allocation they are part of do a very efficient job of keeping housing in the United States highly segregated.[2]

The official surveillance and punishment of people of color is enhanced by the many ordinary white people who informally monitor people of color around them for "suspicious" or unliked activity and report their observations to police, immigration officials, housing authorities, school principals, shopping mall security guards, and social welfare workers.

These routine white interventions into the lives of people of color are assaults not just on individuals, but on families and communities. The combination of racism in the school, child welfare, criminal/legal and immigration systems devastates young people and adults, literally separates and destroys families, and makes strong neighborhood, extended family, and community networks fragile and unsustainable. Massive societal intervention in the lives of people of color perpetuates intergenerational patterns of disadvantage, vulnerability to violence, and economic exploitation.

In communities of color, the fate of individuals, families, and communities are linked. When individuals are harassed, profiled, or beaten by the police, when individuals are denied benefits by immigration officials, when children are disproportionately disciplined by school authorities, when children are unnecessarily taken from families and placed in foster care, family and friends are traumatized, normal human relationships are disrupted, and the social and economic capital[3] of the community is seriously diminished. No one is unaffected.

When the media use the negative impact of such community attacks to further reinforce negative stereotypes and justify discriminatory policies by blaming those under attack, such racial mistreatment is seen as normal and acceptable to white people. For example, even though there is much evidence African American and Latinx youth are systematically pushed out of schools, the media portray the problem as lack of family support, violence in the community, or lack of personal effort, reinforcing stereotypes of people of color as uncaring, violent, and lazy. Teachers and administrators can then avoid responsibility for their contribution to a school system operating in a racially discriminatory manner.

White people are almost never subject to reprimand, much less more severe consequences for regular, routine, and pervasive patterns of racial discrimination they personally commit. Even police officers who murder innocent and unarmed black youth rarely receive serious consequences. Whatever level of racism a white person exhibits, we are generally quick to minimize and individualize the damage done, and to attribute their action to inexperience, a temporary lapse in judgment, or extenuating circumstances so we can exonerate and forgive them. This allows us to avoid holding wrongdoers accountable and avoid examining their role (and ours) in maintaining the web of control over communities of color.

The cumulative impact of the pervasive, everyday web of surveillance, control, and enforcement on people of color should not be underestimated. They always have to operate within white organizations and institutions, are subject to white authority figures, and are vulnerable to disrespect or worse from white people around them. Our compassion and our anti-racist action should be guided by our understanding of how this web of control works.

Buffer zone jobs comprise a large category of working and middle-class jobs and are necessary in our society. People go into the helping professions to serve people, and they provide needed services. Police officers, nurses, teachers, and social workers are routinely honored for their work and dedication. But just because the intent of social service providers and others in buffer zone jobs is well-meaning does not exclude them from accountability for their impact. Racism is currently built into the structure of the buffer zone, and therefore those white people without an explicit anti-racist commitment and practice, despite their best intent, will be acting as agents of the ruling class in maintaining the racial and economic *status quo*.

- *Are you an agent of the racism that reinforces the racial hierarchy, do you work as an ally to people of color, or are there elements of both roles in your work? How can you become more of an ally and less of an agent?*

To quote Taiaiake Alfred (and substituting the word *racism* for *colonialism*):

> The challenge, and the hope, is for each person to recognize and counteract the effects of [racism] in his or her own life, and thus develop the ability to live in a way that contests [racism]. We are all co-opted to one degree or another, so we can only pity those who are blind or who refuse to open their eyes to the [racial] reality, and who continue to validate, legitimate, and accommodate the interests of that reality in opposition to the goals and values of their own nations.[4]

3.4. The Buffer Zone

1. Is the work you do part of the buffer zone—either taking care of people at the bottom of the pyramid, keeping hope alive, or controlling them?

2. Historically how has your job, career, profession, or occupation developed in relationship to communities of color? What impact has it had on different communities of color at different times?

3. How have people in your line of work protected white power and privilege and excluded people of color?

4. Have you noticed individual acts of racism or patterns of racism in the organization or system in which you work?

5. How have individuals and communities of color resisted these actions either from within your work/occupation/profession or from the community?

5. Who are white people who have challenged racism in your work?

6. Who benefits from the work you do—people at the top of the pyramid, people in the buffer zone, or people at the bottom?

7. How can you take into account the impact of the web of control (the entire system of racism) on people of color when you interact with them and when you look at organizational and institutional policies?

8. What will you do to act less as an agent of the wealthy and more as an ally to people of color?

PART IV

The Effects of History

Histories of Racism

THIS PART OF *Uprooting Racism* explores how white racism has defined and controlled specific other groups. All the sections are about white people and what we have done to people of color, even though they seem to focus on people of color. I include this information for several reasons. First, most of us are woefully misinformed about the actual history of interracial relationships, particularly their more devastating aspects. We have been taught lies beginning with the benign story of Columbus's "discovery" of America.

Second, our history affects our current situation and experience. The effects of slavery, the genocide of Native Americans, the conquest of Mexico, and the banning of Chinese and later all Asian immigration continue to influence our lives and the lives of people of color.

Third, we cannot build trust and an honest commitment to creating equality if we ignore the injustices of the past. Our well-intended efforts to change the system will not be taken seriously if we continue to deny or distort the record of white racism.

Fourth, the past, even with all its horror, can give us hope for the future. The United States ended legally sanctioned segregation and broadened its democratic base. We can easily be defeated by the challenges of the present if we don't understand the progress we made in the past.

Finally, we have a long history of white people speaking out for economic and political justice, and we need to reclaim and learn from those role models.

Unfortunately, when we focus on white racism and its effects on people of color, it can seem as if the lives of people of color are determined by racism, that they are simply victims of injustice. Nothing could be further from the truth. They are creators of their own lives and cultures. Racism is one of the social constraints that influence how people of color live, but racism does not determine how they lead their daily lives.

Because the focus of *Uprooting Racism* is on white racism, there could be the false perception that I am ignoring the cultural, political, economic, and personal achievements of people of color. To counter this tendency, it is important for you to supplement the information in this part with the writing, music, dance, speeches, and history of people of color themselves in all the diversity they represent.

If we keep this emphasis in mind, each chapter will help us think more creatively about how to become better allies to Native Americans, African Americans, Asian Americans, Latinx, Arab Americans, Jews, Muslims, recent immigrants, and people of mixed heritage, as well as groups not specifically discussed here, such as South Pacific Islanders and South Asians.

People of Mixed Heritage

NOTHING CHALLENGES white perceptions of race more than the millions of people of mixed heritage in the United States.[1] Still largely invisible in our culture, their presence is in sharp contradiction to our expectation that racial difference is simply binary. People of mixed heritage pose difficult challenges not only for white people, but for people of color as well. Many people of color have minimized the complexities of their own identities and cultures for strategic reasons. Researchers have found that, on average, African Americans have 22% European ancestry, with the range being between 10 and 34%.[2] Virtually all Latinx and Filipinos are multiracial, as are the majority of American Indians and Native Hawaiians. In the United States, a person is considered a member of the lowest status group from which they have any heritage. Therefore it is unsafe for most white people to acknowledge having a mixed racial heritage.[3] Although the numbers are substantial, we do not know how many people who are perceived to be white fall into this category.

The myth of biological race and the desire to maintain the boundaries (and attendant divisions of wealth) between white people and people of color sustain white people's fear of interracial relationships and mixed-heritage young people. Often the justification for discrimination and persecution of interracial couples is that the difficulties of living "like that" are so bad because of the racist response of other white people. Present racial prejudice becomes the justification for continued racist practices against people of mixed heritage.

Only in 1967 did the US Supreme Court rule remaining miscegenation laws illegal.[4] Even today it is commonly assumed members of interracial relationships and mixed-heritage young people lead harder lives, meet more prejudice, and have higher rates of divorce, suicide, and other personal problems. On the contrary, there are indications such people are more resilient and have higher self-esteem than monocultural people.[5] One survey found that a majority of multiracial adults are proud of their mixed-race background (60%) and feel their racial heritage has made them more open to other cultures (59%).[6]

Racism is resilient. It would perfectly possible to replace the racial hierarchy of discrete groups in the US with a racially continuous hierarchy, such as is found in Brazil, still with white people on top. Unless we eliminate white power and privilege, people with lighter skin, regardless of racial heritage, will continue to be more highly valued than people with darker skin.

In reading the following chapters, keep in mind there are people of mixed heritage in all these groups. This shows how inaccurate it is to believe any group of people is single and coherent.

Native Americans

I GREW UP WATCHING Roy Rogers, Gene Autry, and the Lone Ranger kill Indians on television. I played cowboys and Indians every chance I had. We fought over who got to be the cowboys because they always won. Native Americans, for me, were reduced to one generic Indian male who was worth about ¹⁄₂₀ of a white cavalry officer. I "knew" what Indians looked like, what they wore, where they lived, and how sneaky, brave, and clever they were. I knew part of my responsibility as a white man in the past would have been to protect white women from them.

Most of all, I knew Indians were all dead. It was precisely because they were history that we dressed up as our stereotypes of them on Halloween and in Thanksgiving plays. I had no understanding I was recreating a distorted and painful history, and I certainly had no idea Native Americans were still alive in the United States. For many of us still, Native Americans are largely invisible in our daily lives, and real people have been replaced by slogans, chants, mascots, historical replicas, and new age imitations.

Today there are over 500 federally recognized Native American nations and numerous unrecognized ones in the United States. When Columbus arrived in the West Indies, there were approximately 15 million Indigenous people in North America.[1] Today, after reaching a low point around 1900, 6.6 million people identify as some percentage of either American Indian or Alaska Native in the United States, about 2% of the population.[2]

The population of the Taino people and other local inhabitants of the West Indies decreased from several million to 22,000 by 1514, only 22 years after Columbus arrived. The population of Native

Americans in the continental United States dropped from 12 million to 237,000 during the first four centuries of US history. During that time, white people stole 97.5% of Native American land,[3] including (if you are in the Western Hemisphere) the land you are on at this moment.

Please read these last two paragraphs again and consider the magnitude of this genocide and land theft.

The Catholic Church officially justified the destruction of Native Americans in papal bulls of 1452 and 1493. The bull of May 4, 1493, *Inter Cetera*, states that "barbarous nations" be "subjugated and over-thrown" as a means of converting them to the Catholic faith and Christian religion.[4] There is currently an international movement to get this papal bull rescinded.[5]

But the Church did more than sanction the destruction of Native Americans. For example, the missions set up along the California coast were slave labor and death camps for the Indians captured and imprisoned in them. Between 1779 and 1833, twice as many deaths as births occurred at the missions, often prompting padres to call in Spanish soldiers to raid distant villages for replacements. An early ethnologist, Alfred Kroeber, remarked, "The brute upshot of mis-sionization, in spite of its kindly flavor and humanitarian root, was only one thing: death."[6]

The Church was just one of many participants in the process of destroying Native American peoples. In 1783 George Washington ordered that those remaining within the areas of the initial thirteen states be "hunted like beasts" and a "war of extermination" be waged against Native Americans barring US access to certain desired areas, notably the Ohio River Valley.[7] Washington himself fought for the British against the Indians, and as payment he received thousands of acres of Native land. He also owned shares in the Mississippi Company, a land speculation group that claimed 2.5 million acres of land in the Ohio Valley where Native people were still living. On May 31, 1779, Washington wrote to General Sullivan, who was leading an expedition against the Iroquois: "The immediate object is their total destruction and devastation and the capture of as many person of every age and sex as possible...ruin their crops...and prevent their planting more.... Lay waste all settlements around that the country may not be merely overrun, but destroyed."[8]

Or, as Thomas Jefferson put it in 1812, Euro-Americans should drive every Indian in their path "with the beasts of the forests into the stony mountains"; national policy should be to wage war against each Native people it encountered "until that tribe is exterminated, or driven beyond the Mississippi." Andrew Jackson characterized Indians as "wild dogs" and supervised the mutilation of about 800 corpses of Creek people—the bodies of men, women, and children he and his men had massacred. "Scalp bounties paid better than buffalo hides for 'enterprising citizens' in Texas and the Dakotas until the 1880s."[9]

Americans have talked about "manifest destiny" as if there were not real white people involved in the process of killing Native Americans and appropriating their land, as if white people were not manifesting and manufacturing that destiny.

White people also justified the genocide by saying Native Americans died from diseases they were biologically unable to resist. However, we know at times white people introduced diseases to Native American populations intentionally and systematically as part of a policy of extermination. For example, "In 1763 Lord Jeffrey Amherst ordered a subordinate to distribute items taken from a smallpox infirmary as 'gifts' during a peace parley with Pontiac's Confederacy.... Upwards of 100,000 Indians died of smallpox in the ensuing epidemic."[10]

Yet another justification white people have used for their violence is that Native Americans were simple and unsophisticated, and by implication, their culture was not really a loss because they were unable to compete in the modern world. In fact, there were long-term, stable, complex, and sophisticated cultures in all parts of the US including the Southwest, Northwest, South, Southern Mississippi Valley, Northeast, and the Great Plains. Furthermore, a people's right to exist, control their land, and maintain their culture should not be contingent on others' judgment of their sophistication.

Native American societies were so developed, colonists continually took their ideas and practices and incorporated them into their

institutions. White American settlers exploited Native American agricultural, medicinal, hunting and various craft techniques, land use
patterns, trade routes, and the genetic development of foods. Colonists were also heavily influenced by Native American social and
political arrangements. Early political leaders, including Thomas
Jefferson, Thomas Paine, and Benjamin Franklin, acknowledged
the Native American origin of many of the ideas they incorporated
into the Articles of Confederation and the US Constitution.[11] Early
women suffragists such as Elizabeth Cady Stanton, Matilda Joslyn
Gage, and Lucretia Mott were inspired by the respectful gender relationships, the lack of violence against women, and the strong role
women played in Native American societies to challenge the lack
of women's participation in social and political life in the US and
Canada.[12]

Today young people are not taught, and few adults even know
about, the achievements and contributions Native Americans have
made to our lives. Contemporary Native American healing, spiritual,
medicinal, agricultural, and land use practices continue to be exploited by corporations and individuals with no recognition of their
source, no compensation to their originators, and continued attack
upon the Native American communities that produced them.

Throughout the United States today, Native American lands are
being mined, logged, hunted, and developed without permission
or adequate compensation. Native Americans are fighting for recognition of their sovereignty, return of appropriated cultural artifacts and the bodies of their ancestors, recognition of their status
as Native Americans, protection of sacred religious sites, an end to
police and military interference with traditional hunting and fishing
rights, culturally appropriate education for their children, and the
end of stereotyping, inaccuracies, and lies about US history and the
present realities of Native American life.

After centuries of vilifying and committing genocide against
Native Americans, white people have more recently constructed a
mythologized image of them. We hold them up as natural, ecologically wise, at one with nature, enduring, skillful, brave, and in possession of rituals, stories, and beliefs we need to adopt to counter the

destructiveness of our modern industrialized lives. Boy Scouts and Camp Fire Girls, men's lodges and men's movement retreats, new age spiritual groups all mimic a generic version of Native American culture. The movie *Avatar* and the exceedingly popular *Twilight* series of books and movies are just two examples of this phenomenon.[13]

There are many simple and immediate ways we can counter the continued attacks on Native Americans in our society. The following questions suggest some places to start.

4.1. Questions and Actions: Native Americans

1. What people lived on the land you presently inhabit? How were they removed? Where do they live now? Are there any land or tribal recognition claims still pending? Where else in your state are these struggles going on?
2. Do Native Americans have full access to jobs, social services, and community resources in your community? For example, what is the unemployment rate for Native American adults and young people?
3. Are Native Americans in your area harassed for exercising or prohibited from exercising traditional hunting and fishing rights?
4. Is there corporate mining, logging, or other land devastation occurring on Native lands in your region? Are toxic dumps located on Native lands?
5. Is there a climate of hatred toward Native Americans in your area? Is there police harassment or brutality directed toward them?
6. What forms of government, foods, medical treatments, products, names, and customs have white people appropriated from Native Americans? How much has their contribution been recognized? How has it been exploited?
7. Are local Native American historical sites, relics, and burial grounds preserved in your community? Are museums being

asked to return sacred Native American objects to the people from whom they came? If so, how do they respond?

8. Are you part of a spiritual or growth community that has appropriated Native American rituals, artifacts, or customs? How might it feel to Native Americans when people from different religious backgrounds take their sacred rituals and use them as recreational activities or mix them in with traditions from other cultures?

9. Do you hear people refer to Native Americans in derogatory ways or make jokes about "Indians"? How can you respond when someone does a tomahawk chop, war whoop, or otherwise contributes to perpetuating caricatures of Native Americans?

10. Do your children play with toys and video games or watch TV shows or movies where Native Americans are stereotyped, portrayed as the enemy of white people, or otherwise degraded? Are there books, pictures, or artifacts in your house that degrade, make fun of, or stereotype Native Americans?

11. Do textbooks in your local schools accurately and truthfully describe what white settlers and armies did to Native Americans? Do any romanticize them? Do any speak of a generic Indian? Is the full story of Columbus's and the colonists' practices and policies told?

12. What do you and your children know about Native Americans in the contemporary US?

13. When talking about Native peoples, do you refer to Native Americans generically, assuming there are valid generalizations you can make about all Native Americans, or do you name the nation or culture you are referring to and give specific examples?

14. How could Columbus Day and Thanksgiving activities be changed so they did not disguise the genocide of Native Americans in the West Indies and New England?

I currently live on Chochenyo and Karkin Ohlone land in the Oakland/Berkeley area. Indigenous women in the area have created the Sogorea-te' Land Trust. Local non-Native residents are invited to pay an annual shu'umi land fee for our living here. This land tax directly supports the land trust "to acquire and preserve land, establish a cemetery to reinter stolen Ohlone ancestral remains and build a community center and round house" so Indigenous people can thrive in the Bay Area."[14] If you don't live in the Bay Area, think about other proactive and creative ways to show up as allies to Indigenous people in your area. The following are suggestions for white-Indigenous solidarity work.[15]

- *Strengthen* Indigenous-led efforts for the return of land and resources from illegitimate settler states and corporations.
- Support Indigenous self-determination/sovereignty, cultural preservation, and healing.
- *Develop* new ways of listening.
- *Shift* your understanding of time frames and how things "should" function in a movement.
- Build your capacity to sit with discomfort, hear difficult feedback, be challenged in various ways, and stay committed.
- Stay grounded in your own sense of dignity, humanity, interconnectedness, and radical vision.
- Address your own internalized superiority and colonial mind-set.
- *Know whose land you are on.*
- Know your family's history.
- Learn together. Encourage learning that is personal, emotional, spiritual, embodied, and communal.
- Ask permission.
- *Learn where your water, heat, electricity, etc. come from.*
- *Take responsibility for Christian hegemony/Doctrine of Discovery.*
- *Engage in local struggles and build relationships*

African Americans

AS WITH ANY OTHER "racial" identity, the term *African American* hides tremendous diversity. In the United States, there are Africans, native-born African Americans, and immigrants from the West Indies and South America. There are African Americans with hundreds of years of history as free blacks and others whose great grandparents were enslaved. Differences in class, gender, sexual orientation, physical ability, and geographically specific cultures are also vitally important in the African American community. There are no biological, economic, cultural, or physiological generalizations that hold for them except for the existence of racism itself, which they must all deal with. Even here they are vulnerable in different ways.

The first Africans were brought to what is now the United States in 1619. In the earliest days of the colonies, most Africans and 75% of white Europeans were indentured servants and were treated similarly if not equally.[1] Many whites and Africans fraternized, some intermarried and others worked together to revolt against or escape from servitude.

By and large, in the early days of the colonies, Africans were seen by whites as different, but not innately inferior. Differences in economic status were explained by reasons of class and religion, the result of qualities related to being poor and non-Christian.

By the early 1700s, there were over a million Africans enslaved in the West Indies and South America, as well as a long tradition in Christian Europe of treating non-Christians and darker-skinned people as inferior. These factors, combined with a decrease in the number of indentured servants arriving from Europe, led to the gradual expansion of slavery and increasingly rigid distinctions between white servants and Africans in the colonies. After the scare of Bacon's Rebellion in 1676 (in which white and African workers united in arms to challenge the landowning class), those in power moved quickly to consolidate slavery in the mid-Atlantic region. The white landowning class systematically codified the separation of Africans and poor European settlers by legalizing lifetime servitude (slavery) to control the former and by using the latter as a buffer to protect themselves from rebellion by allowing them to be armed and to serve on slave patrols. As historian Ronald Takaki described the process, "the Virginia elite deliberately pitted white laborers and black slaves against each other. The legislature permitted whites to abuse blacks physically with impunity: in 1680, it prescribed thirty lashes on the bare back 'if any Negro or other slave shall presume to lift up his hand in opposition against any Christian.' Planters used landless whites to help put down slave revolts."[2] These tactics created some of the original forms of white privilege in the US.

From 1619 until slavery ended officially in 1865, 10 to 15 million Africans were brought to North America, and millions more died en route from their villages to their final destinations. Probably 2 million died while crossing the Atlantic—a journey called the Middle Passage.[3] In all, 30 to 45 million Africans were abducted or killed by our white US and European foreparents.[4]

Please pause a moment and take in the magnitude of these numbers.

Most of the early leaders of what became the United States, including Washington and Jefferson, owned slaves. During the 18th and 19th centuries, the slave-based agricultural prosperity of the South fueled the industrial expansion of the North. New waves of immigrants came to a land of opportunity partly supported by the jobs this prosperity generated. For example, jobs in the textile mills and shipbuilding companies of New England and the clothing sweatshops and trading centers of New York and other large cities were dependent on cheap cotton produced by enslaved labor in the

South. White immigrants prospered not only while African Americans were enslaved, but because they were, benefiting from jobs in the many trades from which African Americans were excluded.

Not all white people supported slavery. There was a long-standing minority tradition of public outcry for the abolition of slavery, particularly among white women in the 19th century. There were also individual white people such as Robert Carter, who freed their slaves. Carter was the largest landowner and possibly the richest man of his time. Friends with Washington and Jefferson, in midlife he came to see the immorality of being a slaveholder. At tremendous financial and personal cost, he freed all of his nearly 500 enslaved Africans. Others, such as Thomas Paine and John Adams, were abolitionists.

The US Civil War was a complicated political, economic, and social event, and while the extension of slavery was a key issue, the abolition of slavery was not a strong concern in the country. As Lincoln wrote in a letter to Horace Greeley:

> Dear Sir: I have not meant to leave any one in doubt...My paramount object in this struggle is to save the Union, and is not either to save or destroy Slavery. If I could save the Union without freeing any slave, I would do it; and if I could save it by freeing all the slaves, I would do it; and if I could do it by freeing some and leaving others alone, I would also do that. What I do about Slavery and the colored race, I do because it helps to save this Union.[5]

Putting the injustice of slavery behind us is one of the tactics of white resistance we looked at in Part I of this book. We don't talk about the horrors of the Middle Passage, the systematic attempt to eradicate African culture and the everyday participation of common white folks in supporting slavery. We still refer to slavery as something most people survived. We don't talk about the millions dead, the maimed, the tortured, the broken families, the rape, and daily violence. It was not until 2016 that the Smithsonian National Museum of African American History and Culture opened on the Mall in Washington, DC.[6]

Although slavery was officially abolished by the 13th amendment to the US Constitution in 1865, these elements of slavery continue into contemporary times:

- economic and cultural exploitation
- everyday violence including lynching, rape, and physical attack
- political disenfranchisement
- mass incarceration
- almost total segregation in the South and the North

We have enjoyed over 350 years of economic and cultural enrichment of the white community at the expense of African Americans.

It is even more of an affront and part of our denial when we hold onto symbols and reenactments that extol white supremacy. The Confederate flag, for example, was the flag of the army that defended slavery. By continuing "military reenactments" of the defense of slavery, we admit we are unwilling to acknowledge, and in fact continue to deny or minimize, the pain and horror of those whose families and communities were scarred by hundreds of years of enslavement.

Most white people living in the US today have supported and benefited from segregation during our lifetimes. Many of us are still resisting the integration of schools, country clubs, recreation centers, neighborhoods, and businesses. Until we have enough integrity to acknowledge our role and the role of our families, friends, and neighbors in these injustices, we will continue to stand in the way of progress toward full equality. Until we deal with the past, we will not lessen its overpowering influence on the future.

With the end of slavery and the beginning of large-scale migration to Northern cities in the 20th century, the direct assault on African American culture diminished. It was replaced by white society's exploitation of that culture. The appropriation of music, dance, fashion, and various elements of style from African Americans has enriched white culture and individual white people. For example, blues, jazz, rock and roll, and rap are all African American musical forms white people have listened to, copied, and profited from.

In recent decades, intergenerational conflict over patterns of socialization and interracial dating often trigger parents' or other adults' fears of the perceived subversive, scary, or eroticized elements of African American people and culture. White youth manipulate these fears to create more space for their personal autonomy and individual creativity using icons of African American culture (such as music and clothing styles) appropriated and repackaged by white-owned corporations.

National discussions about gender roles and male-female relationships, especially their more difficult and troubling aspects, often use the projected fear of African American men as a framework. In recent decades, national media attention has focused discussion of contemporary issues of male violence on prominent African American men such as Clarence Thomas (sexual harassment), Kobe Bryant and Bill Cosby (rape), Michael Jackson (child sexual assault), and O. J. Simpson (domestic violence). Each of these issues is current, volatile, and contested. Each strikes deep chords of anger, fear, and pain among white people. These African Americans are presumed to represent natural masculinity—but less civilized or controlled sexuality. They are perceived to be clearly outside the boundaries of whiteness. Rarely do white men who commit similar offenses receive the same amount of scrutiny or notoriety men of color do.

The focus on fear of African American male sexuality leaves the lives and concerns of African Americans who are female or transgender unacknowledged. This is despite the fact they have been in the forefront of the fight against racism and for safety and equality for everyone. This lack of respect has meant they have not been acknowledged for the particular needs, concerns, insights, skills, and experience they have consistently provided to the struggles to end racism, sexism, and other systems of oppression.[7]

White women's roles and relationships have been taken as the norm for all women, and therefore African American women's live, are often misunderstood or not seen. For example, we have assumed that because large numbers of white women were falling into poverty (the "feminization of poverty"), so were many women of color.

In reality, most were already living in poverty and had nowhere to fall from. We have assumed that since white women were primarily domestic workers, taking care of children and the home, enslaved women were also. In fact, most enslaved women were field workers and did the same work as men. Since slavery, African American women have continued to work outside the home, often in the homes of white women.

Mistreatment of African American women has also contributed to the exploitation of white women. The wages paid to African American women domestic workers have always put a ceiling on wages paid to white women domestic workers. The expectations and attitudes of white men toward African American women will always limit the respect and equality accorded white women. This relationship between the exploitation of African American and white women has been particularly damaging to poor and working-class white women.

When white people project personal qualities onto African Americans, it reflects our images of who we think ourselves to be. Statements that African Americans are lazy, promiscuous, or stupid are simultaneously statements that white people are hardworking, monogamous, and smart. When we describe African American families as matriarchal and their communities as filled with drugs and violence, we are implying white families are patriarchal and peaceful and our communities are drug- and violence-free.

In recent decades, the social sciences have become a strong legitimizing force for the *status quo* in US society; sociological and psychological explanations of economic disparities between whites and people of color have proliferated. They often offer "explanations" of poverty and violence in the black community using phrases such as "ghetto psychology," "black rage," "internalized oppressions," and lack of "self-esteem" in African American young people. What has remained unchallenged despite these explanations is the dominance of white people, the subordination of African Americans, and policies that keep institutional and structural racism locked into place.[8]

The resistance and resilience of African Americans in the face of racism have been defining characteristics of US history and contemporary life. Ultimately, they force us to see that all our attempts to explain and understand racism fail to change it. These explanatory projects in fact divert our attention from the practical challenge of creating a society in which African Americans have full political, economic, and cultural equality. However critically we analyze the past history of white-African American relationships, our theories reinforce and legitimize white racism by focusing only on African Americans. As James Baldwin noted over 30 years ago, "the Negro in America does not really exist except in the darkness of our minds."[9]

Most white people know little about African Americans because of extensive housing, school, and workplace segregation and because layers of whiteness overlay our perceptions. African Americans have had little opportunity to describe their own experience, and even today we hear the voices of only a few. Those we do hear are generally well educated, successful, and professional. A white-controlled news and publishing network is still the gatekeeper, deciding which African American voices are acceptable. For example, African Americans made up about 4.7% of the total workforce in the newspaper industry in 2014, 5% of television news staff, and just 4% of black news directors.[10] They are rarely in high-level, decision-making positions.

Using social media to break through white media-controlled images and information about black people, the hashtag #BlackLives Matter [BLM] was created in 2012 by three black women, two of whom identify as queer, after unarmed 16-year-old Trayvon Martin's murderer, George Zimmerman, was acquitted. "#BlackLivesMatter is a call to action and a response to the virulent anti-Black racism that permeates our society...Black Lives Matter affirms the lives of Black queer and trans folks, disabled folks, black-undocumented folks, folks with records, women and all Black lives along the gender spectrum. It centers those that have been marginalized within Black liberation movements. It is a tactic to (re)build the Black liberation movement."[11] #Black Lives Matter [BLM] was brought to national attention when 18-year-old Michael Brown was shot and killed on August 9, 2014 by a Ferguson, MO, police officer; Brown's body was left for four hours in the street without medical attention. The ensuing rebellion by African Americans in the city revealed a pattern of exploitation and police violence black residents face on a constant basis. A substantial part of Ferguson's city budget was based on fines and other fees disproportionately collected by the police from the black community. This turns out to be a common practice throughout the US where police and government officials collude in racial harassment for revenue collection to support and justify expanded and militarized policing. These practices terrorize the black community, unfairly drain them of economic resources and lead directly to the hundreds of killings of black adults and young people every year.

Over the last couple of years, cell phone recordings of police killings have increasingly documented a range of extra-judicial police murders of unarmed civilians and a pattern of police misconduct, lack of oversight and accountability that plagues cities across the US. In addition to police killings, black, Latinx, Native Americans, and Muslims of color are routinely racially profiled, disproportionately stopped, harassed, and arrested while driving, walking, wearing the wrong clothes (hoodies), swimming, legally carrying a gun in an open carry state, traveling by plane, and on and on. Overall in 2015, black people were killed by police at over 2½ times the rate of white. About 25% of the African Americans killed were unarmed, compared with 17% of white people.[12]

Black Lives Matter became a movement when African Americans started organizing chapters in various cities to challenge the lack of public outrage at the callous murders of black people. Other black-led formations such as Ferguson Action, Black Youth Project, and the Dream Defenders also joined in the actions. White, Asian, Native American, and Latinx allies started showing up in solidarity. Local groups under a national Movement for Black Lives umbrella have since been working on many local issues relating to racial justice and have engaged in hundreds of non-violent acts of civil disobedience, vigils, and campaigns.

Out of these efforts, a network of more than 50 black-led organizations developed and released a policy and vision platform in the summer of 2016. Its opening lines are: "Black humanity and dignity requires Black political will and power. Despite constant exploitation and perpetual oppression, Black people have bravely and brilliantly been the driving force pushing the U.S. toward the ideals it articulates but has never achieved. In recent years we have taken to the streets, launched massive campaigns, and impacted elections, but our elected leaders have failed to address the legitimate demands of our Movement. We can no longer wait.... It is our hope that by working together to create and amplify a shared agenda, we can continue to move toward a world in which the full humanity and dignity of all people is recognized."[13]

The document covers six major areas: End the War on Black People, Reparations, Invest-Divest, Economic Justice, Community Control, and Political Power. The entire document is visionary yet very specific in its analysis and policy proposals. I encourage you to read through it and think about how you can join the efforts to move a visionary racial justice agenda forward.

There is much white people can do to end racism against African Americans. Below are some questions and activities to use as a starting point.

Many of these suggestions are specific to African Americans; others apply to being an ally to Latinx, Asian Americans, Arab Americans, and Native Americans as well.

4.2. Questions and Actions: African Americans

1. List ways you or other members of your family have down-played, minimized, or denied the effects of slavery and post-slavery Jim Crow segregation on the African American community.

2. List ways your family or foreparents may have colluded with or benefited from the economic exploitation of African Americans.

3. Which contemporary national problems are blamed predominantly on African Americans?

4. Analyze your community. Which parts—neighborhoods, schools, recreational facilities, job sectors, clubs—are presently *de facto* segregated?

   a. Which of these do you participate in?

   b. Notice specific racist institutional practices (for example, redlining, real estate covenants, school district borders, suburban incorporation). List one you are going to work with others to change.

5. Notice what kinds of individual acts of discrimination keep segregation in place (decisions by landlords, real estate agents, employers, teachers). What is one thing you can do to support public policies against discrimination and their strong and consistent enforcement?

6. Work to make sure the police are adequately supervised and monitored.

7. Listen to African Americans define their own lives and problems, and push for their involvement at every level in every situation you are involved in. Support their leadership.

8. Find out what you can do to work against the dismantling of affirmative action and other anti-discrimination programs and policies.

9. Notice the sports you watch and the music you listen to. Are there any in which African Americans are major performers?

   a. Who benefits financially and who benefits culturally from the performances of African Americans in these areas?

   b. What are the economic factors that led African Americans to be major participants in those areas?

   c. What stereotypes do white people use to justify these concentrations?

   d. Support the efforts of African Americans to become more powerful in these arenas through participation in management, through ownership arrangements, through less exploitive recruitment practices.

10. How can you challenge other white people's stereotypes of African Americans? What information or other preparation do you need to be able to do this well?

11. Work for reparations for African Americans.

12. Introduce your children to the complexities, history, and accomplishments of African Americans.

13. Make sure schools and programs for youg people in your area are multicultural and African American youth are not singled out for punishment, disproportionately tracked into lower-level academic classes, or harassed.

Asian Americans

ASIAN AMERICANS have emigrated from over 20 countries and an even greater number of distinct cultures. Like every other referent for a racial group, the term *Asian American* lumps together vastly different cultural groups and subsumes the class, gender, and diversity of millions of people.

The status of Asian Americans has always been ambiguous in a country that sees race as a polarity between black and white. Although we have viewed Asian Americans as inferior for much of US history, at times we have accorded honorary white status to those who have assimilated most completely. For example, white ambiguity about the racial status of Chinese immigrants (the majority of Asians in the West and South in the late 19th century) was reflected in constant shifts in how they were officially categorized. Historian Gary Okihiro describes Louisiana's census:

> In 1860, Chinese were classified as whites; in 1870, they were listed as Chinese; in 1880, children of Chinese men and non-Chinese women were classed as Chinese; but in 1900, all of these children were reclassified as blacks or whites and only those born in China or with two Chinese parents were listed as Chinese.[1]

White people's relationship to Asian Americans is deeply anchored in Eurocentric beliefs. The West has a nearly 3,000-year-old history of relations with Asia. Early Greeks such as Hippocrates, Herodotus, and Aristotle had negative things to say about Asians, and these were commonly accepted stereotypes in their time.[2]

White people have seldom been able to step far enough out of a Eurocentric focus to understand Asian Americans as part of Asian history and culture. Europeans and Americans who invaded Asia in the 19th and early 20th centuries met peoples who had 3,000 to 5,000 years of highly sophisticated and continuously recorded history. Despite this history, we only acknowledge Asians from the time they arrived in North America; we only accept them once they give up, renounce, or betray their broader historical culture.

Current anti-Asian rhetoric claims "we" are under attack or being besieged. We cite Japanese or Chinese imperialism to feed our fears Asian Americans have come to overrun the United States and take away our jobs and industries. Asians, it must be remembered, did not come to North America; the United States went to Asia. It is best to remind ourselves we forcefully opened up Japan and China to US trade in the 19th century after those countries refused to have anything to do with us. Asians did not come to take the wealth of America; in the last two decades, industries from the United States have gone to Asia. And we might add, more recently, Vietnamese, Cambodians, and Laotians did not come to invade the United States, but to escape the invasion and disruption of their countries by US military and economic forces.

Business interests in the mid-19th century encouraged substantial numbers of Chinese to immigrate to the US to replace African Americans after slavery was abolished and African Americans began to gain power during Reconstruction. Later on, when African Americans organized the Brotherhood of Sleeping Car Porters in 1925, Filipino men were brought in and were given jobs African Americans had formerly held. The struggles of African American and Asian workers intertwined, and white business leaders played one group against the other, employing Chinese and other Asian workers when they needed them and excluding them when they didn't.[3]

Beginning in 1882 with the Chinese Exclusion Act and only ending with the 1965 Immigration Act, Asian immigration to the US from Japan, Korea, Southeast Asia, the Philippines, South Asia, and the Pacific islands was either illegal or so sharply limited as to be virtually nonexistent. During periods in which immigration was allowed, often only men were permitted entry. Because of this policy and our male dominant society, we tend to see Asian Americans primarily as men, while portraying Asian women as passive, dependent, sensual, and obedient. This perspective has distorted our understanding of Asian family structure, male life here, and the lives of female family members who remained in Asia.

The US government did not permit Asians who were living in the country to become naturalized citizens for long periods of time. In the late 19th and early 20th centuries, whites passed more than 600 separate pieces of anti-Asian legislation limiting or excluding persons of Asian ancestry from citizenship.[4]

Non-citizens had no legal rights and could not vote or participate in the political process. They were excluded from a variety of occupations and in many states could not own land. Whites could kill Asians with impunity because Asians could not testify against them. Asians throughout the West were socially stigmatized and subject to periodic massacres, expulsions, murders, and the burning of houses, farms, and even entire neighborhoods. It was only in 1952 that the last bars to Asians becoming US citizens were lifted.

White immigrants benefited tremendously from the restriction of Asian immigration. In addition, they benefited from the expanding industrial economy in the Northeast and Midwest based on tin, rubber, and other raw materials arriving from European and US colonies in Asia such as Malaysia, the Philippines, China, and India.

We like to think white people are modern and forward-looking. We often describe Asian cultures as tradition-bound. We think innovations and "progress" come from us, and resistance to change comes from Asians. When Asian Americans propose different ways of approaching problems, we reject their ideas and describe their communities as more traditional than ours.

We have also done the opposite, taking these same stereotypes of other cultures and turned them into virtues. We may describe Asians as hardworking, patient, industrious, meditative, and steady. US business leaders have held up the Japanese as innovative and hardworking and used them as examples to pressure US workers to work harder and be more adaptable to the needs of business. These stereotypes have also been used to justify quotas on Japanese products and "Buy American" campaigns.

Different groups of Asian Americans have often been held up to prove the US is a country where even recent immigrants can get ahead. Koreans are one of the more recent groups to be used in this way.

In media portrayals of the 1992 uprising in Los Angeles, Koreans and African Americans were pitted against each other in the media. This opposition distorted the reality of what took place. It also shifted attention away from the huge role white society had in creating the conditions that sparked the uprising. The biggest immediate obstacles to success in both the African American and Korean communities were then and continue to be the exploitation and oppression experienced as a result of white social practices such as housing and job discrimination, and the restructuring of the economy by large corporations—not the actions or personal prejudices of blacks and Koreans toward each other's communities.

For example, structural discrimination and anti-immigrant bias force well-educated Koreans to become small shop owners in African American and Latinx communities, where they face small profits and vulnerability to violence. Deteriorating economic conditions, coupled with media attention to their "success," directed people's anger toward them rather than toward economic policymakers. Koreans were clearly set up to be sacrificed to rioters. Their calls to the Los Angeles Police Department and to state and local officials for protection were unanswered.[5]

White people, on the other hand, could sit back and watch the show, perhaps temporarily uneasy about things getting out of hand, but nevertheless buffered from the direct effects of the violence and assured of protection. When rioters attacked major shopping malls in white Culver City, they were quickly stopped by police.[6]

A good illustration of how white people's lack of acceptance, suspicion, and fear of Asian Americans can lead to violence and discrimination is the death of Vincent Chin in 1982. Chin was a Chinese

American living in Detroit who was killed by two white unemployed auto workers who believed that he was Japanese. He had lived in the United States all his life. His killers had been led to believe they couldn't get work because of the import of Japanese cars. They believed Japanese corporations were responsible for their unemployment, and every Japanese American was complicit with the Japanese government. And they couldn't tell a Japanese American from a Chinese American. The sentence they each eventually received for killing Chin was barely a reprimand—three years' probation and a $3,000 fine.[7]

Wen Ho Lee was a Taiwanese American nuclear scientist who, while working at Los Alamos in 1999, was accused of releasing classified nuclear documents. He was held in solitary confinement for nine months by the government and then released, without having been charged for espionage. In 2006 he won a settlement from the government of nearly $900,000.

More recently there have been cases similar to Wen Ho Lee's. Guoqing Cao and Shuyu Li, scientists at Eli Lilly, were arrested in October 2013, accused of passing $55 million worth of secrets to a Chinese drug company. They were jailed and then placed under house arrest; the charges were changed to wire fraud and then dropped in December 2014. The proprietary information they allegedly passed was not proprietary after all.

Sherry Chen, a hydrologist at the National Weather Service, sent publicly available info to an old classmate in China and referred them to a colleague for further information. The colleague reported her as a potential spy, and she was arrested in October 2014. Charges were dropped in March 2015, but the National Weather Service has refused to give Chen her job back.

Xiaoxing Xi, then chair of the Temple University physics department, was arrested in May 2015 for allegedly sending plans to a device used in semiconductor research, known as a "pocket heater," to China. The plans were not for a pocket heater; investigators without the proper scientific background had mixed them up. The charges were eventually dropped.[8]

Wen Ho Lee and others have been vindicated, although not fully compensated. Vincent Chin is dead. All of them are among many Asian Americans blamed for economic problems, targeted for being dangerous immigrants, and then attacked.

White people have used the "success" of some Asian Americans[9] to demonstrate the lack of racism in the US and the opportunity African Americans have supposedly had and not used. Some white people label Asians a "model minority," a racial code phrase (see Part I) implying Asian Americans are hardworking, industrious, thrifty, future-oriented, and law-abiding, as all good white Christians are (or at least should be). However, this is just another example of projecting white stereotypes onto Asian Americans.

Many Japanese Americans were highly "successful" in the Western United States, but were still attacked, locked up in concentration camps, and subjected to mob violence during World War II.[10] Economic success may offer some protection against the worst effects of racism, but as long as white Americans consider Asian Americans (and other people of color) different and inferior, no amount of economic success will protect Asian Americans from continued attack and injustice. Vincent Chin could have been rich or poor, a citizen or non-citizen—what mattered to the two men who killed him was that he was Asian American. We must ask ourselves how many decades, generations, centuries even people must live here before they are accepted as "all-American" if they are not white.

White people need to be considerably better informed about the particular histories and complexity of Asian American communities in the US. We need to break down our simplified stereotypes by going beyond awareness of the Chinese New Year and Japanese internment and realizing that within particular Asian American communities there is great vibrancy, creativity, diversity, and much resistance to racism. There have been a constant exchange and mutual influence between many different Asian American cultures. The complexity of these dynamics defies simple generalizations about economic success or model minorities.

4.3. Questions and Actions: Asian Americans

1. What specific Asian American cultural communities live in your area? How can you find out more about the uniqueness of each particular community?
2. List four key Asian American concerns.
3. Are different Asian American groups represented in your city and county governments, school boards, and other local political institutions?
4. What are some of the "positive" stereotypes you hear about Asian Americans? What complexities and problems do these stereotypes cover up? What can you learn about white self-images from these stereotypes?
5. How have different Asian American groups been scapegoated for economic problems in your community? How have non-American Asians been blamed?
6. What do white people expect Asian Americans need to do or be in order to be accepted into the white community? Are there hidden reservations or conditions for that acceptance?
7. How are Asian American and Asian culture and history represented in the schools in your community?
8. Do you and your children have accurate knowledge about the struggles for independence from colonialism of the Filipino/as, Chinese, Koreans, Vietnamese, and Indians?
9. How has the relationship of the US with particular Asian countries affected the immigration of Asians and their treatment once here?
10. What are ways China is currently being portrayed as an archenemy of the US? How does that portrayal limit our ability to negotiate and cooperate with China?

Latinx

In 2014, the US Census Bureau estimated Hispanics made up 17.3% of the population in the United States, over 55 million people.[1] They comprised 38% of the populations of California and Texas, 18% of New York's and New Jersey's populations, 23% of Florida's, 30% of Arizona's, 47% of New Mexico's, 27% of Nevada's, and 21% of Colorado's.[2]

The variations of Spanish spoken are many, and the differences between communities of Latinx are large. Some groups, such as Cuban Americans or Puerto Ricans, have kept strong national identities. The families of others have lived in the US for hundreds of years and have Spanish-derived cultures but no connection with another country.

The very terminology used to describe Latinx has been in dispute over the years. I use *Latinx* because, when speaking in very general terms, it is broadly inclusive and some version of "Latino" tends to be preferred over "Hispanic" by Spanish-speaking people. However "Hispanic" and "Latino/a," and "Latinx" derive their meaning from Spain, and these words conceal the connections to North and South American land struggles and the intermingling of Spanish-derived culture with Native American cultures.

I also use the term *Spanish-speaking* because most Latinx in the US are connected to long-standing and complex Spanish language cultures spanning the hemisphere, even if they don't personally speak the language. This term also reminds us that racism plays out in cultural as well as economic and political arenas.

There is no national identity or set of interests uniting Latinx except their concern for the end of racism toward them. Many Latinx prefer to be called Cubano/as, Mexicano/as or Puertoriqueño/as/ Boricuans. These are the three largest groups of Spanish-speaking people in the United States; many Latinx identities are formed primarily within these communities.

Part of the white US *creation story* (told on Thanksgiving) relates how white roots are deep, how we were the original European settlers. Contrary to our story, descendants of Spanish colonists have lived in the Southeast, Southwest, and West for considerably longer than most English and French-speaking people. The first permanent European settlement within current US borders was established at St. Augustine, in what is now Florida, in 1565. From settlements in Florida, Mexico, and the West Indies, approximately ⅓ of the present territory of the continental United States was invaded by Spanish soldiers and missionaries and conquered in most brutal ways. A combination of Spanish administrators, conquistadors, ranchers, and missionaries killed, tortured, and enslaved most of the Native American men and killed, raped, and intermarried with the Native American women in the colonial South and Southwest.

When anyone's ancestors arrived in the United States—whether 400 years ago or last week—should not be important. Ironically, in some states with strong anti-immigrant organizing like Arizona, the majority of white people have family histories of less than 70 years in the area. Cracking down on immigrants without papers promotes police harassment, job and housing discrimination, and denial of health and educational services to anyone whom a white person "mistakes" for someone without documentation.

The 1823 Monroe Doctrine was the first attempt to articulate the US claim that all of the Western Hemisphere was "our backyard," and we could control what happened there in order to protect ourselves from "outsiders." Since then the US has initiated hundreds of invasions and interventions in Central and South American countries, leading to the deaths of tens of thousands of people; the US has supported military dictatorships, creating havoc in the lives and economies of local populations.

For example, in 1830, when the Mexican government outlawed slavery and prohibited further American immigration into Texas, whites were outraged and thousands continued to move into Texas as illegal aliens. They rose against Mexican rule in 1836 and, although initially defeated, were eventually victorious, claiming independence as the Lone Star State. Texas was annexed by the United States in 1845. Then the US instigated border skirmishes in order to justify a brutal invasion of Mexico in 1846, resulting in the 1848 Treaty of Guadalupe Hidalgo in which Mexico was forced to hand over all of California, New Mexico, Nevada, and parts of Colorado, Arizona, and Utah. As one member of Congress wrote at the time about our "manifest destiny" to rule the hemisphere, "This continent was intended by Providence as a vast theatre on which to work out the grand experiment of Republican government, under the auspices of the Anglo-Saxon race."[3]

In 1898, the US declared war on Spain and took over the war of independence Cubans had started in 1895. Within three months, the US defeated the Spanish forces and required them to turn over control of Cuba, completely ignoring the Cubans who had been fighting for their freedom. The US also took over Puerto Rico, annexed Hawaii, occupied Wake Island and Guam in the Pacific, and claimed the Philippines. Filipinos had been engaged in a long-term war of independence with Spain, and in 1899 they rose up against US rule. President McKinley sent in 70,000 troops. Three years later, ⅙ of the Philippine population was dead and the war was over.[4]

More recently, many Spanish-speaking people have arrived from Cuba, the Dominican Republic, and many Central and South American countries. These immigrations have been connected with US foreign policy and economic expansion. Groups of refugees came to the United States seeking asylum and economic opportunity. US government and corporate policy also directly encouraged migration through the Bracero Program, which brought more than 5 million Mexican workers to the United States between 1942 and 1964 as low-waged agricultural labor.[5]

Our politicians and leaders are clearly hypocritical when they blame recent Spanish-speaking immigrants for our economic problems and try to enforce a rigid border separation between Mexico (or Cuba or Haiti) and the United States. Corporate interests demand cheap labor and free movement of capital and resources throughout the Americas and have pushed through the North American Free Trade Agreement (NAFTA), the General Agreement on Tariffs and Trade (GATT), and other policies conducive to their ends. Then they encourage us to blame poorly paid Mexican and Central American workers for the lack of jobs and economic dislocation resulting from those policies.

White elites in the US have long been concerned with both expanding and maintaining our national borders. Expansion is seen as economic opportunity, while the maintenance consists of keeping Spanish-speaking people on the fringes of society and not allowing them into centers of power and control. The struggles of many Latinx have therefore been focused on the borderlands, both physical and figurative, between Anglo and Spanish land and culture.

Latinx have occupied various positions in the racial hierarchy of the United States depending upon economic and cultural factors. After the annexation of the Southwest in 1848, Mexicans had enough economic clout and "civilized" habits that they were accepted as white and given the rights of citizenship in California.[6] This was in contrast to the few blacks there, who were ranked far below Mexicans; to the Chinese, who were ranked slightly above Native Americans and had no rights; and to Native Americans, who were considered barely human and were killed indiscriminately.[7] California's racial hierarchy still has white people on top, but today Spanish-speaking people are considered, along with African Americans, to be at the bottom, and some Asian Americans are held up as closer to white and treated far better.

Latinx are underrepresented, undercounted, and underestimated. Their lives, culture, and the deprivations they have suffered are invisible to us. For example, in the Los Angeles uprising in 1992, from the media coverage you never would have known that the greatest number of people killed from any ethnic group were Latinx. The greatest damage done was to property owned by Latinx. Immediately following the uprising, there was an immigration crackdown and hundreds of Spanish-speaking Los Angeles residents were deported, most without trials or legal recourse.[8] Similarly in the aftermath of hurricane Katrina, the media barely mentioned the impact on the significant immigrant Latinx (and Native American and Southeast Asian) communities.

Spanish-speaking people can participate in literary, musical, dramatic, political, and popular developments throughout the Spanish-speaking world, a major international culture largely invisible to monolingual white people. White people have fought against the use of Spanish in schools and workplaces and have ignored, made fun of, and attacked Spanish language culture as being inferior, uncivilized, rural, traditional, monolithic, subversive, and dangerous. What are white people trying to maintain, and what do we fear, when we attack a vital international culture of which we are ignorant?

We are saying English is the exclusive global language of culture and achievement. We are, in addition, demonstrating that white racism is not only about economic and political domination, but is also about cultural hegemony. It is about white people and white institutions being able to define what culture is, who gets to participate in it and what language, literature, art, and music are included.

It is crucial for us to understand the importance of racism as a system of cultural domination. White people have long denied or minimized the importance of culture to people's everyday lives. We have appealed to universal, international, and "human" standards and values in our politics, science, and philosophy. This makes it very difficult for us to recognize the value of culture in our own lives, much less in other people's. We fail to see the inspirational role culture plays in resistance to domination by people of color. Using music as an example, when we are unfamiliar with the contributions of Reuben Blades, Lila Downs, Mercedes Sosa, Tito Puente, Carlos Santana, Flaco Jimenez, Los Lobos, Selena, and Villa-Lobos, we deny ourselves access to the richness, creativity, and inspiration their culture could provide us. Instead of maintaining cultural borders, we need to become much better at crossing them.

Use the following questions—along with suggestions in the chapters on Native Americans, African Americans, and Asian Americans—to guide your work as an ally to Latinx.

4.4. Questions and Actions: Latinx

1. Which groups of Latinx people live in your town, city, or rural area?

2. Which groups of Latinx people provide labor or services on which you personally or the economy are dependent (farm workers, low-wage manufacturing workers, or workers in factories near the Mexican border)?

3. What do you gain and what do you lose when workers are poorly paid, work in unsanitary conditions, are exposed to dangerous chemicals, and have unsafe working conditions?

4. How well are Latinx communities represented in your local governments?

5. Are there adequate support services for Spanish-speaking families and Spanish-speaking youth in your area? How could you find out?

6. How has the history of US involvement with Mexico, Cuba, Puerto Rico, and El Salvador influenced the status and position of the immigrant communities that arrived here from those countries?

7. How have stereotypes of Latinx helped prepare for or justify invasions and control of South and Central American countries?

8. Have you been involved with solidarity work with Spanish-speaking countries? How might that work have been connected to the exploitation of Latinx communities closer to home?

9. Did your foreparents speak a native language that has been lost in your family or community? What other losses accompanied the pressure to be a monolingual community?

10. How has the emergence of English as the language used in international communication affected people whose primary language is not English?

11. Do you speak Spanish? If not, what might be reasons for learning to do so?

Arab Americans

ON MAY 24, 2001, months before the bombings of the World Trade Center and the Pentagon, I came across the following sentences in two different articles on front pages of the *New York Times*:

> Like most Afghan men he wore a turban coiled around his head like a holy bandage.
>
> Afghanistan, known these days as a womb for global jihad...

In the US, images of Arabs and images of Islam are generated by a Western media lens filled with stereotypes, disrespect, misinformation, and emotionally laden descriptions. Arabs and Islam are conflated, producing a confusing and distorted picture of both. For example, despite the common perception that Arab Americans are Muslim, the majority are Christian.[1]

Stereotypes of Arab and Arab American men as untrustworthy and deceptive businessmen, terrorists, fanatics, sheiks, and traders riding camels—and of women as seductive or submissive are still so pervasive sometimes I find it difficult to form other images. Have you seen images recently of:

- an Arab American father playing catch with his son or daughter?
- an Arab American woman in a business suit?
- Arab American youth doing community service?
- an Arab American community celebrating a birth, marriage, or college graduation?

In one panoramic survey of Arab characters and images in 900 films, 12 were positive, 50 were balanced, and all the rest negative.[2] How can we treat Arabs respectfully and inclusively when they are portrayed as exotic or erotic, sinister and threatening, totally alien and dangerous to white Christians?

Arab Americans come from Algeria, Egypt, Iraq, Jordan, Kuwait, Lebanon, Libya, Palestine, Mauritania, Morocco, Qatar, Saudi Arabia, Yemen, Sudan, Syria, Tunisia, and the United Arab Emirates. (Iran and Turkey are not Arabic-speaking countries, and their citizens are not considered Arabs.) There are probably around four million Arab Americans in the US today, living in communities throughout the country. The majority were born in the US, and over 80% are citizens.[3]

The first wave of Arab American immigrants came to the Western Hemisphere beginning around 1880 through the end of World War I. They were mostly from what was called the Greater Syria area, which included Lebanon, homeland to many of the early immigrants. These immigrants were primarily Christian, and substantial numbers of this first generation became peddlers, shopkeepers, and traders. Later waves of immigrants came from a variety of Arabic-speaking countries and were mostly Sunni Muslims.

Early Arab American immigrants were yet another group the legal system attempted to place within its rigid yet arbitrary racial classification system. In the early 20th century, they were denied citizenship in the US and Canada because they were labeled Asian and therefore were not considered white. For example, in 1914 George Dow was denied permission to become a US citizen because he was a Syrian of Asiatic birth, and the law (a 1790 US statute) stated that only free white persons could become citizens. The following year, a different court ruled that 19th-century laws allowed Syrians, because they were so closely related to "white persons," to become citizens.[4]

In 1942, the difficulty with arbitrary racial classifications was again apparent in divergent court rulings based on race and religion. One court decision ruled that Yemenis were not eligible for citizenship "especially because of their dark skin and the fact that they are 'part of the Mohammedan world,' separated from Christian Europe by a wide gulf." Two years later, another Arab was granted citizenship because the judge considered Arabs to share an Aryan culture with whites.[5]

Diverse US presidential candidates—George McGovern in 1972, Jimmy Carter in 1976, Ronald Reagan in 1980, Walter Mondale in 1984, and Hillary Clinton in 2000—rejected political and financial support from Arab Americans and even returned contributions that had been previously received, denying them the opportunity as citizens to support the candidates of their choice.[6]

A climate of anti-Arab racism was much in evidence during the first Gulf War against Iraq. For example, in a nationally televised news briefing on NBC, February 27, 1991, General Norman Schwarzkopf, head of US military operations, stated that the Iraqis "are not part of the same human race we are."[7] *Time* magazine, the *New York Times*, and many other media carried editorials, articles, and cartoons describing Arabs as less than human.

Harassment and violence only increased after 9/11. Anti-Arab hate crimes rose dramatically, including beatings and murder. Racial profiling and surveillance by law enforcement became routine. Housing, job, and others forms of discrimination no longer even needed to be justified. And the negative portrayal of Arabs on TV, in the movies, and in video games continues to reinforce American hatred and violence against them. The constant negative portrayal leads to hate crimes and sometimes murder, as when Lebanese American Khalid Jabara, 37, was shot and killed on his front porch in Tulsa, Oklahoma, in August, 2016. His killer had previously shouted phrases such as "dirty Arabs," "filthy Lebanese," and "Ayerabs" when he harassed the family.[8]

Arab Americans have reached the highest levels of professional achievement throughout the United States and Canada, have been political and social leaders, and have contributed to the arts and sciences. However, they continue to be vilified in the media, left out of mainstream political and social affairs, misrepresented in textbooks, and excluded from multicultural curricula. They are also readily blamed for the actions of Arabs or Muslims in any part of the world and are vulnerable to verbal and physical attack simply for being of Arab descent.

The targeting of Arab Americans for violence makes all of us less safe in two ways. First, we do not respond to the extreme violence of white men as quickly or as thoroughly as we should because our attention is on "Arab terrorists." The United States has a long history of home-grown white male terrorists, including the Ku Klux Klan, the assassins of John Kennedy and Martin Luther King, Timothy McVeigh, the anti-abortionist murderers of Dr. Bernard Slepian, Dr. George Tiller and others, the Columbine High School massacre, the Sikh Temple shooting, and the murder of nine churchgoers at Emanuel AME Church in Charleston, SC.

Since the Oklahoma City bombing by white men, white extremist groups have hatched conspiracies to bomb buildings, banks, refineries, utilities, clinics, and bridges; to assassinate politicians, judges, civil rights figures, and others; to attack Army bases, National Guard armories, and a train; to rob banks and armored cars, and to amass illegal machine guns, missiles, and explosives.[9] Yet a disproportionate amount of our funding for anti-terrorism prevention focuses on Arab Americans and Muslims, not on much more prevalent white terrorist individuals and groups.

We are also put at risk because, in the name of combating "Arab terrorism," the civil liberties of every citizen are compromised through legislation like the Illegal Immigration Reform and Immigrant Responsibility Act of 1996, the Antiterrorism and Effective Death Penalty Act of 1996, and the so-called Patriot Act of 2001. This latter legislation created a new class of persons who are vulnerable to being deported simply because of their alleged association with a list of "terrorist groups."

Finally, consider how anti-Arab racism allows us to be manipulated around foreign policy issues. In the last decades, the US has invaded Iraq, Afghanistan, Pakistan, and Somalia; bombed Yemen, the Sudan, Libya, and Syria; and provided arms and other supplies to Israel, which has invaded Lebanon and Palestine. At the same time, our government has supported dictatorships and ruling elites in Saudi Arabia, Egypt, Jordan, Kuwait, and the United Arab Emirates. Without a high level of anti-Arab feeling in the United States, popular support would surely be lacking for military aggression in clear breach of international law. White US citizens will continue to be manipulated by government and military propaganda until we understand the complexities of Arab societies, understand the distinctions between Islamic cultures and Arabic ones, and overcome our anti-Arab racism so we can see Arab peoples and Arab Americans as distinct, fully human members of our communities.

4.5. Questions and Actions: Arab Americans

1. What are cultural traditions, community organizations, and political issues of the Arab American communities in your local area?
2. Who are national Arab American leaders, and what organizations are prominent nationally?
3. How can you respond when people around you make anti-Arab comments?
4. Have there been anti-Arab harassment, racial profiling, or hate crimes in your area? How can you join efforts to combat such harassment and hate crimes?
5. How can you join with others to challenge media stereotypes, misinformation, and lack of positive media coverage of Arab Americans?
6. Western nations contribute billions of dollars a year in arms and other resources to Saudi Arabia, Egypt, Israel, Iraq, and other countries supporting war and repression and, ultimately, fueling anti-Western feeling and terrorism. How can you work to insure money is directed to build a foundation for peace?

Muslims

IN THE UNITED STATES, on February 10, 2015, three young Muslims—Yusor Abu-Salha, her husband, Deah Barakat, and her sister Razan Abu-Salha—were murdered by their white neighbor in Chapel Hill, North Carolina. On February 13, a man started a fire at the Quba Islamic Institute in Houston, Texas. On the 14th, the Islamic School of Rhode Island was vandalized. On the 15th, the Hindu Temple and Cultural Center in Bothell, Washington, was vandalized. On the same day, also in Bothell, Skyview Junior High School was vandalized. On the 28th of the month, Mukhtar Ahmed, a Pakstani man, was shot in the head and killed while driving on interstate I-71 in Kentucky. On March 5, Ahmed al-Jumaili, newly arrived in the US as an immigrant from Iraq, was shot and killed as he was taking pictures outside his apartment.[1]

These kinds of attacks, while not always this frequent, are constant. Like all hate crimes and Islamophobic comments, they are a reminder to the Muslim community they are under siege, seen by many white Americans as dangerous outsiders and therefore vulnerable to violence.

Anti-Muslim oppression—often referred to as *Islamophobia*—is a combination of religious, racial, and cultural oppression targeting the presence, dress, behavior, job and educational opportunities, and institutions of anyone perceived to be not only Muslim but Arab or even generally from the Middle East or South Asia. Muslims are racially profiled in airports and in urban settings, routinely discriminated against in job and housing situations, and portrayed as dangerous fanatics in the popular media—particularly in books, movies, and video games. Islamic organizations are under intense surveillance by the government, are denied access to some of the funding and other opportunities Christian and Jewish groups enjoy, have their charitable activities challenged, are routinely denied building permits, and have their mosques and cultural centers attacked.

Popular culture does not reflect that most Muslims are neither Arab nor from the Middle East. Of the over 1.6 billion Muslims in the world (about 23% of the world's population), the majority live in countries as diverse as Indonesia, Malaysia, Pakistan, Sudan, China, Nigeria, Kenya, India, and the Philippines. The countries with the largest Muslim populations are (not in order) Indonesia, Pakistan, Bangladesh, India, Turkey, Iran, Egypt, Nigeria, and China. Each of these countries has between 50 and 100 million Muslim citizens.[2] Despite the dramatic religious and cultural variety of the Muslim world, Islam is often portrayed in the US as a monolithic, militaristic religion, unchanged since the 7th century, hostile to Christianity, and inimical to all things modern and Western. Muslims themselves are often assumed to be mindless adherents, devoid of any individuality: fanatical, blind followers of extremist clerics.

These biased attitudes have historical roots. Muslims have been treated as the prototypical enemy of Western Christendom since the first crusade was announced by the Pope Urban II in 1095. He launched this expedition to unite the fighting rulers and people of southern Europe under a new common identity as Christian. In his proclamation, the Pope denounced Islam as an abomination and enemy of God and declared that every Christian had a moral obligation to march to the Holy Land and claim it from "the Moors." The subsequent war to claim the areas of Spain and Portugal for Christendom was also labeled a crusade.[3] Over the following centuries, Christian secular and religious leaders forged a common European identity whose defining characteristic was defence against spiritual and physical threat from Islam.

During the 15th century, in the first process of racial (as opposed to ethnic) cleansing, Spanish rulers began persecuting Moors as well as Jews in their attempt to create a racially and religiously pure country, expelling the Moors entirely from Spain in 1609. The Spanish Inquisition was established to hunt down *conversos* (Moors and Jews who were suspected of falsely converting to Christianity) so they would not pollute the blood of a new national identity. During this period, the religious identity "Christian" began to take on a racial component, signifying *white Christian*, and the word *European* began to be equated with both *white* and *Christian*.[4] Emerging nation-states such as Spain claimed legitimacy from a unity of faith and a common pseudo-scientific racial heritage encapsulated in the Spanish phrases *sangre puro* and *limpieza de sangre*.[5]

During this period of nation building and emerging national identities, the word *Moor* was used as both a religious and a racial signifier and a general term to describe the Other—the perennial enemy of Christendom anywhere in the world who, by rejecting Christianity, "remains outside the Western economic, cultural, and political consensus."[6] As one commentator has written, "the term 'Moor' was used interchangeably with such similarly ambiguous terms as 'African,' 'Ethiopian,' 'Negro,' and even 'Indian' to designate a figure from different parts or the whole of African (or beyond) who was either black or Moslem, neither, or both... characterized alternately and sometimes simultaneously in contradictory extremes, as noble or monstrous, civil or savage."[7]

In contrast, there have been brief periods in US political history when Islam was not treated as an enemy of Christendom and relations between the US and Muslim nations were friendly. Washington, Franklin, and Jefferson respected and had generally positive things to say about Islam. In 1777, Morocco was the first country in the world to recognize the new United States government, with Tunisia following suit the next year. Even in the period of the Barbary War against pirates off the coast of North Africa, Islam was referred to with respect, and a political alternative to war was pursued by the US. At the same time, however, stereotypes about Muslims as infidels were promulgated by Christian priests and ministers and expressed in popular culture.[8]

Islam was first brought to the United States by enslaved Africans. It has been estimated that 20–30% of the men and 12–15% of the women were Muslim.[9] However, Christians made practicing Islam difficult, and many were forced to convert to Christianity.

Throughout the 19th and 20th centuries in the United States, various immigration laws favored Arab Christian communities and worked to restrict the arrival of Muslims.[10] With the collapse of the Ottoman Empire after World War I, the US began to play a larger role in West Asia. However, it was only after the British Empire collapsed, the state of Israel was created, and the US's dependence on oil began to grow that the US began seriously intervening in Middle East countries and heavily funding right-wing regimes such as the Shah in Iran and the Saudi royal family in Saudi Arabia.

After World War II, immigration from Muslim countries increased. At the same time, the African American Muslim community continued to grow, now about ¼ of the Muslim population in the US. Besides 4% who are Hispanic, the rest of the US Muslim population is primarily first- or second-generation immigrants from South Asia (India and Pakistan), various West Asian countries such as Iraq and Afghanistan, Turkey and Iran, and Indonesia, Bosnia, Kenya, Somalia, and Malaysia. Estimates of the total Muslim American population in the US range widely, but it is probably somewhere between four to five million. As a Pew Research Survey title suggests, most Muslims in the US are well-educated and middle-class. This report concluded that Muslim Americans are "largely assimilated, happy with their lives, and moderate with respect to many of the issues that have divided Muslims and Westerners around the world."[11]

The target of present-day Islamophobia is Muslims not as they are, but as they have been imagined for centuries in the Western imagination: dark, menacing, non-Christian others, intent on destroying Western civilization. These stereotypes become justification for public policy targeting individual Muslims and Muslims as a group.

Recent controversies over the siting of Mosques and Islamic cultural centers are indicative of deep-seated Islamophobia and racism.

There have been protests against the building of mosques in such diverse places as Murfreesboro, TN, Sheboygan, MI, and Temecula, CA, as well as in Brooklyn and Staten Island, NY. In Columbia, TN, a mosque has been burned down, and in Cedar Rapids, Jacksonville, Detroit, and Seattle, mosques have been smeared with animal feces, defaced with graffiti, vandalized, attacked with pipe bombs, and set afire by arsonists.[12] In Columbia, in a powerful act of solidarity with the Muslim community, the local pastor of the Presbyterian Church gave the Muslim community the keys to the church and said they could use it as their house of worship.

The 2010 protest against the Park51 Islamic cultural center proposed for a site two blocks from the location of the 9/11 bombings is indicative of Islamophobia. Protesters assumed that because Al Qaeda is a Muslim organization, all Muslims are terrorists, there were no Muslims who died in the 9/11 attacks or who played roles in the rescue of people caught in the buildings—and an old Burlington Coat Store could suddenly be "hallowed ground." These protestors also assumed Muslims should not enjoy the same religious freedom as Christians or Jews, even while many Muslims were risking their lives fighting as US soldiers in Afghanistan and Iraq.

The controversy over whether President Obama is a Muslim is another example of Islamophobia. Underlying the disbelief Obama is a Christian is an assumption that African Americans cannot be true Christians and will always be outsiders. This disbelief is enhanced by the stereotype that Muslims and people of color are dangerous and cannot be the equals of law-abiding white Christian Americans.

Anit-Muslim hatred is stirred up by conservative political leaders like President Trump and mainstream corporate media. It is also fueled by the Islamophobia industry. There are five key individuals and seven foundations that provide tens of millions of dollars to various entities for development and dissemination of misleading propaganda about Islam and the American Muslim community.[13] All of this activity taps into widespread underlying beliefs that must be taken seriously. In September 2015, a Pew poll showed that 29% of the population still believe Obama is a Muslim.[14] A more general

2015 YouGov poll found 55% of respondents had an unfavourable opinion of Islam and 40% supported a national registry of Muslims.[15]

Like the impact of any form of oppression, the toll on Muslims is tremendous. In the words of Darakshan Raja, co-founder of the Muslim American Women's Policy Forum, "For some of us, organizing and resisting against this system of anti-Muslim violence is survival.... It is emotionally exhausting and traumatizing to live in a world where a core part of our identity, Muslim, is consistently dehumanized." Raja continued, "I would like for the broader U.S. society to recognize that anti-Muslim violence is structural...It is an extension of the systems of oppression that America is built upon." She continued, "It is codified in policies and laws that make up the War on Terror, which we all fund through our tax dollars.... The collective blame, hate violence, and dehumanization Muslims experience must be seen as an extension of state violence. These systems of violence can only sustain themselves if we continue to accept the dehumanization of communities. A simple start to rejecting anti-Muslim violence is rejecting our dehumanization."[16]

Just as with racial profiling and discrimination directed against other groups, Islamophobia threatens our collective safety when resources are selectively and inappropriately directed at entire communities rather than at criminal behavior which is prevalent in all communities. The civil and religious rights of everyone are threatened when any group is singled out as not entitled to them. When we speak out and stand strong as allies to the Muslim community, we challenge violence and injustice, increase our safety and freedom, challenge age-old Christian stereotypes and myths, and uphold legal rights to freedom of religion, freedom of assembly, and freedom from discrimination and attack. Now is the time to work with Muslims to challenge Islamophobia.

4.6. Questions and Actions: Muslims

1. What are cultural traditions, community organizations, and political issues of the Muslim communities in your local area?
2. Who are national Muslim leaders and what organizations are prominent nationally?
3. Do you know the fundamental beliefs of Islam and something about the major organizational branches? Where can you find out more about Islam?
4. How can you respond when people around you make anti-Muslim comments?
5. Have there been anti-Muslim harassment, racial profiling, or hate crimes in your area? How can you join efforts to combat such harassment and hate crimes?
6. How can you join with others to challenge media stereotypes, misinformation, and lack of positive coverage of Muslims?
7. Western nations spend billions of dollars a year supporting war and repression and, ultimately, fueling anti-Western feeling and terrorism in such Muslim countries as Indonesia, Sudan, Yemen, Pakistan, Afghanistan, and Iraq. How can you work to insure money is directed to build a foundation for peace in those countries?

4.7. Suggestions for Confronting Islamophobia

1. Oppose all national and state anti-Muslim legislation.
2. Engage with your local mosques.
3. Organize faith leaders to write a joint letter to the editor of local newspapers.
4. Create kits for allies to respond to Islamophobia.
5. Host a multi-faith weekend to dispel anti-Muslim misconceptions.
6. If you see a Muslim being harassed—intervene.
7. Be friendly to Muslims you encounter.
8. Support your Muslim friends, colleagues, and neighbors.
9. Talk with young people about what they see/experience.
10. Call out hate speech.
11. Organize a "Learn about Islam" forum.
12. Write op-eds.
13. Challenge US military aggression and intervention aimed at predominantly Muslim countries.
14. Challenge media misrepresentations, stereotypes, and lies about Islam and the scapegoating of Muslims in the media and by public figures.

Jewish People

WHEN I'M IN a workshop on racism, and the facilitators tell every-one to break up into a white group and a people of color group, I immediately want to say, "Wait a minute. I'm not white." There are many white people in the United States and throughout Europe who would immediately agree: "Of course you're not white. Jewish people are part of the contamination of the white Christian race, along with people of color, Roma, Native Americans, and Muslims." These at-titudes are based on the conjunction of whiteness with Christianity.

Christians have long considered Jews to be inferior and a threat to Christians because they rejected Jesus as the son of God. In ad-dition, Jews have been falsely accused of killing Jesus because of stories in the New Testament. These stories are still read for Good Friday Easter services and considered true today by hundreds of millions of Christians. They are also promulgated by popular media such as on Christian broadcasting networks and in the wildly popu-lar Christian film *The Passion*.

Various anti-Jewish stereotypes were disseminated by early Church leaders such as St. John Chrysostom, who wrote:

> The Jews are full of hatred for the rest of mankind and are the enemies of all gentiles: they are parasites on the gentile societies that harbor them; they are addicted to money, and through the power of money, they aspire to be rulers of the world.[1]

Early Christian leaders continually attacked Jews on theological grounds and condoned the actions of Christians who vandalized synagogues and killed Jews. When Christianity became the official religion of the Roman Empire in the 4th century, Jews became even more vulnerable to violence from Christians. Jews were banned from public office and from many occupations, and some were forced to become tax collectors (because Christians weren't allowed to participate in the sinful activity of usury). Jews were subject to special taxes, prohibited from practicing their religion and building or repairing synagogues, not allowed to intermarry with Christians, and prohibited from holding any civil or economic position higher than any Christian. They were subject to forced conversions and commonly referred to as a source of religious pollution, contagion, and disease, setting the stage for later racially based anti-Jewish oppression.[2]

Large-scale attacks on Jews by Christians occurred during the Crusades, when Jews were seen as the European agents of the Muslim/Arab "infidels" who controlled the Holy Lands. Although the goal of the church was to attack Muslims and reclaim Jerusalem, most crusaders never left Europe. As they pillaged their way toward Jerusalem, they rounded up and killed thousands of Jews and destroyed their communities.

In subsequent centuries, Jews were forced to convert or were banished from such regions as England (1290), France (1306, 1322, 1394), Hungary (1367), Strasbourg (1381), Austria (1421), and Cologne (1426). Jews fought to defend themselves, fled, converted, or looked for protection from secular rulers, but were generally not powerful enough to protect themselves from Christian violence.[3]

On March 31, 1492, the Spanish monarchs, pressed by the Inquisition, gave all Jews four months either to convert or to pack up whatever they could and leave the country they had lived in for centuries.[4] Even after the Spanish expulsion, the Inquisition continued to persecute those suspected of "idolatry." Under the laws of purity of blood, any person with even one drop of Jewish blood was condemned. To prove their innocence, suspects had to display genealogical charts proving they had no Jewish ancestry. In other words, the Inquisition, drawing on anti-Jewish stereotypes from early church teachings, combined religious and biological justifications for persecution, setting the stage for the later development of biologically based theories of racism and the German genocide against Jews.

Many Jews fled from Spain to Portugal, but within a few years were forced to flee again after being given the choice of forced baptism or death. Subsequently they faced persecution and expulsion from the Italian peninsula and from many German cities and principalities in the 16th century, as well as pogroms in the Ukraine in the mid-17th century.[5]

Meanwhile many Jews who emigrated from the Khazar Empire in Central Asia when it collapsed in the 12th and 13th centuries had moved into Poland, Hungary, and western Russia and came under increasing attack from Christians in eastern Europe.[6]

Anti-Jewish hatred became rooted in Protestant Christianity during the "Enlightenment" through the writings of such key figures as Martin Luther. In 1543 Luther wrote "Against the Jews and Their Lies" in which he accused the Jews of being not only the bloodthirsty murderers of Christianity, but also of the German people:

> We are at fault in not avenging all this innocent blood of our Lord and Churches and the blood of the children which they have shed since then, and which still shines forth from their Jewish eyes and skin. We are at fault in not slaying them.[7]

Luther went on to suggest Germans burn the houses and synagogues of the Jews, ban their rabbis under pain of death, withdraw Jewish safe-conduct on the highways, prohibit usury, institute manual labor for young Jews, and finally, confiscate their wealth and expel them from Germany.

Most Christians believed Jews were a nation of outcasts who had killed Christ, rejected Christianity, used the blood of Christian children in Passover rituals, and prevented the Second Coming by their failure to convert. Even before biological theories of race, Jews were believed automatically to pass on these traits to each succeeding generation regardless of where they lived, what they practiced, and even, in many cases, whether or not they converted to Christianity. These beliefs were also reflected in the official policies of the

Catholic Church and many Protestant denominations. It was only in 1965, for instance, that Vatican Council II voted to absolve contemporary Jews of any guilt for the crucifixion of Jesus and to repudiate the belief that God rejected the Jews because they refused to accept Jesus as the savior.[8]

Jews today are part of many cultural groups on several continents. Jewish people are not only not a race—we have seen how this is not a meaningful concept—but they also come in many shades and colors, from nearly black Ethiopian Jews, to dark brown Jews from the Cochin coast of India, to light brown Jews from Argentina and Morocco, to blond and light-skinned Jews in Denmark and England. While this diversity is a refutation of racial stereotypes, it can make Jews more vulnerable when another group of people is claiming some kind of national identity, religious unity, or genetic purity. The membership application of the Invisible Empire of the Knights of the Ku Klux Klan requires one to answer the question "Are you a White, native-born, non-jewish [sic], American citizen?"[9]

When light-skinned Jews walk down the street, their skin color is immediately visible, while their cultural practices and religious beliefs may not be. If they can *pass* for white Christians and don't voluntarily give away that they're Jewish, they can enjoy the same respect and privilege given other white people in our society. Their presence is accepted, their words are listened to, and they have more police and judicial protection. In order to pass, Jews have to give up, minimize, or downplay any visibly Jewish aspects of their life and appearance. They can't say or do anything that will mark them as different. Since being Jewish, at its core, is inherently a range of ways of being, talking, and doing things that are not Christian, the more they pass, the less they are true to themselves. At any time, they might be found out and face mistrust, discrimination, or outright abuse.

In the United States, besides the threat of violence and the constant pressure to assimilate, one of the prices all people pay to be accepted as white is to collude in perpetuating racism. This is a price many southern and eastern Europeans as well as assimilated white

Ashkenazi Jews have paid. Passing leads people to believe economic improvement for themselves is different than economic justice for everyone. Today in US society, there is some privilege attached to being white, or, we might say, accepted as white on condition you support the racial hierarchy that keeps people of color on the bottom.

Many Jewish people have accepted this racial hierarchy in exchange for feelings of safety and acceptance. Consequently, they have established, in this country and in Israel, racialized hierarchies within the Jewish community. Jewish people of color constitute around 20% of the US Jewish population, including African, African American, Latinx, Asian, Native American, Sephardic, Mizrahi, and mixed-race Jews by heritage, adoption, and marriage.[10] They are a majority of Jews in Israel. Despite these facts, European-descended Jews dominate culture and politics in the Jewish communities of both Israel and the United States. This has rendered Jewish people of color invisible and made it seem racism is an issue Jewish people are separate from. Yet we carry the pain, violence, and confusion of racism within our own bodies and in the distribution of economic and cultural power within our Jewish communities.

Ruling classes have always used cultural differences to exploit people and to determine the roles outside groups would play in the economic system. Ruling classes use *systems of oppression* such as anti-Jewish oppression:

- to divide people, exploiting some groups more heavily than others
- to strengthen white cultural solidarity and chauvinism
- to make white Christian workers feel lucky they have some privilege or status no matter how heavily exploited they are
- to divert working and middle-class attention from the wealthy by focusing on scapegoats "above" them (Jewish bankers) and "below" them (African Americans, Latinx, and immigrants of color).

There are other complex strands in *anti-Jewish oppression*. Stereotypes, lies, and misinformation leads many people who are fighting racism, whether they are people of color or white, to downplay the importance of anti-Jewish oppression and not respond vigorously when Jews are attacked. Whenever the stereotypes of Jewish money or power go unchallenged, the power of the predominantly Christian ruling class is strengthened and racism continues. Colluding with anti-Jewish oppression, even through silence, contributes to inequality and racial injustice.

With some exceptions, Jews have lived for long periods of time in Muslim-controlled areas (such as medieval Spain and in the Ottoman Empire) in relative peace and respect. In Europe and the US, Jews and Moors have been categorized together as infidels, threats to Christianity and to Western societies. Although it is beyond the scope of this book, we have much to learn about how racism operates by analyzing the ways anti-Arab and anti-Muslim racism is related to anti-Jewish oppression, how European-descended white sectors of Jewish-American and Israeli society have contributed to anti-Arab and anti-Muslim racism, and how white Christian-dominated Western societies, for instance through the work of Christian Zionists, have set up Jews and Arabs to fight each other in Israel and Palestine.

Looking in detail at how anti-Jewish oppression operates gives us further insight into the dynamics of racism. It helps us see that racism is not simply a religious, biological, or cultural persecution. It rests, instead, on institutionalization of power and violence.

I'm white *and* I'm Jewish. Acknowledging my white privilege allows me to challenge racism both within the Jewish community and in the larger society. And when I, as a Jew, challenge anti-Jewish oppression, it does not distract from the struggle to end racism; it enhances it, making it clearer how dominant Christianity is a cornerstone of racism. I work for racial justice by drawing on my Jewish identity, Jewish values, and our collective knowledge and experience of Christian dominance, racism, institutionalized violence, and economic injustice. My greatest effectiveness as an ally to people of color comes from my history and experience as a Jew.

4.8. Questions and Actions: Jewish People

If you are Christian or of Christian background:

1. What did you learn in religious school or church or from the Bible about Jewish people? What did you learn about people of color?

2. What non-explicit messages did you receive about both groups from your Christian heritage?

3. In what ways is it true and in what ways is it not true to say "The United States is a Christian country?" How would you respond if someone said this in your presence?

4. What are some of the ways Jews are blamed for social problems?

5. How can you respond when people say Jews own or control everything?

6. Beginning with the fact that Jesus and Mary were Arab Jews, how has Christianity whitewashed its origins?

7. How can you challenge anti-Jewish oppression expressed within your own church and by other Christians?

If you are Jewish:

1. Are you generally treated as white or as non-white in Jewish society? In gentile society?

2. What forms does racism take within the US Jewish community?

3. What kind of support do you need from Christian allies when anti-Jewish statements or actions are being committed?

4. How can you draw on your Jewish identity, history, and experience to be an ally to (other) people of color?

5. When you or other Jewish people raise issues of racism, do you find yourselves attacked? What support do you need from Christians when this happens? What support do you need from other Jewish people?

6. How could you challenge racism within the Jewish community?

Recent Immigrants

IMMIGRATION IS A racial issue. US Immigration and Customs Enforcement (ICE) officials do not stop and interrogate white people or conduct raids to stem the flow of large numbers of illegal Canadian, British, and eastern European immigrants. There are not hundreds of miles of barbed wire fencing between Canada and the US. Vigilante groups do not patrol that border.

Obviously, one of the great strengths of Canada, the United States, New Zealand, and Australia as nations has been their ability to welcome the presence and contributions of new immigrants. But not all immigrants and not all the time. (And always at the expense of Indigenous people.) Recent immigrants have always been both feared and disdained by older residents. And immigrants of color, during short periods when they have been allowed to enter these countries, have always been treated differently than lighter-skinned arrivals.

Many of us in the West like to think of our countries as magnets for immigration because of the opportunity to be found here. Many of us believe our countries are the most civilized in the world, with coveted resources everyone else is desperate to share. This misperception has allowed us to construct a fantasy about "alien invasion"— hordes of people massed at our borders, frantically trying to sneak across only to overrun our communities, take our jobs, and use up our social services. To complement this image, we have constructed metaphors of immigrants as carriers of disease, infection, vermin, or simply as invaders. These may be a stories we tell ourselves, but they are not accurate.

Most immigrants from dedeveloped countries migrate to other

dedeveloped countries, not to industrialized ones. Less than 2% of the world's migration ends in the United States.[1] Many factors fuel immigration including war, natural disaster, famine, and lack of work. The United States is a major cause of migration around the world because its foreign policies have disrupted stable social and economic systems in many countries. There are many Southeast Asians in the US because we invaded Vietnam, attacked surrounding countries, and then welcomed those who supported our cause. There are immigrants from Cuba and Haiti here because we have supported dictatorships in those countries in the past, and US-based corporate exploitation and trade embargos have led to these countries' impoverishment. There are Mexicans and Central Americans here because corporate agribusiness, manufacturing, and extraction industries have invaded and severely disrupted rural and urban economies, concentrated wealth among an elite, and forced people to migrate to urban areas or out of the country in search of work to support themselves and their families.[2]

In addition, the US has promoted International Monetary Fund (IMF) structural adjustment policies, World Bank loans for large-scale agricultural modernization projects, and "free trade" agreements forcing millions of people to move from rural areas into cities and from one nation to another in search of food, work, and safety. (This is an international aspect of the neoliberal agenda described in Part V.) Women in developing countries have been particularly hard hit by these practices. When women are displaced from their land or unable to continue farming because of policies emphasizing export agriculture, they end up migrating to cities to work in textile, manufacturing, or electronic industries, or traveling to other countries to do nursing, domestic, textile, or sex work.[3]

The United States has generally not been against immigration as much as it has been against the long-term development of non-white immigrant communities. English and Irish immigrants were brought over to clear and settle the East Coast, Chinese laborers were brought over to build the railroads, and Mexican labor, through the Bracero program, was brought in to work the fields of the Southwest.

The labor of all groups was exploited, but there was still a color line at the border. People of color were not expected or encouraged to stay. During the limited period when Chinese men were given permission to immigrate, no Chinese women were allowed into the country, and even during great labor shortages, Mexicans were only given short-term visas. No such restrictions applied to English and Irish immigrants.

Once they arrived in the US, why did white immigrants fare better than immigrants of color? Immigrants from Ireland, Italy, Spain, Greece, and various regions of eastern Europe faced violence, discrimination and social prejudice, and limited access to jobs, housing, and education, just like immigrants from other regions of the world. However, immigrants from southern and eastern Europe, both men and women, were able to come in significant numbers. Although they faced discrimination, these immigrants were not driven out of trades, professions, and other occupations the way African Americans and immigrants of color were. "White" immigrants were able to become citizens, could vote, and therefore were able to develop political strength. There were few laws preventing them from participating in civil society or from owning land and businesses. The government established public schools, hospitals, and other services specifically to help them assimilate into US society. And while they did occasionally face violent attack, it was nowhere near as brutal and sustained, nor was it supported by the government as was the violence experienced by immigrants of color. Immigrants of color had as little status and government protection as African Americans and Native Americans, and therefore were subject to discrimination, hate crimes, and mob violence. They were often killed with impunity, oftentimes with state or national government collusion or active participation.[4]

Today the selective control of immigration to serve economic needs continues, as technology workers from South and East Asia enter the US on special visas to serve the interests of the computer industry, and women of color are imported from economically exploited countries as nurses under the Nursing Relief Act of 1989.

Large communities of Mexican, Central American, and Asian immigrants provide the labor force for the textile, computer, food harvesting, and service sectors of the US economy. Businesses are not interested in eliminating illegal immigration—heavily exploited immigrant labor is a source of great profit to them. They are interested in controlling it, using the system to undermine immigrants' ability to organize against workplace exploitation and keeping citizen workers alienated from and unable to unite with immigrant workers. As writer and historian Grace Chang notes, "immigration from the Third World into the United States doesn't just happen to a set of factors but is carefully orchestrated—that is, desired, planned, compelled, managed, accelerated, slowed, and periodically stopped—by the direct actions of U.S. interests, including the government as state and as employer, private employers, and corporations."[5]

Studies show that high levels of immigration do not increase joblessness even among the lowest-paid workers, and there is little correlation between immigration and wage level. While immigrant labor does bring down wages in low-wage sectors by about 5%, this impact is more than offset by the increased demand for goods and services they create which creates more jobs and a subsequent increase in wages.[6] Nor do immigrants bring disease or reduce health standards. Even though most immigrants come from countries poorer than the United States, recent immigrants are healthier than the US-born population in general, and babies born to immigrant mothers are healthier than those born to US-born mothers.[7]

Immigrants do not drain our social services. In fact, just the opposite is true. In general, young people, the elderly, the infirm, and those with disabilities do not emigrate. Immigrants come as adult workers, having been raised and educated at the expense of their country of origin. In addition, language barriers, fears of deportation, and the generally poor level of social services offered in the United States result in immigrants using fewer public services than comparable groups of citizens. Immigrants without documentation in the US collectively contribute nearly $12 billion each year to state and local tax coffers, primarily in the form of income, property, and sales or excise taxes.[8] Undocumented immigrants also pay sales taxes, gasoline taxes, and all the taxes everyone else pays. US citizens of all races benefit significantly from the economic and cultural contributions of recent immigrants, including the undocumented.

Despite the presence of 19,000 Immigration and Customs Enforcement (ICE) officials with a 2016 budget over $6 billion, many employers do not generally comply with immigration laws or report workers without papers unless those workers are demanding higher wages, safer working conditions, basic benefits, or the right to form a union. ICE is used as the threat and enforcement tool to deport workers who are asserting workers' rights. If immigration laws were vigorously and consistently enforced, much of the most dangerous and poorest-paid agricultural fieldwork, manufacturing, textile, food processing, and maintenance work throughout the US would immediately come to a halt. The intent of immigration laws is not to stop the work, but to maintain the highly exploitive conditions under which it is done.[9]

Many white people say they are in favor of legal immigration and only against undocumented immigration. Today's immigration laws favor those who have family who are US citizens or permanent residents. This means most people of color in the world are permanently excluded. Those who arrive here without documents are no more "illegal" than people of color were who could not vote or use public facilities before the Civil Rights movement. Racially discriminatory laws arbitrarily designate the actions of people of color illegal when they try to access the same rights and opportunities as white people.

Because ICE is part of Homeland Security, under the Secure Communities program, 287(g), and other programs, local law enforcement agencies are being pressured to enforce immigration laws, something they are ill-prepared to do and which diverts much-needed resources from routine law enforcement activities. In addition, when local police become ICE agents, it seriously compromises their relationships with immigrant communities and makes normal crime prevention and criminal investigations more difficult. Under these programs, hundreds of thousands of immigrants who have no criminal record and pose no identifiable threat to anybody have been detailed and deported.[10] Deporting busboys, gardeners, domestic workers, and car wash workers for not having legal papers with them when they are stopped by officials leads to broken families, separation of parents and children, and fearful and devastated immigrant communities. It does nothing to protect the US from terrorism. Laws like Arizona's SB 1070 go even further, mandating local law enforcement officials to stop anyone who they have reasonable suspicion might be an unlawful immigrant. Although parts of this bill were declared unconstitutional by the courts, other states have passed similar legislation.[11]

Like all attempts to monitor, control, and punish communities of color, current immigration policies target individuals and communities and throw up further racial barriers to full participation in US society. These policies lead to insecure communities, disrupted lives and families, and further hardship. They provide convenient scapegoats for economic problems, leaving the real causes and culprits unnoticed. They make a mockery of our claim that all people in the US are treated equally.

The only way fully to incorporate immigrants into our communities is to normalize their status and provide them with full rights and benefits. Until this occurs, employers' ability to exploit them will continue to depress wages, and set working people against each other, contributing to the further exploitation of all workers and the continuing harassment of Latinx, African, Asian, and South Asian communities under the guise of immigration enforcement.

We are heavily indebted to immigrants, both those with and those without legal documents, for our daily well-being. At the same time, these workers are some of the most highly exploited people in our society. To change this, we can begin to work for full rights and protections for them. All immigrants and refugees should enjoy:

- Full legal rights regardless of status
- Access to education and health care programs regardless of status
- Access to permanent residency
- Clear and uniform standards for the granting of refugee status regardless of country of origin

- Criteria for refugee status should include vulnerability to domestic violence, femicide, and female genital mutilation
- Elimination of employer sanctions and an end to visas tied to employment
- Release if they have been held without charges or denied legal rights

We should also work for:
- Resolution of the backlogs of visa applicants
- Demilitarization of the US-Mexico border
- Non-governmental oversight of Immigration and Customs Enforcement
- The end of arbitrary and unnecessary detentions and deportations that break up families
- A general amnesty for those presently in the country
- An end to the use of private companies for housing, detention centers, or providing services for immigrants
- An end to individuals and militia groups patrolling the borders

There are many immigrant-led organizations fighting for safety, dignity, and civil and human rights in the US. Supporting these organizations leads toward a society in which all people are valued and included. Some of these organizations are:
- Mijente: action.mijente.net
- National Domestic Workers Alliance (NDWA): domesticworkers.org
- National Day Labor Organizing Network (NDLON): ndlon.org
- #Not1More: notonemoredeportation.com
- Presente—Strengthening the political voice of Latinx communities: presente.org
- United Farm Workers Union (UFW): ufw.org
- Coalition of Immokalee Workers: ciw-online.org
- Restaurant Opportunities Centers United: rocunited.org
- Cosecha: movimientocosecha.com

4.9. Questions and Actions: Recent Immigrants

1. Were your foreparents legal immigrants to the US when people of color were excluded?
2. In what ways do you benefit from the work of immigrants (including those who are undocumented) for clothes, meat, vegetables, fruit, electronic goods, and other household items?
3. In what ways do you benefit from the work of immigrants for services such as domestic work, gardening, childcare, elder care, nursing, transportation (taxi, bus, and van services), hotel room services, and restaurant work?
4. What are the largest communities of recent immigrants in your area? What challenges are they facing? What kind of marginalization or exclusion?
5. How can you get to know and support those communities?
6. How can you challenge those who argue that immigrants are dangerous to our communities and deserve to be racially profiled, criminalized, and punished?
7. In what ways can you support just, non-racist immigration reform?

We All Stand to Gain

IN THIS PART, we have seen that racism has been established and maintained by the ruling class to exploit the land and labor of people of color and to preserve white supremacy.

Yet people of color are not just the result of what white people have done to them or even of how they have resisted racism. The lives and cultures of people of color can only be conveyed through their own voices, and I encourage you to listen to those voices. Your life will be changed as a result.

To broaden the narrow thinking which constrains white people's worldview and understanding, we need to promote the thinking, creative expression, and leadership of people of color. We have systematically controlled, exploited, and stymied such expression for hundreds of years. We have a historic responsibility to work for the end of white cultural, political, and economic exploitation.

In return, the burdens of guilt, blame, shame, and sadness will be lifted from our shoulders. We will no longer be standing on the backs of other people with all the precariousness that position entails. We will have an active role to play in ending injustice. We will gain immeasurably from the contributions people of color make to the world without exploiting them for it. And we will have a more accurate assessment of the contributions of white people. We will better see that leadership, wisdom, and creative expression have nothing to do with racial groupings, but result from the rich interplay between individual creativity, culture, circumstances, politics, and history—and defy any categorization. Most importantly, we will end our collusion in exploitation and violence and reclaim our humanity and moral integrity.

PART V

Fighting Institutional Racism

Institutional Racism

RACISM IS NOT JUST the sum total of all the individual acts in which white people discriminate, harass, or otherwise mistreat people of color. The accumulated effects of centuries of white racism have created institutional racism more entrenched than individual people's racial prejudice. In fact, institutional racism is barely touched by individual changes in white consciousness. We often find it difficult to see or to know how to challenge it because we are so used to focusing on individual actions and attitudes.

The following chapters examine ways racism plays out in some of our major institutions during this period of neoliberal capitalism. As you read, recall the web of control described in Part III. Each institution mentioned here reinforces others and contributes to the web of surveillance, control, and punishment under which people of color live. Each institution denies them the rights and benefits of full participation in US society and at the same time demeans, harasses, and attacks them, their families, and communities. *Institutional racism* is a mechanism for shifting material resources (land, money, the fruits of their labor) from people of color to white people, particularly those in the ruling class.

Land and Housing

IN CAPITALIST SOCIETY, land is wealth. It is the foundation for housing, the source of food and water, wood, minerals, oil, gas and other resources, the location of industry. For indigenous people, the land is also sacred—a source of wisdom, inspiration, community, and relationship to all life. The history of racism in the United States can be traced to people's possession of and dispossession from land. Racism today is still inscribed with those practices and patterns of dispossession.

When settlers arrived on the continent, Native Americans used all of the land to sustain themselves and their communities. Steadily and with extreme force, white people pushed Native Americans off their land. The church had ruled (see the chapter on Native Americans in Part III) that those who set out to "discover" land were acting under a god-given mandate to steal it from its non-Christian residents. This legal "Doctrine of Discovery" is still cited in contemporary land use cases involving Native Americans.[1]

Early settlers stole vast tracts of land, contradictorily claiming it was both uninhabited and that its inhabitants were not using it productively. Native Americans were routinely forced to move from area to area to land white people did not want—until whites decided that they wanted it after all. Nor could Native Americans claim title to land in courts because they had no legal standing. By the end of the colonial period, the US ruling class had accumulated most land into vast farms and estates, enshrining their power in the Constitution by granting voting rights only to white Christian men of property, i.e., those who owned land.

In 1862, the first section of what eventually amounted to

270,000,000 acres of land was opened up to homesteading by primarily white Christian men (you had to be a citizen or intended citizen to qualify). After the US army had violently driven Native Americans off their land, over 10% of the land area of the United States was ultimately given away for free to white settlers who "made improvements" to the land. Today, 46 million white people or 20% of the white population are direct beneficiaries of the Homestead Act.[2]

In 1887, the Dawes Act broke up Native American tribal holdings into small individual properties and allowed the US government to claim the "surplus," thus facilitating white people acquiring even more Native American land. At the same time, the federal government took responsibility for collecting fees from anyone who used tribal land, with the money to be held in a trust fund. Although the fees were consistently undervalued by the government, over decades billions of dollars were paid into this trust by mining, oil and gas companies, ranchers, and others who degraded the land through extraction and pollution. Even now over $350 million is collected annually by the Bureau of Indian Affairs, part of the Interior Department. The money was supposed to be given to the descendants of the original Indian landowners, but every audit since 1928 had found billions missing from the trust fund.[3]

In 1996, in the largest ever class action lawsuit against the US government, more than 300,000 Native Americans asked for $27.5 billion in settlement. The government delayed, often claiming vital records couldn't be found. It was later discovered that boxes of documents were being destroyed even as lawyers from the government said they were searching for them. The director of the Bureau of Indian Affairs and the Secretary of the Interior were eventually held in contempt of court and fined, but no restitution was made and the amount owed continued to accumulate. After some time, the total amount owed Native Americans was calculated to be close to $50 billion, but despite repeated audits reporting massive government fraud and incompetence and several court rulings in favor of the plaintiffs, the government delayed payments and refused a settlement.

In December 2009, after 13 years of litigation and 122 years of outstanding claims, US Attorney General Eric Holder reached an agreement with Native American groups to pay plaintiffs $3.4 billion, $2 billion of which would be set aside for a land consolidation scholarship program to benefit Native American investments. The settlement was finalized in 2011.[4] There are currently over 100 similar lawsuits pending.

The mismanagement of the Indian land trust fund is certainly the biggest and longest-standing financial scandal in the history of the United States. Institutional racism seems obviously present when one compares the $3.4 billion settlement in this lawsuit with the US government's $180 billion bailout for insurance giant AIG or $10 billion bailout for Goldman Sachs during the same period.

Many white people are resentful that Native Americans are able to run casinos on their land, yet 60% of federally recognized tribes have no gaming operations and most of those that do have operations that are barely profitable.[5] But every year the federal government deprives Native peoples of billions of dollars in legitimate land use fees, keeping Native communities in poverty.

In general, African Americans could not own land in most of the US until after the Civil War. After the war, blacks could buy land if they had the money, and a few were able to purchase farms and urban home sites. Some were even able to become prosperous from land, work, and businesses. However, eventually, no matter how long established or successful, whites found ways to dispossess them of their land and possessions, usually forcing them to vacate their homes in what can be called a process of ethnic cleansing that no part of the country was immune to.

White people used a variety of means to carry out black ethnic cleansing. There were large-scale race riots that destroyed entire city sections of prosperous black communities such as Tulsa, Oklahoma, and Rosewood, Florida. There were smaller-scale murders, threats, and intimidation that pushed blacks out of towns and counties in fear of their lives. In hundreds, probably thousands, of places across the US, black populations declined precipitously, often within days or weeks because African Americans were murdered, warned to leave, or burned out. They lost their land, homes, and possessions, everything they could not carry with them.

Most of those towns and counties have stayed white. For example, Forsyth County, Georgia, is now a white commuter area in the Atlanta metropolitan area. In 1912, there was a racial cleansing in which its white residents drove out 1,000 black residents. Forced to flee within days, most blacks lost everything, and whites quickly took over their land and possessions. Nearly a century later in 2000, out of a population of 98,000, there were only 684 blacks, most living on the county's border.[6]

Today, when a cross is burned in a yard or graffiti is written on a doorway, wall, or fence, people of color understand it as a warning that they are not wanted—and if they do not leave, more serious violence will follow. African Americans have a century and a half of evidence that white people will burn out or kill them if they ignore or are ignorant of these warnings. They also know that few other whites will try to protect them and they will have little legal redress, can hope for little more than an apology decades or even a hundred years later.

The support of farming in the US is another land use issue demonstrating massive racial disparity. The US government has systematically supported white farmers by providing subsidized loans, agricultural colleges, extensive networks of rural agricultural support, crop supports, and subsidies. Recently it was revealed that access to credit and other government support was systematically denied to black and Native farmers in the 1960s, 70s, and 80s causing thousands to lose their farms. In a massive settlement in 1999, the government admitted long-standing policies and practices of racial discrimination. In 2011, President Obama signed a bill settling the claims.[7]

As a result of these and many other land policies, white people own 98% of all privately owned agricultural land in the US.[8]

Asian Americans have also been targeted for widespread violence and exclusion, particularly in the West. Although their immigration to the US was prohibited for extended periods, those who had already settled here or who arrived with documentation faced an inability to buy land and periodic mob violence that burned down houses, stores, and entire communities up and down the West Coast. Several times the entire Asian population of a state was required to leave the state on short notice. Most infamously, 120,000 Japanese Americans were rounded up and sent to concentration camps at the beginning of World War II. Given six days to leave their homes and businesses, they lost their land, homes, and almost everything they owned. They spent years living impoverished in prison camps in desert areas of the western US.[9]

Although main targets of exclusion and discrimination have been Native Americans, Asian Americans (primarily Chinese and Japanese), and African Americans, other groups such as Jews and Latinx (primarily Mexicans) have also been subject to racial cleansing and exclusion in both urban and rural areas. Historian James Loewen estimates there may have been 10,000 white-only areas at their height in 1970, and millions of people live in or grew up in sundown towns and neighborhoods.[10]

When civil rights laws made formal segregation illegal in the 1960s, white people began moving out of urban areas into the suburbs, recreating whites-only neighborhoods. This was facilitated by federal housing subsidies for roads, schools, and other infrastructure. Real estate agents might steer white clients and people of color to different neighborhoods, quote higher rents or house prices to people of color, or use selective advertising to fill vacancies or promote properties.

As Loewen emphasizes, very few segregated white towns or suburbs are that way by accident. Although today the means of enforcement are usually more subtle (and clearly illegal), white people in the US continue to flock to all-white enclaves. Threats, intimidation, past reputation, tacit agreements, and subtle pressure all maintain white segregation. White people, when deciding where to live, may not even be consciously aware they are being steered or that they themselves favor white-only areas, camouflaging their interests with such racially coded phrases as "safety," "good schools," or "nicer neighborhoods." As sociologist Eduardo Bonilla-Silva observed, "although a variety of data suggest racial considerations are central to whites' residential choices, more than 90 percent of whites state in surveys that they have no problem with the idea of blacks moving into their neighborhoods."[11]

Meanwhile, vibrant communities of color that had flourished in the postwar era continue to be demolished. Funded by the federal government and cleared through the use of eminent domain laws, large public projects such ports, post offices, airports, convention centers, and sports stadiums, as well as freeways and rapid transit systems designed to service suburban areas, have destroyed housing, communal networks, small businesses, cultural centers, and generally thriving communities created by people of color in urban areas. Remaining communities have little economic infrastructure left as corporations moved manufacturing facilities overseas and new businesses locate their offices and stores in the suburbs. White city governments often placed garbage dumps and toxic waste facilities in communities of color.[12]

The current cycle of white displacement of people of color from the land continues as older white people decide the suburbs don't meet their needs and younger white people look for inexpensive housing in culturally diverse urban areas. Labeled *gentrification*, this process is fueled by local development policies that emphasize high-end condos, boutique businesses, high-tech jobs, and the advantages of "environmentally friendly" living. The overall effect is to destroy intact, if vulnerable, communities of color by raising rents and housing prices, pushing out local ethnic businesses, and diminishing job opportunities; small-scale manufacturing is replaced by "more profitable" land uses.[13]

The land you live on was surely stolen from Native Americans, but it is also likely to have been either subsequently stolen from African Americans or other people of color, or just maintained as white-only space by systematic racial policies and practices.

5.1. Questions and Actions: Land and Housing

1. Whose land are you on and how did white people gain control of it?
2. How was white ownership maintained?
3. What means have white people used to keep people of color out? How do they still maintain control?
4. How is where you live different, in environmental quality, safety, infrastructure, or beauty than places where people of color live?
5. Even if where you live is currently integrated, it might have racial discrimination or violence as part of its history. Find out about the history of the community you live in. What impact does that history continue to have on land use or land accessibility today?
6. Is displacement of long-time residents of color by younger and more affluent white people occurring in your or surrounding neighborhoods? How are people organizing to resist this process? How can you get involved in naming and resisting the displacement of people of color in your area?

Public Policy

PUBLIC POLICY refers to government planning, decision-making, and allocation of public resources. Government officials are constantly confronted by an array of issues affecting our communities. Which issues are addressed, how they are addressed, who gets to participate in discussions, and what solutions are considered viable are all influenced by racism. Any informed, active citizen can influence the nature of public policy discussion and decisions, although here again, white people, particularly those with money and connections, have long had greater political influence. The Movement for Black Lives vision and platform lays out a number of issue areas and the public policies needed to increase racial equity.[1]

People can influence public policy at several levels. We are most powerful when we organize around particular issues or programs and create pressure public officials must respond to. The civil rights, women's liberation, disability rights, and other movements are examples of large-scale organizing that led to new laws, executive orders, funding appropriations, federal guidelines, and other specific results.

Another way to influence public policy is by electing officials who represent our interests. This is always complex because candidates run on a platform of interests, some of which may be progressive and others of which may not be. They also make promises during elections and then do not or cannot follow through. Unless there is public pressure and support while elected officials are in office, they alone don't have the leverage to fight entrenched interests.

People are also able to respond to proposed legislation, state initiatives, nominations of public officials, and public planning documents. Concerted mobilization of people dramatically leverages our power in influencing policy decisions. Unless we analyze issues carefully and critically, keeping a focus on how they affect racism and race relations, we will not be able to marshal our forces effectively.

Public policy issues change over time, but every public policy issue in the United States is at least partly an issue of race. We must always pay attention to the racial consequences of any issue being considered, even economically "progressive" ones, so new policies don't have racist effects.

Public action through educational and organizing efforts is what influences and shapes public policy debate. During the first part of the 19th century, enslaved Africans, freed Africans, and their white allies worked to make abolition an issue that could not be avoided. Civil and voting rights for African Americans became public policy issues as a result of grassroots organizing during the Civil Rights movement. Japanese Americans organized, lobbied, and advocated for many years until reparations for the internment of Japanese American citizens during World War II became an issue the government had to address. These are the kinds of campaigns we can support. This is the kind of public action we need to take.

Pick a current public policy issue and ask yourself the following questions.

Any public policy issue can be analyzed using these and other questions. They stimulate our critical thinking so we do not mistakenly collude with an agenda that benefits a few and keeps the class, racial, and gender *status quo* in place.

5.2. Questions and Actions: Public Policy

1. How is the problem being defined? Who is defining the problem? Who is not part of the discussion?
2. Who is being blamed for the problem? What racial or other fears are being appealed to?
3. What is the core issue?
4. What is the historical context for this issue?
5. What is being proposed as a solution? What would be the actual results of such a proposal?
6. How would this proposal affect people of color? How would it affect white people?
7. How would this proposal affect the rich?
8. How would it affect women? Young people? Poor and working people?
9. What are other options?
10. How are people organizing to address this problem in a more progressive way? How are people organizing to resist any racial backlash this issue might represent?
11. What is one thing you could do to address this problem?

Reparations

WE WILL NOT GET VERY FAR in the struggle for racial justice unless we have significant national public support and leadership to address racial injustice directly and forcefully. This calls for no less than massive *reinvestment* in communities of color to redress the long-term effects of racism. Some might call it reinvestment for what was taken out of communities of color by white people. Others might call it restorative justice. The concept is often referred to as reparations.

The 20th century has seen national and international examples of reparations. The German government paid reparations both to individual Jews who suffered losses during the Holocaust and to the state of Israel. The US government paid reparations to Japanese Americans for the losses they suffered from the confiscation of their property and their forced relocation during World War II.[1]

Particularly within the African American community, the demand for reparations for slavery and its aftermath has been gaining momentum. Over the years, John Conyers, a Democrat from Michigan, introduced bills to put the issue before the US House of Representatives. There have also been public conferences, books, talks, and lawsuits. The Movement for Black Lives platform has an entire section on reparations.

The idea of reparations for African Americans has a long history. On January 16, 1865, General William T. Sherman issued Special Field Order No.15, which awarded all the Sea Islands south of Charleston, South Carolina, and a significant portion of coastal lands to newly freed slaves to homestead. Each freedman was eligible for 40 acres of tillable ground. The order became a proposed law passed by both houses of Congress but ultimately vetoed by President Andrew Johnson.[2]

The principle under which Germany paid reparations was stated in the 1952 Luxembourg Agreement, which said a state that victimized inhabitants on the basis of group membership has an obligation to compensate that group on the same basis. Slavery was a system legitimized in the US Constitution and enforced through local, state, and federal statutes. The genocide of Native Americans, the destruction of their cultures, and the establishment and failure of the treaty system were acts of the US government. In both cases, individuals were targeted simply because of their membership in a particular group, and the damage from those systems continues to this day.[3]

One form reparations for Native Americans could take would be the return of land. For example, there is much federal land no longer used for military bases. The government has promised to give priority to the claims of Native Americans for such land, but in practice this policy has not been carried out. Cleaning up and returning unused land could be a first step in providing a meaningful land base to Native communities.

Specific examples of reparations includes the 1988 bill providing $20,000 to each Japanese interned by the US in World War II; the state of Florida's reparations to the living survivors of the white riot that destroyed many lives in the black community of Rosewood; the state of North Carolina's reparations to the living survivors of the state's eugenics program, and the City of Chicago's 2015 ordinance allotting $5.5 million for cash payments, free college education, and a range of social services to 57 living survivors of police torture by the Chicago police department.[4]

Whether we call it reinvestment, restoration, redistribution, or reparations, US society should, through public policy, take responsibility for killing millions of people, stealing land, and exploiting the labor and culture of Native Americans, African Americans, Latinx, and Asian Americans during the last 500 years of European settlement in North America. Public reinvestment needs to be focused and accountable. Reparations should include acknowledgement of harm done, restitution addressing the economic, psychological, educational, and health impacts of the harm done, and closure.

People of color do not want handouts. They say they want an end to racial exploitation; they want the same opportunities white people have. As Professor Eric Yamamoto has observed (in relationship to the Japanese American redress movement), "Reparations, if thoughtfully conceived, offered and administered, can be transformative. They can help change material conditions of group life and send political messages about societal commitment to principles of equality."[5]

How do we pay for reinvestment? It is no secret, but still little discussed among us, that wealth is concentrated among a relatively few in the United States. In 2015 the top 10% of the population owned 76% of the total wealth of the entire country. They averaged over $4 million per household.[6] Over 90% of the total wealth of the country is owned by white people, with Latinx holding 2.3% and blacks holding 2.6%. At the same time, the bottom 32.1% of white families have an average net worth of $0. In other words, economic inequality dramatically affects both poor and working-class whites and people of color, with race being a crucial factor.[7]

In the last two decades in the US, income, capital gains, and inheritance taxes have been significantly cut, allowing those with the most wealth to pass on even greater amounts to their children. We have corporate welfare policies, for example: unlimited deduction for interest on corporate debt, intangible asset write-offs, foreign tax credits, and write-offs for the banks' foreign debt losses.

Such government policies favor the rich over the rest of us, and white people over people of color. We need to tax the income and accumulated wealth of the small percentage of individuals, families, and corporations controlling our economy and communities so we can reinvest money in community-controlled and racially just development. Poor, working-, and middle-class people of all races, women and men, young and old, people with disabilities, rural, urban and suburban dwellers would benefit if we did so.

The tax structure of the United States is complex, at least partly to protect the tremendous accumulation and concentration of wealth. A detailed analysis of this is beyond the scope of this book. We could make the entire system simpler and substantially more just with a few major changes. Here are some suggestions:

- Eliminate all tax credits and exemptions except the personal exemption
- Eliminate all itemized deductions
- Lower the lowest rates and raise the highest rates in a simple scale
- Eliminate special treatment for capital gains
- Impose the income tax on the increase in value of all holdings at death
- Withhold taxes on all income, regardless of source
- Have a means test for all individual government benefits such as social security
- Impose a 1% excise tax on all securities and options trading
- Eliminate corporate tax preferences and increase corporate taxes to generate about 31% of total income tax collection
- Tax income earned in the United States regardless of the filer's country of residence
- Eliminate write-offs for taxes paid to foreign governments
- Raise taxes on overseas investors
- Raise taxes on foreign companies earning money in the United States[8]

Voting

MANY OF US HAVE COME to take our right to vote for granted, forgetting our foreparents' long struggles to achieve it. People fought for hundreds of years to extend the right to vote, first from rich white men to poor and working-class white men, then to men of color and finally to women.

In this chapter, I deal primarily with the situation in the US because of the widespread and well-documented practice of disenfranchising voters of color. However, all white-dominated countries have histories of denying people of color the right to vote.

Preliminary data for the 2016 presidential election in the United States show whites constituted 79% of Donald Trump's total vote, while 79% of people of color voted for Hillary Clinton. But were people of color adequately represented? Did all of their votes count?[1]

Denying people of color the right to vote is a practice deeply embedded in the US political system, and we need to understand that history so we don't consider the present practices anomalous. Our Founding Fathers, in a compromise to ensure Southern states would participate in the union, agreed that slaves, although they could not vote, would count as ⅗ of a person for the purpose of calculating the number of Electoral College representatives allotted to each state. The number of representatives was, in turn, used to calculate the number of electoral votes each state would have. This compromise gave the Southern states a political advantage so powerful the US had Southern slave-owning presidents for 50 of the first 72 years of the country's history.[2]

African American men received the right to vote with the passage of the 15th amendment to the US Constitution in 1870. But even today the two-party, winner-take-all Electoral College system continues to discriminate against and marginalize people of color. In the 2000 election, Bush won the electoral votes of every Southern state and every border state except Maryland, despite the fact that 53% of all blacks (over 90% of whom voted for the Democrats) live in the Southern states. There are more white Republicans than black votes in each of those states, so the electoral college discounted the votes of over ½ the people of color in the country. Millions of Native American and Latinx voters who live in overwhelmingly white Republican states like Arizona, Nevada, Oklahoma, Utah, Montana, and Texas have been equally unrepresented by Electoral College voting.

A further dilution of the votes of people of color occurs because of the way electoral votes are unequally distributed between rural and urban states. For example, in Wyoming in 2016, one Electoral College vote corresponded to 195,000 voters, while in California, with more voters of color, the ratio was one Electoral College vote to over 711,000 voters. Another way to understand this impact is that, nationally, African American votes weigh 95% as much as white votes, Latinx votes are on average 91%, and Asian American votes 93% as much as a white vote.[3]

Representation in the US Senate is similarly skewed. Vermont's 625,000 residents have two United States senators, and so do New York's 19 million. A Vermonter has 30 times the voting power in the Senate of a New Yorker just over the state line. The nation's largest gap, between Wyoming and California, is more than double that. The 38 million people who live in the nation's 22 least populated states (including Wyoming) are represented by 44 senators. The 38 million residents of California are represented by two senators. The US Senate may be the least democratic legislative chamber in any overdeveloped nation in the world.[4] This gap in representation is widening and has major racial implications. By 2025, the four states of New York, California, Texas, and Florida will have non-white majorities and 25% of the nation's population but will have the same

Senate representation as the four states of Wyoming, Montana, Idaho, and North Dakota.[5]

The Electoral College system is not the only way people of color lose voting representation. After emancipation and the passage of the 14th and 15th amendments, the Southern states worked to exclude newly enfranchised black voters. The white ruling class of the South was very explicit about what it was doing. For example, in Virginia, US Senator Carter Glass worked to expand disenfranchisement laws along with poll taxes and literacy tests. He described the state's 1901 convention this way:

> Discrimination! Why that is precisely what we propose. That, exactly, is what this Convention was elected for—to discriminate to the very extremity of permissible action under the limits of the Federal Constitution, with a view to the elimination of every Negro voter who can be gotten rid of legally, without materially impairing the numerical strength of the white electorate.[6]

In Alabama, the criminal code in the state constitution of 1901 was, according to the chair of the convention John Knox, designed to "ensure white supremacy," and crimes worthy of disenfranchisement were classified depending in large part by whether delegates thought blacks were likely to commit them.[7] The state was also focused on excluding poor whites. Delegates "wished to disfranchise most of the Negroes and the uneducated and propertyless whites in order to legally create a conservative electorate," wrote historian Malcolm McMillan.[8]

Historically, another way white people disenfranchised voters of color was by disenfranchising felons—but not just any felons.[9] Many states disenfranchised criminals even before the Civil War. But after the Civil War and Reconstruction in the South, legal codes were created to limit the effects of the 14th and 15th amendments that gave blacks equal protection under the law and gave black men the right to vote. In Mississippi, the convention of 1890 replaced laws disenfranchising all convicts with laws disenfranchising only people convicted of the crimes blacks were supposedly more likely to commit. For almost a century thereafter, you couldn't lose your right to vote in Mississippi if you committed murder or rape, but you could if you married someone of another race. In Florida, the constitution drafted in 1868 disenfranchised ex-felons as well as anyone convicted of larceny, a crime whites considered ex-slaves were most likely to commit.

The provisions implemented during those post-Reconstruction conventions, from poll taxes to grandfather clauses[10] to literacy tests, were almost all struck down by the Civil Rights Act of 1965. The only ones still standing are felony provisions, which leaves 5 million people, including 2.2 million black men (approximately 1 out of 13 African Americans) currently denied the right to vote because of incarceration or past felony convictions.[11] In Florida, Kentucky, and Virginia, more than 1 in 5 African Americans can't vote for these reasons.[12]

As journalist Nicholas Thompson of the *Washington Monthly* noted, "Three out of every five felony convictions don't lead to jail time, and there's no clear line you have to cross to earn one.... Stopping payment on a check of more than $150 with intent to defraud makes you a felon in Florida. Being caught with one-fifth of an ounce of crack earns you a federal felony, but being caught with one-fifth of an ounce of cocaine only earns a misdemeanor."

Besides being arbitrary, racially biased, and a continuation of historic patterns of discrimination, Thompson wrote, "denying felons the right to vote...runs against both the idea that people can redeem themselves and one of the nation's most important principles, the right to choose who governs you." Thompson quoted neoconservative social theorist James Q. Wilson: "A perpetual loss of the right to vote serves no practical or philosophical purpose."[13]

Bob Wing, former editor of *ColorLines* magazine, described how even people of color who can vote are marginalized due to the two-party political system in the US. To win elections, both parties must take their most loyal voters for granted and focus their messages and money on winning over so-called undecided voters. The undecideds are mostly white, affluent suburbanites; both parties try to position their politics, rhetoric, and policies to woo them. The interests of people of color are ignored or even attacked by both parties as they pander to a white center.[14]

There are, of course, other strategies white people use to keep people of color from voting or to keep their votes from counting: at-large elections, gerrymandering, failure to redistrict when called for, *packing* (drawing electoral districts so the majority of a group is packed into one area, which therefore gives it only a single representative), and its opposite *cracking* (spreading out voters of color over several districts so their votes are diluted). Since 2010, a total of 10 states have more restrictive voter ID laws in place (and six states have strict photo ID requirements), seven have laws making it harder for citizens to register, six cut back on early voting days and hours, and three made it harder to restore voting rights for people with past criminal convictions.[15] Voters in the 2016 US presidential election faced long lines (at least 10 states reported waits of over an hour), malfunctioning voting machines (at least 13 states), confusion over voting restrictions (14 states), arbitrary and illegal removal of names from the voter rolls, and voter intimidation in several states.[16]

Finally, because the Electoral College vote distribution is tied to the census and we know the census undercounts communities of color, those communities lose political representation. The Census Bureau has refused to adjust the 2010 census results to account for a known undercount that leaves out at least 1.5 million people, all of whom are poor and many of whom are people of color. These data errors also have serious repercussions in the distribution of federal and state funds for social programs and community development grants.[17]

White people often complain people of color don't vote in large enough numbers. I've heard it said, "They must not care enough." But how many white people would vote if we were harassed on the way to the poll and, after we traveled over an hour to get there and then waited a couple of hours in line, we were told we weren't listed or that we needed to show extra identification or the voting machines were broken? How many would vote if, when we tried to make a complaint, there was no one who spoke our language to help us, and all the complaint lines were busy and understaffed? How many would vote if we discovered later that many of our votes were thrown out because of "irregularities" in the ballots and voting machines? What if this had been going on for over 150 years?

There are numerous places to begin overhauling the US voting system:

- Eliminate the Electoral College system
- Develop a system of proportional representation for elections (a system already in place in many municipalities and counties; various forms are used throughout the world)
- Institute federal monitoring of elections
- Allow for district voting in local elections
- Develop a multi-party system of government
- Redistrict by population, supervised by widely representative bodies of citizens from each community
- Remove restrictions on ex-felons' voting and set up programs to help them register, as Canada does
- Install modern, easy-to-use, transparent voting machinery that produces a paper record; keep polls open 24 hours or more; declare voting day a national holiday
- Institute election-day registration

There are already community groups working on many of these issues. By becoming active on this issue, you are strengthening democracy and making sure *all* votes count.

Affirmative Action

AFFIRMATIVE ACTION is designed to eliminate institutional discrimination in situations where decisions, policies, and procedures that may not be *explicitly* discriminatory have had a negative impact on a specific group of people. Yet today a vocal white minority says we should stop affirmative action not only as a legal remedy, but also as a social commitment. These people say we have gone too far in correcting racial injustice.

Affirmative action is practiced in many areas of our society. We have hiring and recruiting preferences for veterans, women, and the children of alumni at many universities; special economic incentives for purchase of US-made products; import quotas against foreign goods and agricultural and textile subsidies. These practices have led to a huge over-representation of white people, men, and people of middle-, upper-middle-, and ruling-class backgrounds in our universities, in well-paid jobs, and in the professions.

Many forms of discrimination in our society are illegal. The federal government put in place affirmative action programs to redress racial inequality and injustice in a series of steps in the 1960s as a response to the tremendous mobilization of African Americans and white allies pushing for integration and racial justice.[1]

However, racism, rather than being self-correcting, is self-perpetuating. Disadvantages to people of color and benefits to white people are passed on to each succeeding generation unless remedial action is taken. The disadvantages to people of color coalesce into institutional practices adversely affecting people of color even though the intent of individual actions may be race-neutral. We have to take positive steps to eliminate and compensate for these institutional effects, even when there is no discernible discriminatory intent. Affirmative action policies serve as a corrective to such patterns of discrimination. They keep score on the progress toward proportional representation and place the burden of proof on organizations to show why it is not possible to achieve it.

An argument raised against affirmative action is that individual white people, often white males, have to pay for past discrimination and may not get the jobs they deserve. It is true that specific white people may not receive specific job opportunities. We tend to forget that millions of specific people of color have lost specific job opportunities as a result of decades of racial discrimination. To be concerned only with white applicants who don't get the job, while ignoring the people of color who don't get it, shows racial preference.

Affirmative action is not a cure-all. Affirmative action programs cannot direct us to the social policies we need to pursue so we do not have to compete for scarce resources in the first place. In the larger picture, we must ask ourselves why there aren't enough well-paying, challenging, and safe jobs for everyone. Why aren't there enough places in universities for everyone who wants an education? Expanding opportunity for people of color means expanding not only their access to existing jobs, education, and housing (affirmative action), but removing the obstacles that cause these resources to be limited (tremendous inequality and concentration of wealth in the ruling class).

In 1996, confronted with Proposition 209 (which would have eliminated affirmative action programs in California if it were passed), a group of white men in Oakland came together to discuss ways we could add our efforts to those of people of color who were defending affirmative action. We were angry racism continued, angry affirmative action was being curtailed, and angry that white men were being portrayed as the victims of affirmative action programs. As a group, we felt that since we had benefited so directly from affirmative action programs, it would be hypocritical to deny these benefits to people of color just when they had finally gained access to them. We named ourselves Angry White Guys for Affirmative Action and began a campaign to address white people on the issue. We chose the name to challenge the conventional thinking that all white men were racist, reactive, and resentful of affirmative action.

When we gathered for meetings of Angry White Guys for Affirmative Action, our goal was not to understand our privilege, but to use our status as white men to counter the racist attacks on communities of color. Working closely with organizations led by people of color, we mapped out a strategy to reach white people in the urban and suburban areas around us. We gave talks and conducted workshops, wrote editorials, stood on street corners with our banner, conducted a walk of hope between urban and suburban churches and synagogues, educated white people about the history of affirmative action and about the deceptive and manipulative tactics being used to attack it. And we talked about our own experiences as beneficiaries of affirmative action, challenging the myth of a level playing field. (See the chapter on white benefits in Part II of this book for my personal account.)

Just like reparations mentioned earlier, affirmative action has been a symbol of white people's acknowledgement of and serious commitment to eradicating racial discrimination. It has been interpreted as such by most people of color. The hypocrisy is clear when white people who say they support equal opportunity attack affirmative action, yet want to leave intact the basic economic and racial injustices it is designed to correct. Ask people who oppose affirmative action how they propose to eliminate racial discrimination. You can learn a lot about their underlying beliefs from their answers.

5.3. Questions and Actions: Affirmative Action

1. List some of the obvious and subtle ways people of color may be discriminated against in the hiring, promotion, and benefits processes at your workplace or other workplaces you encounter in your daily life.
2. Which of these areas do you control? In which do you participate (as a worker, manager, or client/consumer)?
3. What is the role of any labor organizations related to your workplace regarding affirmative action?
4. How are people recruited to the organizations you are involved in?
5. How might these recruitment practices discriminate against people of color?
6. Have there been charges, lawsuits, or public action against discrimination in any institution you use (a bank, school, city government, retail store, or manufacturer)? How was it resolved? Did you ignore or feel angry about the disruption? Did you support the action against discrimination by:
   a. Joining the action?
   b. Boycotting the store or product?
   c. Writing letters of support?
   d. Encouraging your friends, family, or co-workers to be supportive?
7. What would the composition of your workplace look like at all levels if it truly reflected the racial diversity of your community?
8. Affirmative action is a tool for full inclusion and equal opportunity for all people, not only people of color. Go back through these questions and substitute women, people who are lgb, transgender or gender queer, people with disabilities, seniors, or young people for people of color.

9. What fears, doubts, questions, or concerns do you have about affirmative action? Where do your fears come from? What could you do to answer your questions? Who could you talk with about your concerns?

10. Have you ever been chosen for a job, training program, college-level program, or housing opportunity for which you were less qualified than others? Have you ever been given preference because of family connections, economic background, age, race, or gender?

11. Think again about Question 10 and try to understand ways family connections, economic background, race, age, or gender may have given you benefits compared to other applicants.

12. Besides numerical goals, what measures would you suggest be used to monitor racial and other forms of discrimination?

13. How are you going to respond to people who say affirmative action unfairly discriminates against white males?

14. List three things you can do to defend or strengthen affirmative action programs in your workplace, community, or state.

15. Choose one you will start doing.

At Work

WHITENESS HAS LONG BEEN related to racism in the workplace and economy. As Historian David Roediger explains in his book *The Wages of Whiteness*, part of the campaign to entice white male workers into industrial jobs during the 19th century was to rationalize that at least they were not slaves. They could keep their white masculinity intact, even while giving up their economic independence, because (they were told) being a worker in a factory was not the same as being a slave working for a master.

Male industrial workers eventually borrowed the language of slavery to describe their "waged slavery." They played on similarities between their work situation and that of slaves, at the same time trying to keep the differences clear so they could preserve industrial and craft jobs for whites. Business and political leaders used racism to manipulate white industrial workers by instilling in them a false sense of pride which they then relied on to hold themselves separate from male workers of color.[1]

W.E.B. Du Bois was one of the first historians to note the impact racism had on both blacks and whites in the South. Because of slavery, there was no major labor movement to protect the region's five million poor whites, who owned no slaves, from being heavily exploited by the 8,000 largest slave owners. The availability of cheap slave labor undermined white workers' ability to bargain for higher wages and better working conditions. More recently, Michael Reich demonstrated that where the gap between the wages of blacks and whites is greatest, wages of whites are the lowest and profit to the wealthy the highest. He described how racism works in the work-place:

> Wages of white labor are lessened by racism because the fear
> of a cheaper and underemployed Black labor supply in the
> area is invoked by employers when labor presents its wage
> demands. Racial antagonisms on the shop floor deflect atten-
> tion from labor grievances related to working conditions, per-
> mitting employers to cut costs. Racial divisions among labor
> prevent the development of united worker organizations
> both within the workplace and in the labor movement as a
> whole. As a result union strength and union militancy will be
> less the greater the extent of racism.[2]

Work in the United States is still highly segregated by class, race, and gender. The overall economy, as well as most large organizations, is vertically segregated as well. Upper-middle- and upper-class white men have access to the jobs with the most money, power, and status. Women, working-class whites, and people of color are strung out on the economic hierarchy, but are found disproportionately at the bottom in the least secure, most unsafe, poorly paid jobs.

The immediate impact of racism on working people of color is economic. Profits from racism, or *super-exploitation* as economist Victor Perlo described it, are the profits employers make when they underpay workers of color. In other words, super-exploitation is the wage differential between white workers and workers of color, mul-tiplied by the number of workers in private enterprises. Perlo notes that the profits from racism against all minorities grew from $56 bil-lion in 1947 to $197 billion in 1992 (expressed in 1995 dollars). When the earnings of white workers are compared with those of specific other groups, we find the profits from super-exploitation (the gap in earnings between the groups) more than doubled from African American workers, and increased tenfold from Latinx, Native Ameri-can, and Asian American workers.

In addition, racism benefits employers and hurts white workers because any low-waged segment of the workforce exerts significant downward pressure on *all* wages. Perlo concluded his chapter on racism and work by stating that the extra profits employers gained from racism—either directly at the expense of minority workers, or indirectly at the expense of white workers—came to approximately $500 billion in 1995.[3]

Winning the broader struggle for economic democracy is crucial for truly ending racism, and a key to achieving economic justice is solidarity between white workers and workers of color, between US workers and workers from other countries. Racism undermines both levels of solidarity.

One way to challenge these patterns is to organize against new attempts by US financial interests to further consolidate their dominance through such trade agreements as the Trans-Pacific Partnership trade agreement (TPP) and the Transatlantic Trade and Investment Partnership (TTIP). The TPP and TTIP, like their predecessors, do not create jobs, protect the environment, or ensure safe imports. Rather they make it easy for companies to move production to locations with the lowest wages, lowest labor standards, and least environmental regulation. Neoliberal governments sign trade agreements to offer such concessions to companies operating in the international arena. These trade agreements, negotiated secretly, falsely encourage us to believe our own (white) US jobs will be protected at the expense of people of color in other countries. In reality, US workers get traded off against foreign workers and are able to exert almost no control over labor-related and environmental policy in the US.

Through economic policies instituted by the World Bank, International Monetary Fund (IMF), and World Trade Organization (WTO), white-dominated companies and governments have created an *international* racial hierarchy of wealth, power, and control that mirrors the US domestic one. We are not powerless against multinational corporations if we overcome our training in racism to work together with people from other countries. We can challenge the dumping of toxic waste and unsafe products in other countries; the exploitation of foreign workers by US companies; the sexual exploitation of women of color overseas by US tourists, corporate, and military personnel; the economic policies of the IMF and the World

Bank; the scapegoating of foreign workers for US-generated problems and the scapegoating of Chinese, Arab, and Japanese capitalists while British, Canadian, and German capitalists go unmentioned.

Many of us work for large corporations and can challenge their policies from within. We all have specific opportunities to confront racism where we work.

To identify where you have the most leverage related to your work, it is important to make an assessment of your workplace. Use the following questions. Talk with others, particularly people of color, to help you do the assessment.

Look to the leadership of the people of color you work with (if there are any). They know where the racism lies in your organization. People of color already in your workplace may be quite clear about what kind of solidarity they need from white coworkers. Ask them how they see things and what their priorities are.

You will need to work with other white workers, building a core group dedicated to eliminating racism. Many of your white coworkers may not have questioned the racism in your workplace. They need information and support for making changes in workplace practices and environment. You may meet with solid resistance from others who feel they have something to lose from eliminating racism. Challenging them will require strategic thinking.

Many workers have such pressing financial and emotional needs they may not understand at first why racial equality and economic justice need to be a priority. The information provided in this book can help you devise effective strategies to show them the costs of racism in their lives.

A good way to begin, once you have the information you need, is to ask questions:

- Why is this person of color paid less than a white person who was hired more recently?
- Why aren't there any people of color at management level?
- Why don't people of color stay with this organization very long?
- What effect does that kind of comment (e.g., a racial put-down) have on other people around here?

5.4. Assessment: At Work

1. Who, by race, gender, and class, has the power to make decisions about hiring, firing, wages, and working conditions in your workplace? Who gets promoted and who doesn't? Are there upper levels (glass ceilings) beyond which some groups of people (i.e., people of color, white women) cannot go?

2. Is hiring non-discriminatory? Are job openings posted and distributed? Do they attract a wide variety of applicants? Are certain groups excluded? Does the diversity of your workplace reflect the diversity of the wider community?

3. Do layoffs, reassignments, workplace closures, or other cutbacks disproportionately affect people of color?

4. What are the salary differentials between the lowest- and highest-paid workers? Are salaries for comparable work equal?

5. Are there *invisible workers*—people who cook, clean, or do maintenance, for example—who are not generally noticed or not paid well?

6. Do the board of directors and the top-level management of your employer include significant numbers of people of color?

7. What is the racial composition of the group of people that actually owns your workplace? Who makes money from the profits of your work?

8. Are there jokes, teasing, put-downs, or harassment of people based on race, gender, sexual orientation, age, religion, or other differences?

9. Has there been or is there any racial or sexual harassment or discrimination, or charges of such or investigations by any outside agency about such things? Do people of color describe discrimination or harassment at your workplace?

10. Does your organization provide products or services to people of color? If it does, is the clientele treated with respect and dignity? Do staff members make racial comments about clients? Is there any discrimination in how people are served or treated?

11. Do the advertising and publicity images your employer produces convey a multiracial image or do they reinforce racial or sexual stereotypes?

12. Are there any workplace groups such as unions or affirmative action committees that monitor or respond to racial discrimination? Are they effective? Are they supported or hindered by management? Do they challenge or do they support racism?

13. Is your employer part of a larger organization, with manufacturing or other facilities at other sites? Are those sites in communities of color? If they are, are workers paid the same as, and treated equally to, workers at your site?

14. Has your employer closed down or moved facilities to areas of the United States or to other countries in order to pay workers less or to avoid unionization, workplace safety regulations, or other oversight?

15. Does your company produce any kinds of toxic waste? If so, in which communities is the waste dumped?

Asking questions raises issues for people to think about. Sometimes that alone will encourage other people to make some changes. Often you'll get excuses, justifications, or cynicism in response. Those responses will let you and others see how white people are thinking about racism and what level of awareness they have. It will also help you map out where you'll meet resistance to further actions.

It is generally not useful to label people as racist. If you attack people personally, they will probably become defensive and counterattack, and it makes it seem like racism is all about personal conduct.

Everyone within the organization will feel unsafe. You will do better to document racism within the organization, build alliances, and propose concrete changes. You want to focus on policies, practices, and procedures.

- What is the mission of the organization or business you are working for?
- What is the relationship of the mission to communities of color?
- What are the needs of those communities?
- What is the relationship of the company to workers of color in this country and in others? Where are they, what are they paid, what are their working conditions?
- How do white people hold power in your organization?
- The most important question to ask might be, what long-term changes will be made in who holds power and how decisions are made?

Eliminating racism is not a question of economic cost but of injustice. However, when you organize against specific forms of racism, it can be a useful short-term strategy to point out the economic benefits of the changes desired or the economic costs of the old patterns:

- What does it cost an organization when there are high turnover rates for personnel who are people of color, when clients of color are not well served, or when the leadership talent of people of color is not used?
- What does it cost when there are discrimination lawsuits, strikes, boycotts, or government investigations because of racism within the organization?

Organizations have different levels of vulnerability to such costs.

Each particular fight against racism is part of the long-term struggle. Even when one initiative is unsuccessful, it can educate and organize other workers. Our long-term goal is to create a broad movement of people committed to eliminating racism in all aspects of our lives.

I am not going to romanticize the power of workers; in most circumstances, multinational companies can play off workers from
multiple sites against each other. However, keeping the issue of
race- and gender-based exploitation on the table in every workplace
struggle will further the move toward economic justice. Doing so
keeps people of color and white women in leadership positions,
demonstrates the interconnected ways people are exploited, and
produces the informed solidarity essential to the success of any
struggle for economic justice.

At School

A PRIME EXAMPLE of the power and wealth behind the neoliberal race/class agenda is the US educational system. The Bill & Melinda Gates Foundation (Microsoft), the Eli and Edythe Broad Foundation (KB Home and SunAmerica), and the Walton Family Foundation (Walmart), Howard Rich, Art Pope, the DeVos Family Foundation (Amway), David Tepper and Alan Fournier, Michael Bloomberg, Laura and John Arnold, and Reed Hastings (Netflix) and Mark Zuckerberg (Facebook)—a network of multimillionaires and billionaires, think tanks, foundations, and private corporations—have been pushing an educational agenda that emphasizes standardized testing, No Child Left Behind, Race to the Top, moving public funding to vouchers and Charter Schools, and attacks on teachers' unions.[1] Over the last 25 years, each of these educational strategies has demonstrably failed to improve educational outcomes but has succeeded in transferring huge sums of money from already underfunded public schools to for-profit corporations.

Most students in the United States go to schools highly segregated by race—because of discriminatory housing and lending practices and estate tax laws which promote the transfer of wealth through generations (the white privileges I described in Part II). This institutional racism has created a racially segregated educational system as unequal as it was before the US Supreme Court's *Brown v Board of Education* ruling outlawed intentional school segregation in 1954. Even within "integrated" schools, students are segregated by race and tracked by class or by smaller divisions of economic difference. Segregation and tracking limit most students to low-income job options in their adult lives.

Differences in public school funding by race are another example of institutional racism. Although in most states there is a standard reimbursement per student to school districts, the actual amount spent on students' education depends on many factors including local property taxes, contributions from parents, volunteer hours from community members, business and foundation contributions. The average spent per pupil can vary by thousands of dollars even in the same metropolitan area.

Predominantly white schools spend much more per student than schools in which the majority are students of color. The average difference in spending is probably about 2 to 1, although in many areas the greatest differences can run 8 or 10 to 1.[2] The top 10% of school districts (primarily white and suburban) spend 10 times more than the bottom 10% (primarily urban, where students of color are congregated). As just one example, the city of Greenwich, CT, spends $6,000/year per pupil more than the city of Bridgeport, CT, in the same county. In a classroom of 25, that equals a $150,000 difference.[3]

When any per-pupil difference is multiplied by the number of students in a school, the impact is enormous. Funding determines the number of students per teacher; the quantity of classroom necessities like books and computers; the availability of art and music classes; recreational equipment; teachers' aides, special events and field trips, and—in the long run—the best teachers. Without a single overt act of discrimination, the educational opportunities of most children of color in the US are greatly deficient when compared to those of white children.

Given the economic and educational realities of this society, it makes sense for us to give young people the best education possible. That is why, when white parents can afford it—and sometimes even when we can't—we move to school districts with better schools, work hard to get our children into the best schools within the district, or send them to charter or independent schools. We shouldn't feel guilty for doing so. But insofar as many children of color and poor and working-class white children are abandoned to the disaster of inadequately funded public schooling, our individual actions do contribute to the overall gap between white young people and young people of color and between rich and poor.

- Find out per student expenditures in your district and neighboring ones.
- What differences do you find? Where does the extra money come from?
- How can you work with others to develop new school-funding strategies?

However, education is more than money. It includes teachers, curricula, school buildings, safety to learn, and many other factors. Racism affects the quality and quantity of each of these resources. Although students of color made up more than 45% of the student population in 2012, the percentage of teachers who are white is increasing and presently approaches 83% (of that approximately 75% is female).[4] This means few students of color have role models of their own ethnicity, and few white students have contact with people of color in positions of authority. Changes in educational policy, such as the National Teacher's Exam and longer teacher education courses present unnecessary obstacles to teachers of color and contribute to their increasing exclusion from our classrooms. Many white teachers carry with them subtle and not-so-subtle biases against youth of color. Researchers have found teachers give higher grades to young people of their own race, and white teachers give significantly lower grades to black and Latinx students.[5] White teachers may also exhibit greater aggression, overt friendliness coupled with covert rejection, avoidance or simply offer less assistance to students of color while being completely unaware of their implicit bias.[6] This is *interpersonal racism*.

- Who is teaching in our schools?
- How are they trained?
- What do they do in the classroom?
- How does racism in schools affect teachers of color?

We see another aspect of the neoliberal political agenda in schools: surveillance, control, and punishment. Our public schools have become increasingly militarized; there are armed police and private security guards in many. Zero tolerance policies leading to racialized discipline coupled with high suspension rates create a school-to-prison pipeline specifically targeting students of color. Students of color do not drop out of school; they are actively pushed out by the multiple levels of racism embedded in our educational institutions. This is *structural racism*.

We also need to eliminate racism in the curriculum. School curricula in the United States have a European/US historical focus emphasizing the development of ideas and political processes from Greece through Rome and Europe to the United States. The Greeks themselves acknowledged the sources of their learning and made many references to their Egyptian mentors.[7] Textbooks often present other world civilizations as if they only became significant when they were discovered by or interacted with white Westerners. Cultures from other geographic regions are presented superficially (through food, holidays, traditional clothing, and little else), particularly in the lower grades.

Our curricula also omit the history of white colonialism as colonialism, and they don't address racism and other forms of exploitation. People of color are marginally represented as token individuals who achieved great things despite adversity rather than as members of communities of resistance. The enormous contributions people of color have made to our society are simply not mentioned.[8] For example, Arab contributions to mathematics, astronomy, geology, mineralogy, botany, and natural history are seldom attributed to them. The Arabic numbering system, which replaced the cumbersome and limited Roman numeral system—along with trigonometry and algebra, which serve as cornerstones of modern mathematics—were all contributions from Muslim societies.[9]

As a result, young people of color do not see themselves at the center of history and culture. They do not see themselves as active participants in creating this society. The roles played by their foreparents have simply been written out of history, giving both white young people and young people of color distorted understandings of their own heritages. This is *cultural racism.*

We need to challenge all aspects of racism in educational curricula, including, but not limited to, literature classes in which only white authors are presented; the exclusion of poor and working people from written histories; the exclusive use of white cultural examples for math problems, and the omission of racism as a pervasive and central component of lessons in history, social studies, and other subjects.

There are further questions we need to ask:
- How are students treated in school?
- Are students of color systematically harassed, disciplined, or tracked by teachers or administrators?
- Does the school have anti-racist policies in place, and are these known and enforced?
- How are students prepared to deal with racism?

Social scientists once thought that if white students and students of color just had contact with each other, prejudice would diminish. They have since found that contact by itself doesn't necessarily eliminate prejudice. White people often simply claim the people of color they know are "different." In any case, most white students in the US don't go to school with students of color. Because of tracking, even those who may study in the same building do not share the same classes or social networks.

The neoliberal educational agenda is to emphasize individual achievement, family choice, the measurement of learning through high-stakes standardized testing, and the punishment of students and their teachers and schools when they don't "measure up." So-called failure is then used to justify closing schools, disciplining teachers and principals, and shifting money to corporate-run charter schools and voucher programs (private school choice programs.) Marketed as a way to fix failing schools, particularly in low-income black and Latinx communities, vouchers give (predominantly white) families subsidies from the public education budget to attend a school of their choice. Much of voucher and charter school funding comes out of the public education budget and ends up either in the pockets of Christian organizations who run private schools or with large national for-profit corporations who run schools and provide a variety of support services. The corporations are accountable to their shareholders but not to students, families, or communities—and it shows in the results. Charter schools have consistently been found to achieve mediocre educational results.[10]

Many people are already involved in the struggle to make our schools more democratic, safer, and less racist. These efforts include two kinds of interventions.

The first approach is to help individual students of color succeed in spite of the limited opportunity provided by their school or community. Tutoring programs, scholarship funds, special training programs—these are sometimes effective in helping individuals acquire higher education or better jobs.

However, as David C. Berliner explained, "virtually every scholar of teaching and schooling knows that when the variance in student scores on achievement tests is examined along with the many potential factors that may have contributed to those test scores, school effects account for about 20% of the variation in achievement test scores.... On the other hand, out-of-school variables account for about 60% of the variance that can be accounted for in student achievement. In aggregate, such factors as family income; the neighborhood's sense of collective efficacy, violence rate, and average income; medical and dental care available and used; level of food insecurity; number of moves a family makes over the course of a child's school years;...provision of high-quality early education in the neighborhood; language spoken at home; and so forth, all substantially affect school achievement."[11]

Individual achievement programs may lift a few young people of color into educational opportunities and professional careers, but they do not address the systemic inequality between the educational opportunities of white students and students of color (and between poor and working-class white students and those from professional and ruling-class families). On the contrary, the results of these programs—a few successful people of color—are often used by whites to put down the rest of the community and blame those who don't succeed.

The second approach is to attack the structural roots of inequality. People are organizing around the issues of school funding, curriculum development, resource allocation, teacher training, and the control and administration of school districts and educational programs. Parents, students, teachers, and community members are challenging standardized and high-stakes testing, school closings, attacks on teachers' unions, the militarization of campuses, and the transfer of educational funding to charter schools, vouchers, and privately run corporations. Such activity is probably already occurring in your community, and you can join. If it isn't happening, get together with concerned parents, teachers, and educational activists to get something going. The questions we must keep asking ourselves as we analyze the *status quo* or evaluate changes we want to make are:

- What are the effects of these policies on students of color?
- Who is going to benefit from the changes?
- How can we achieve equitable opportunities and outcomes for all students and their families?

Health Care

THE US HEALTH CARE SYSTEM is so riddled with racism that tens of thousands of people of color die needlessly every year. Others are permanently disabled, live with remediable conditions, or suffer seriously inferior quality of life. The impact of race is felt in every area from basic accessibility to health care, through adequacy of insurance coverage, prescribed treatments, prenatal care, cultural sensitivity of care, availability of specialized treatments, and physical proximity to hospitals, to under-prescription of routine diagnostic tests and painkillers and over-prescription of amputations and sterilization. Former US Surgeon General David Satcher labeled these disparities "institutionalized racism."[1]

The cumulative impact is devastating to people of color. To give just one example for the African American community, which is the best documented, it is estimated blacks suffer over 91,000 excess deaths a year—that is 37% of all black deaths.[2] *Excess deaths* are deaths from preventable or treatable health conditions and are therefore unnecessary or avoidable.[3] In other words, all other factors being equal, 91,000 black people die each year because of racism. Because of this, African Americans have a life expectancy four and a half years less than white Americans.[4] For parts of the Latinx and Southeast Asian communities, life expectancy and health care status are equally low, and in many Native American communities, they are even lower. Obviously not all deaths of people of color are attributable to racism, but it is well documented that tens of thousands are.

Race and gender clearly make a difference in how patients are diagnosed and treated. In one study, medical residents viewed a video showing a white male and a black female patient (the students did not know they were actors), who described identical systems of chest pain indicative of heart disease. Seventy-four percent of the students believed the white male had heart disease, but only 46% believed the black female did.

Another study of Medicare patients found only 64% of black patients receive potentially curative treatment for early stage lung cancer, while 77% of white patients receive it, leading to survival rates (after five years) of 34% for whites and just 26% for blacks. A UCLA study found Hispanics in emergency rooms in Los Angeles are twice as likely as white people in comparable circumstances to end up with no pain medication—not even a Tylenol. Over 30 years' worth of studies show that because of racial implicit bias on the part of white medical personnel, people of color who arrive at a hospital while having a heart attack are significantly less likely to receive everything from aspirin, beta-blocking and clot-dissolving drugs to angioplasty or bypass surgery.[5]

Racism in the health care system is also an international problem. Drug development and pricing policies demonstrate how people of color in economically exploited countries suffer needlessly from policies that ultimately benefit white people in overdeveloped ones, and financially benefit an even smaller number of the white Western elite.[6]

Pharmaceutical companies do not develop many treatments to cure diseases that primarily affect people in economically exploited countries (and kill millions of people annually). Of the 1556 new drugs marketed between 1975 and 2004, only 21 were indicated for neglected diseases (including malaria and tuberculosis, but not HIV), and a mere 10 were directed at neglected tropical diseases which affect over a billion people annually.[7] The main emphasis of drug company research programs is "lifestyle drugs" for conditions like obesity, baldness, face wrinkles, and impotence. Although the companies complain that, otherwise, research would be unprofitable, the total revenue of the pharmaceutical industry in 2014 was $1.6 trillion.

Drug companies defend their profits at the cost of millions of lives in Africa, South America, and Asia. For example, GlaxoWellcome threatened legal action against the Indian company Cipla for trying to provide Ghana and Uganda with a cheap version of Combivir, two drugs developed in the US with public funding. Nearly 40 companies took the South African government to court to prevent its making low-cost generic equivalents of certain AIDS drugs available to people who could not otherwise afford to be treated for AIDS. This lawsuit was dropped only after there was a large international outcry in response to the fact that many of the 5.7 million South Africans who are HIV-positive will die much sooner without access to low-cost drug treatments.[8]

All people should have a basic right to adequate health care regardless of economic factors, and we need to address the concerns of many white people who suffer from lack of medical insurance or inadequate care. Race is an independent variable, and any improvements to US health care will need to include race-specific remedies to address the systemic ways people of color are denied, have limited access to, or experience inadequate medical care, leading to needless suffering and death.

The Police

JUST AS TEACHERS have the buffer zone function of training young people for their future roles in the economic hierarchy, police officers, security guards, prison wardens, and immigration officials have the function of disciplining those who don't follow the rules. They do this through racial profiling, racial harassment, intimidation, violence, and the creation of terror in communities of color through their constant surveillance, disruption, and aggression. Teachers are primarily women because women have been traditionally trained to be caretakers of young people. Police officers and other security personnel are primarily men because men have been traditionally trained to enforce class, gender, and racial roles. Both occupations are primarily white because their function is also to train people of color to accept their place in society and to punish them when they don't. People in these roles act as buffers between people of color and the rest of the white community.

Of course, for white people economic status also influences our experience with the police; those who are middle- or upper-middle-class are generally more respectful and trusting of them because the police are protecting their property and upholding their values. Those who are poor or working-class have more likely experienced harassment and abuse from the police and have less at stake in their role of maintaining the *status quo*.

As a middle-class white child, I was raised to trust the police and to look upon them as a source of help. The ensuing decades have worn off much of that trust, but in general, I do not expect to be stopped and searched arbitrarily by law enforcement. African Americans, Latinx, and Native Americans are very likely to be stopped and searched by the police for no apparent cause. This doesn't just happen to young men hanging out on the street. If the police think you look suspicious—and to some police, any person of color looks suspicious—you may be stopped even if you are with your family, even if there is no apparent cause for suspicion, even if you are just driving by somewhere.[1] As has been so well documented by observers using cell phones and video cameras in the last few years. Black, Latinx, and Native Americans, female, male, and trans, of all ages and economic class have been arbitrarily stopped, arrested, and every year hundreds are killed by police and vigilantes. Black drivers are 31% more likely to be pulled over than whites; they are more than twice as likely to be subject to police searches as white drivers; and they are nearly twice as likely to not be given any reason for the traffic stop.[2]

In one egregious example, in October 2015, Lawrence Crosby, a black engineering doctoral candidate, had the police called on him by a white woman for "suspicious" activity while he was working on his car. Within 10 seconds of Mr. Crosby getting out of his car with his hands in the air, he was tackled, he was kneed while he was standing up, then he was punched repeatedly by multiple officers, for allegedly stealing his own car.[3] We have also seen how people of color, particularly if they are Black, Latinx, Native American, or Muslim are persecuted (and sometimes killed) for swimming, for talking back to a teacher, for walking home wearing a hoodie, for playing in the park with a toy gun as a 12-year-old, for sleeping in their car, for singing loudly in their church, for drumming in public, for acting suspiciously in their own yard or home.

In neighborhoods where there is large-scale displacement of people of color by new white arrivals with greater financial resources, this dynamic is particularly acute. New white arrivals want clean streets cleared of people who are homeless, and "safe" (which by definition for white people means little presence of people of color). Even neighborhood web-based networks like Nextdoor have become sites for extensive racial profiling by white people, although because of protests, the organization is taking some steps to address this issue.[4] The police are quick to respond and often use violence as a first rather than last resort. For example, 12-year-old Tamir Rice was shot and killed while playing in a park in Chicago within two seconds of the police driving up—before the squad car was fully stopped. No officer was indicted for his murder.[5]

It is hard to underestimate or even convey the level of intense, constant surveillance, harassment, and attack on Black, Latinx, immigrant, and Native American communities. As professor of psychology Dr. Derald Wing Sue has summarized, citing multiple studies, "micro [and macro] aggressions are constant and continuing experiences of marginalized groups in our society; they assail the self-esteem of recipients, produce anger and frustration, deplete psychic energy, lower feelings of subjective well-being and worthiness, produce physical health problems, shorten life expectancy, and deny minority populations equal access and opportunity in education, employment, and health care."[6]

Every year there are hundreds of reports of *police brutality*—the excessive use of force well beyond what is required in a situation. Thirty-six percent of unarmed people killed by police were black males in 2016 despite making up only 6% of the US population.[7] Many people of color are vulnerable to much higher rates of police brutality than white people: in 2016, Native Americans experienced 10.13 deaths per million people, blacks 6.64, Latinx 3.23, and whites 2.9.[8] Although more police officers have been charged for killings in recent years, in 2014 and 2015 not a single police officer was convicted in such cases.[9]

One reason police are so lethal is they are militarized. The US is the largest arms and weapons manufacturer and distributor in the world—providing more weapons than the rest of the world combined. Since the military is constantly upgrading its weapons systems, they have found it useful to unload surplus military-grade weapons to local police and sheriff departments. In addition, the US Department of Homeland Security has provided billions of dollars for the acquisition of military equipment by local police, sheriff and border patrol departments; these departments also buy their own military weapons using hundreds of millions of dollars from asset seizures from motorists and others who have not been charged with a crime.[10] The result of these policies is thousands of police departments nationwide have acquired armored cars and tanks, stun grenades, military grade assault rifles, helicopters, airplanes, drones, machine guns, bomb suits, and other paramilitary equipment. This is the "war on terror" come home to our neighborhoods. The ACLU has concluded this militarization "unfairly impacts people of color and undermines individual liberties, and it has been allowed to happen in the absence of any meaningful public discussion."[11]

The racism behind much police brutality makes people of color unsafe in many ways. For example, they are vulnerable to racial profiling, sexual harassment, extortion, and attack from the police. Second, knowledge of police brutality prevents many people of color, particularly women, from seeking protection from non-racial crimes such as domestic violence. Many women of color are understandably hesitant about handing their men over to a racist and violent police force and a discriminatory criminal/legal system, even though their refusal to do so might increase their own vulnerability. In addition, the fines, court fees, bail fees, and other expenses involved with entanglement with the police drains money from already poor communities and funnels it into city budgets (which fund more police and high-tech weapons).

Many white people are afraid of being robbed, beaten, raped, or burglarized. Some of us have been already. Most of the crime we experience is committed by other white people, often by people we know. When there are racist patterns to police practices, we are even more at risk because the police are looking in the wrong direction.

This is not to say that white people are never robbed by people of color. You may even know someone who was. You have certainly read about someone who was, because the racial bias of the news media presents us with a disproportionate number of these cases, giving them wide publicity, which in turn exacerbates our fears.[12]

We then allow the police to continue their practices, justifying their "excesses" by attributing them to rogue officers who, it is claimed, are the exception.

When we don't respond strongly and actively to police brutality in our communities, we increase polarization and justify the anger of people of color who say the police represent the interests of white people. If we want to deal with racism, we have to rein in, retrain, and redirect the police so they don't initiate acts of violence in our name. More multicultural awareness for police, or more community policing are not enough.[13] How should we redirect the police? White-collar financial crimes, tax evasion, and high-level drug importation and distribution are more devastating to our lives and pocketbooks than petty thievery and small-scale drug dealing and are obvious places to start.

Where do the police devote their time and attention? How do they allocate resources? How well are they trained, including training in racism, domestic violence, community relations, and community

5.5. Assessment: The Police

1. Is there an independent police review board or commission in your community? How effective is it?
2. Are there allegations of police brutality or civil suits against the police or sheriff's department? What is their status, and how have law enforcement officials responded?
3. What is the history of allegations, lawsuits, and police response in your local police and sheriff's departments?
4. How are allegations of police abuse handled? Are there independent investigations? Are criminal charges pursued for criminal conduct?
5. Are the police and sheriff's departments fully integrated? Are members trained to deal with a multicultural

population? How do they respond to different kinds of calls? Do they work well with community agencies and organizations?

6. Is the response to family violence racially biased? Is there a policy of mandatory arrest for incidents of domestic violence? Are reports of the sexual assault and rape of young people investigated and prosecuted vigorously and without discrimination?

7. Is community policing used by the police department? How is the community involved? Are people of color from within the community represented and empowered?

8. Are the police and sheriff's departments in your area currently enforcing or participating in programs that enforce federal immigration laws? How does this impact immigrant communities? How does it impact the ability of police to conduct routine law enforcement activities?

9. White adults and adults of color can collude to blame and criminalize young people for high crime and drug abuse rates. This conveniently ignores the responsibility adults have for youth safety, education, family support, and rec- reational opportunities. Do the police in your area respond without prejudice and undue force to the needs of young people in your community? (Ask young people.) How can young people be more involved in police-community accountability?

building? These are the kinds of questions we need to ask. Here are some places to start.

When you see the police stop people of color, slow down, turn on your cell phone. You have the right to observe and film the police. Let them know you're paying attention. Don't assume that because the detained are people of color, they must have done something wrong. Don't assume that because you respect the police, they respect everyone in the community.

Get together with other concerned citizens to monitor police activities.

The single biggest deterrent to police abuse is accountability to the community. Good community-based policing can help make all our lives safer. Even better is having lots of alternatives to calling the police for intervention in situations involving interpersonal violence, victimless crimes, and mental health situations. Decreasing funding to the police and shifting those resources into community services is the biggest deterrent to needing police services in the first place.

The Criminal/legal System

MOST OF US don't have an active, everyday role in the criminal/legal system, but we do have some influence on what happens within it. Our advocacy for crime legislation, the death penalty, and particular police practices such as immigration enforcement, as well as our funding of prisons, jails, and "wars" on crime and drugs, all play a part in how people are treated on a daily basis by the legal system.

Wealthy white people have controlled the US legal system since colonial times. They wrote our country's founding legal documents based on English common law which itself was based on Christian canon law. These documents limited most legal rights and the ability to use the criminal/legal system to men of property.[1]

When slavery was legally ended after the Civil War, the criminal/legal system took over the role of controlling the African American population (with a lot of help from the KKK and other groups). When Jim Crow laws were passed in the South during the last two decades of the 19th century, they included laws aimed at introducing a new form of slavery, the *convict labor system*. White people criminalized behaviors they believed could be used to ensnare newly freed slaves by intimidating them, and forced freed slaves into debt peonage for white-owned agricultural and industrial enterprises. It became a crime to be hired by an employer without a discharge paper from a previous employer, and even walking down the street without proof of employment was a crime. In a harbinger of the current operation of the child welfare and foster care systems, orphans and the children of black people deemed inadequate parents could be apprenticed to their former masters.

The legal system entrapped blacks at every turn, and then the lo-cal sheriff would lease the prisoner to a farm, corporation, or public employer. Brutally treated, unable to escape, almost always tortured, starved, and often literally worked to death in just a few years, newly freed slaves were re-enslaved—but this time by a system with no economic interest in keeping them alive. Workers were leased, used up, and then replaced by a new round of "criminals." Like tenant farmers and sharecroppers, if people did stay alive, they were con-tinually subjected to never-ending rounds of indebtedness to who-ever leased them. State governments made tremendous amounts of money from this system, and the coal mines, steel mills, timber op-erations, and vast cotton plantations—literally the entire economy of the South—were dependent on their labor. Many of these enter-prises were owned by northern companies and financiers: the steel was shipped to northern manufacturers and the cotton to northern textile mills.[2]

The system of false or flimsy arrest and prosecution of men of color and their subsequent sale for corporate enslavement continued into the 1940s and 50s. Much progress was made to eliminate this system, but even in the 1970s and 80s, people were still enslaved in labor camps in the South. With the passage of the Justice System Improvement Act of 1979, legal barriers to exploiting prisoner labor for profit were removed, and once again prisoners were coerced into working for corporate profits. Looking for workers they could pay less even than those in majority world countries, companies such as Whole Foods, Wal-Mart, Aramark, AT&T, BP, McDonalds, and Victoria's Secret moved into the prison labor employment business.[3]

Two reports released in 2000 showed that at every stage of the US criminal/legal system—from arrest through plea bargaining to sentencing—African Americans and Latinx get tougher treatment than whites.[4]

The total US population under supervision in prison, jail, on parole or probation grew from 1.8 million in 1980 to 6.8 million in 2014.[5] This 400% increase compares with only a 3% increase in the number of violent offenders. Of those 6.8 million individuals,

2.3 million were in prison or jail—67% for non-violent offenses and around 25% percent for non-violent drug offenses.[6] By 2014, private correctional facilities were a $4.8 billion industry with profits of $629 million.[7]

In this vast prison/industrial complex,[8] there are well over one million African Americans behind bars, out of a total prison population of 2.3 million. In 2009, nearly 69% of those arrested for a violent criminal act were white, but we would never know that from looking at the makeup of the prison population because so many people of color are convicted for non-violent drug offenses.[9] African Americans serve virtually as much time in prison for a drug offense as whites do for a violent offense.[10]

In a clear example of racism in the criminal/legal system, an October 2010 report found in California, in the 25 cities surveyed, police arrested blacks at rates between 4 and 12 times greater than they arrested whites for marijuana possession, even though US government data consistently show whites use marijuana at higher rates than blacks do. Young black men, targeted by the police for racial profiling and harassment, end up entangled in the criminal/legal system for low-levels of possession and with a drug offence on their record limiting their future job opportunities in ways young white men who also use marijuana rarely experience.[11] Legalization of marijuana reduces arrest rates across the board regardless of race. But in Massachusetts, after the drug was decriminalized, it was found that in 2014 blacks were still 3.3 times as likely as white people to be arrested for it. Similar results have been found in Washington and Colorado since legalization.[12]

The increased criminalization of communities of color through racial profiling, the "war on drugs," and mandatory minimum sentencing has had a severe impact on African American and Latinx women and people who are transgender—they have become the fastest-growing group of people coming into prison. The number of women in prison has now risen to over 215,000, with over a million under supervision by the criminal/legal system. Over 50% of the women incarcerated are women of color, and up to 80% of these women are there for non-violent crimes, primarily drug possession.[13]

Almost all of them are poor, and 80 to 90% of them have experienced male violence in the form of child sexual assault, rape, or domestic violence.[14]

Subtle racism rooted in the structure of the probation system is another problem with the criminal/legal system. A study by University of Washington sociologists found a consistent bias in probation officers' written reports on young black and white offenders with the same backgrounds, offenses, and ages. The officers routinely described blacks as bad kids with character flaws, while they wrote about white offenders as victims of negative environmental factors such as exposure to family conflict or delinquent friends.[15]

The combination of racially biased perceptions and racism built into the structures of the criminal/legal system contributes to the fact that although blacks under the age of 18 make up 17% of their age group in the US, they comprise 46% of young people arrested, 31% of those sent to juvenile court, 38% of those detained in juvenile jails, and 30% of those found guilty of being a delinquent. Black youths account for 41% of all juveniles tried in adult criminal courts, 38% of those sent to juvenile facilities, and 58% of juveniles confined in adult prisons.[16]

Racism also plays a role in sentencing. White victims are considered more valuable, and those who harm them are given harsher sentences. As Richard Morin, writing in the *Washington Post*, reported:

> A black man is run over and killed by a drunken driver.
> A typical sentence: two years in prison.
>
> A white man is run over and killed by a drunken driver.
> A typical sentence: four years in prison
>
> A white woman is run over and killed by a drunken driver.
> A typical sentence: seven years in prison.

In the same article, Morin concluded, holding constant all other key factors about the crime, the killer, and the victim, "murderers who kill black victims receive 26.8 percent shorter sentences than they would have received if the victims had been white."[17]

In January 2000, George Ryan, the Republican governor of Illinois, put a halt to executions in the state after Northwestern University journalism students discovered several death row inmates were actually innocent. Since 1977, Illinois has exonerated 13 death row inmates and killed 12. The *Chicago Tribune* examined the almost 300 death penalty cases in Illinois since the death penalty was reinstated and found half of the 260 cases appealed were ultimately reversed.[18] The US keeps company with China, Iran, Pakistan, Saudi Arabia, and Iraq as the primary countries who still have a death penalty.[19] Some US states and most countries have long abandoned the need to penalize people with death. The death penalty has been proven ineffective as a deterrent, racially and economically biased, cruel and unusual punishment, and a diversion from the pressing issues of racial and economic justice.

Under the neoliberal agenda, we have become a society under surveillance and policed by for-profit corporations running private security firms, while building and maintaining prisons, jails, and deportation centers. The fastest-growing male occupations are security guards, police, immigration officials, and prison wardens. There are over 800,000 police officers and detectives and another million private security guards in the US.[20] Tens of thousands of police are members of heavily armed, militarily trained SWAT teams deployed primarily in communities of color.[21] In addition, there are over 55,000 armed law enforcement officers inside the US Office of Homeland Security who have practically no public supervision.[22] We now routinely find metal detectors and armed security in airports, government buildings, schools, and other public facilities. This entire prison/industrial complex preys on low-income white people and people of color to create an illusion of safety for the rest of us.

A policed and criminalized society is a tremendous drain on material resources. Incarceration costs run over $74 billion a year and have shifted expenditures away from education and other social services.[23] The state of California, which used to be second in education spending per student in the US and now is 41st, has built 21 prisons in the last 35 years and only one university. It costs, on average, $30,700 a year to incarcerate a prisoner and much less to send them to a university.[24] It is calculated that a reduction by half in the incarceration rate for people with non-violent drug offenses would result in a savings of $16.9 billion, most of which could be invested in public services.[25]

- *Would you want white youth to be treated as harshly as youth of color are now?*
- *What about your own children, grandchildren, nieces, nephews, or the children of friends?*
- *Should 13- and 15-year-olds be treated as adults and imprisoned for life?*
- *What responsibility does our society have for their behavior?*

Young people of color don't grow, make, import, or transport drugs; white adults do. Young people of color don't manufacture and sell guns, nor do they move jobs and businesses out of neighborhoods; white-led corporations do. Young people of color don't keep information about birth control, sexually transmitted diseases, drugs and violence away from young people; white adults do. Young people of color don't decrease funds for education while increasing spending on war and prisons; white adults do. As white adults, we need to take responsibility for the policies and decisions that set young people of color up to fail and then punishes them for their lack of success.

There are many groups working to dramatically transform or abolish the current prison system by moving money from policing and incarceration to rehabilitation; they campaign for transformative justice programs, adequate mental health care, affordable housing, and living wage jobs. Groups are also confronting the substantial political clout prison guard unions have in many states and challenging the huge private prison and detention center corporations reaping enormous profits off inmates and state budgets. Some of the fiercest resistance to the *status quo* has come from prisoners themselves. The national prisoners labor strike in 2016, following a statewide hunger strike in California in 2013, included 20,000 prisoners in 20 prisons in 11 states. The California prisoners and their allies were protesting inhumane, slave-labor-like conditions and treatment including solitary confinement, arbitrary individual and group punishment, sexual and physical abuse from prison guards, lack of adequate and nutritious food (they were asking for a 2,000-calorie diet), lack of education and rehabilitation options. The 2016 strike was specifically focused on slave-labor working conditions for prisoners within a context of the prison-industrial complex and the school-to-prison pipeline.[26]

There are many ways to become involved with groups working to transform our inhumane, costly, and ineffective incarceration system such as:
- prison solidarity work
- becoming a pen pal to an inmate[27]
- working for policy-level change
- building restorative and transformative justice and other alternative programs in communities.

You can also get involved with more specific campaigns to:
- end the death penalty, solitary confinement, and other barbarous practices
- shift funding from prisons to schools and public health programs
- stop the building of new prisons

We also need to look at the broader social context to understand the root causes of violence and criminal behavior. We know what works for crime reduction—well-paid and safe jobs, challenging and supportive educational opportunities, recreational activities, adequate health care, and adequate economic and psychological family support services. We must measure every dollar we spend on prisons and jails, which can never be a long-term solution, against the other ways we know we can reduce the levels of violence we all fear.

Religion

SPIRITUALITY REFERS TO our experience of being connected to a reality greater than ourselves. We are all spiritual beings. *Religions* are the organized social structures in which some of us put spirituality into practice. Many of us are connected to a particular religious institution through our upbringing or through current affiliation.

Most white people who are part of an organized religion in the United States are Christian, so I am going to focus this discussion on Christianity. If you are a white person who is Muslim, Jewish, Buddhist, or pagan, or who belongs to a new age spiritual community, much of this chapter (with some adaptations) will be relevant to you as well.

The major denominations of the Christian church have contributed to racism and anti-Jewish and anti-Muslim oppression in both Europe and the United States for many centuries. Colonization, genocide, and slavery by the Spanish, Portuguese, English, Dutch, Belgian, and French empires were given explicit, divine sanction by official statements from churches.[1] In the US, Canada, Australia, and other white-settler-dominated countries, Christian denominations, religious orders, and individual churches owned slaves and ran boarding schools in which kidnapped Indigenous young people were beaten, molested, and large numbers were starved to death.[2]

Today, Christian institutions promote racist foreign policy on the basis of a US manifest destiny to save other countries by bringing them "freedom," "free markets," and democracy; they support domestic policies that punish people for their sins rather than provide for their needs.[3]

The Christian concept of sin many young people internalize prepares them to accept and enforce hierarchies of class, race, and gender. The socialization doesn't have to be brutal or even overt if young people are taught early on to intuit from the culture around them which beliefs and behaviors are taboo. The sense of crossing the line of what is acceptable (to sin) produces guilt and often even a fear-based paralysis, making it difficult for people to challenge taboos and those who benefit from them. Lillian Smith, a Southern white woman, wrote about how Christian training in the concept of sin enforced racial segregation in the US.

> When we as small children crept over the race line and ate and played with Negroes or broke other segregation customs known to us we felt the same dread fear of consequences, the same overwhelming guilt we felt when we crept over the sex line and played with our body, or thought thoughts about God or parents we weren't supposed to think. Each was a "sin" and deserved "punishment," each would receive it in this world or the next. Each was tied up with the others and all were tied close to God.... The lesson of segregation was only a logical extension of the lessons on sex and white superiority and God.[4]

At the same time, many individual Christians and church leaders have been inspired by Christian teachings to work for social justice. In other words, Christianity and its teachings have been used by Christians both to support slavery, genocide, and economic exploitation and to inspire resistance to them.[5]

This is not the place for a detailed discussion of Christian history or theology. Nor can the important role faith plays in white Christian resistance to racism be addressed. It is important we build on the inspiration our religious faiths give us to work for social justice, while resisting racism in our religious institutions. Use the following questions to guide you in these tasks.

You probably participate in other institutions besides work, school, and church, such as social service agencies, recreational clubs, youth service organizations, or volunteer agencies. Think about these institutions also; ask yourself some of the questions from the previous chapters. What do you notice? Where are you going to become involved?

5.6. Assessment: Religion

1. What did you learn about people of color, Jews, and Muslims in Sunday school or sermons?
2. Is your religious community all-white? Is the leadership all-white?
3. What is the history of your church's practice of establishing missions in or sending missionaries to communities of color or Native American, Jewish, or Muslim communities in the US or to other parts of the world such as Africa, South America, Asia, or Muslim majority countries?
4. What attitudes are expressed about people of color during discussion of missionary work, charity, or social problems?
5. What connections, if any, are made in your church between sin, evil, and the lives or situations of people of color or people who are Jewish or Muslim? What Christian virtues are used to make negative judgments about people of color (e.g., "We are hardworking, but they are lazy")?
6. What religious or historical role do the Jewish people have in your church's teachings? How may that role have contributed to anti-Jewish oppression?
7. What do you know about the history of resistance to racism in your religion or denomination (e.g., abolitionist or civil rights struggles)?
8. What Christian values did you learn that might direct you to work against social injustice? What values specifically inspire or support racial justice work?

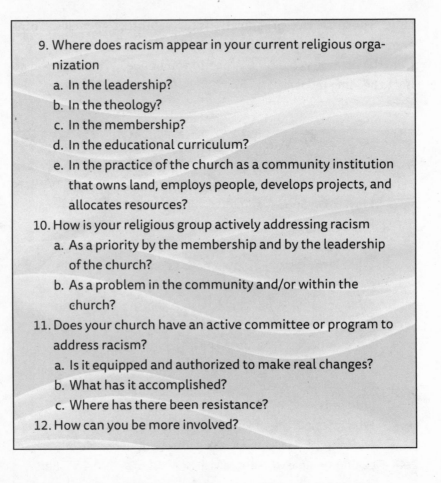

9. Where does racism appear in your current religious organization
a. In the leadership?
b. In the theology?
c. In the membership?
d. In the educational curriculum?
e. In the practice of the church as a community institution
that owns land, employs people, develops projects, and
allocates resources?
10. How is your religious group actively addressing racism
a. As a priority by the membership and by the leadership
of the church?
b. As a problem in the community and/or within the
church?
11. Does your church have an active committee or program to
address racism?
a. Is it equipped and authorized to make real changes?
b. What has it accomplished?
c. Where has there been resistance?
12. How can you be more involved?

Foreign Policy

THE US RULING-CLASS neoliberal agenda is shared by elites throughout the overdeveloped world. This agenda and its major institutions were put into place in the 1960s and 70s during the cold war after most countries in the world won their independence from colonial powers. Neoliberalism has relied on structural adjustment policies, international trade agreements, IMF loans, and "free" market ideology to maintain (neo)colonial rule by the trilateral countries of Europe, North America, and Japan. It has used brutal invasions (for example, Vietnam, Afghanistan, and Iraq), coercive economic policies, and covert intervention to maintain global political and economic dominance.

One of the foundations of Western Christian colonialism was white supremacy, so it's not surprising racism is a mainstay of US foreign policy. During the colonial period, foreign policy was directed against European competitors such as England, Spain, and France and against Native Americans. White Christians saw themselves as Chosen People in a Promised Land, and Native peoples were labeled Canaanites, Moors, and animals—all inferior beings in this Christian worldview.[1]

In the US, this worldview is often labeled *American exceptionalism*—belief that the United States has a higher calling, a moral responsibility, and a providential (God-given) or manifest destiny to conquer and rule over people of inferior races such as Native Americans, blacks, and Latinx.[2] The desire of capitalist leaders for perpetual expansion is easily justified by the racial and spiritual inferiority of the people whose land and resources are desired. People of color are considered to be in the way, hindrances to progress, modernity, and the superior morality and intelligence of the white Christian race.

The US has fought wars against white Christian Europeans only with great reluctance and for specific reasons of defense. It has continually fought wars throughout the rest of the world, believing, as superior people, we must provide other countries with our superior forms of religion, morality, democracy, economic and legal systems. When people refused our generous gifts, we quickly sent in the marines, concluding it was easier (and racially justified) to kill great numbers of them rather than accommodate their own desires for independence and self-sufficiency. Just since World War II, the US has killed or directly sponsored and financed the killing of millions of Asian, Latinx, black and Arab people in countries such as Korea, Vietnam, Indonesia, Laos, Cambodia, Iran, Iraq, Nicaragua, El Salvador, Chile, Brazil, Somalia, the Congo, South Africa, Palestine, Afghanistan—the list seems interminable. The US has been at war 222 out of 239 years since 1776[3] and has spent over $1.7 trillion on war just since 2001.[4] In 2017, the US was bombing seven Muslim majority countries in the Middle East, amounting to an actual Crusade against Islam, while our regional proxy allies (Saudi Arabia and Israel) are waging war against the Yemenis and Palestinians respectively with our sanction and weapons. Because the targets of our violence are people of color, the number of those killed, injured, or displaced is rarely counted and certainly not mourned. The deaths of US soldiers are tracked assiduously, and their lives and sacrifice honored. When Madeleine Albright, then US Ambassador to the UN under Clinton, was confronted with the fact that US economic sanctions against Iraq were estimated to have cost the lives of 500,000 Iraqi children, she replied, "I think that is a very hard choice, but the price, we think, the price is worth it."[5] Could she possibly have made this statement in reference to white children?

Even US foreign *aid* is based on racist assumptions that nations colonized and depleted by Western imperial powers now need us to help them get back on their feet. These "relations of rescue," whether individual or national, are used to justify interventions rarely beneficial to those receiving such "help."[6] An example of this dynamic is the response to the devastating 2010 earthquake in Haiti. The charitable response of individuals in the US was needed, substantial, and well-intended. But the US, after years of economic policies that deliberately impoverished the nation and supported military dictatorships—including participation in deposing the democratically elected president, Jean Bertrand Aristide—used the crisis to send in large numbers of troops, slow down the distribution of international aid, and set the stage for further economic exploitation. When aid was slow in reaching desperate people in need, it was easy to blame the Haitians for lack of infrastructure—infrastructure that had been deliberately sabotaged by US policies.[7] Confirming their sense of the US as a generous Christian nation, people could feel good about their charitable response, blame the Haitians for their problems, and ignore the devastating centuries-long impact of US interventions.

5.7. Assessment: Foreign Policy

1. Do you believe the US is a generous country?
2. How do you think people in other countries such as Haiti, Iraq, Afghanistan, Vietnam, or the Congo see our country?
3. Can you name all the countries the US is currently bombing?[8] All the countries we currently have military bases in? What percentage of the world's military arms and supplies we sell?
4. Consider a country the US has invaded or intervened in during your lifetime. How many people died as a result of our intervention? What were the reasons given for our intervention? How was the belief in manifest destiny and American exceptionalism part of the justification for intervention? What role did racism play?

5. In what ways are the deaths of US soldiers shown greater concern than the deaths of civilians killed by US soldiers in other countries?

6. In what ways does this mirror the way that the abduction and murder of white young people in the US is shown greater concern than the abduction and murder of young people of color?

7. Is there any way, even slightly, that you believe the life of a US soldier is more valuable than an Iraqi woman or young person killed by our troops?

8. Is there any way, even slightly, that you believe the life of a young white person in the United States is more valuable than the life of an African American, Latinx, or Native American young person?

Environmental Justice

ONE OF THE MOST critical national and international issues humanity faces is global warming, including such visible effects as ice cap melting, rising temperatures and sea levels, species and habitat destruction, unsustainable levels of consumption, and increasing numbers of extreme weather events. Neither the problems nor the solutions are race-neutral.

Environmental racism refers to any policy, practice, or directive that differentially affects or disadvantages (whether intentionally or unintentionally) individuals, groups, or communities based on race or ethnicity. It combines with public policies and industry practices to provide benefits for whites while shifting costs to people of color. Numerous studies have shown heavily polluting industries in North America (such as mining and manufacturing, garbage dumps, toxic waste sites, medical waste incinerators, and congested freeways) are located disproportionately in communities of color and on Native American land.[1] Higher levels of air, water, and land pollution lead directly to higher levels of asthma, cancer, and other illnesses, i.e., increased mortality for young people and adults. In addition, people of color are, in general, more likely to have jobs with higher exposure to contaminants such as pesticides, asbestos, lead, and other toxic chemicals.[2] Finally, people of color are most likely to experience lack of access to clean air and water and uncontaminated, affordable, and healthy food.[3]

At the international level, the United States is the largest per capita consumer nation on Earth: with less than 5% of the world's population, the US uses about 25% of the world's annual fossil fuel consumption—including nearly 25% of the coal, 27% of the oil, and 27% of the world's natural gas.[4] US-based multinational oil, mining, agribusiness, lumber, fishing, and manufacturing companies, along with their European, Japanese, and Chinese counterparts, continue to pursue profits at all costs throughout the world. These companies destroy ecosystems and block efforts to cut back on consumption and address global climate change. The US military is the largest and most destructive contributor to global heating through the production of its equipment and armaments, the transport and size of its personnel, its deployment of people—and the use of environmentally destructive weapons such as Agent Orange, white phosphorus, depleted uranium, land mines, and cluster bombs.[5]

As I described earlier, US foreign policy is based on the disposability of people of color for the benefit of white people. Our domestic policy mirrors this practice. Hurricanes Rita and Katrina, winter storm Sandy, droughts and massive forest fires in the western US were devastating but predictable events. Their damage was compounded by inadequately maintained levees and canals, dilapidated housing, poor emergency planning, police protection of white property and harassment of people of color, racially biased media coverage, and racist municipal and state policies that gave priority to rebuilding white neighborhoods and tourist centers over the neighborhoods where people of color lived.[6] Both internationally and domestically, the exploitation and destruction of the environment is intertwined with the exploitation and oppression of people of color.

- *Have you recently consumed coffee, tea, chocolate, bananas, meat, or mono-cultured crops?*
- *Have you recently used transportation or heating systems that relied on fossil fuel?*
- *Have you recently used a cell phone, computer, or other electronic device using heavy metals?*
- *Do you wear clothes from environmentally destructive materials (e.g., cotton or polyester) made by people of color in dangerous and low-waged work?*

We are all directly connected to environmental degradation and worker exploitation involved in producing these products; the hidden consequences include child labor, slavery, highly toxic working conditions and pollution, the destruction of vast areas of the natural environment; pollution of rivers, groundwater systems, and other ecosystems; the extinction of a tremendous number of animal and plant species, and the release of methane and CO_2 into the air.

On the front lines of attack, communities of color have also been on the front lines of resistance. The people of color and Indigenous people-led environmental justice movement, understaffed and poorly funded, have had to work mostly on their own because larger mainstream environmental organizations and funders are run by white people. People of color (and majority world nations at the international level) have been systematically shut out of the conversations and decision-making related to environmental issues. Basic white racist assumptions continue to operate in the environmental movement. Some of these are:

- White people know what's best
- White people know how to get things done
- People without education, money, and connections are not qualified to lead organizations and organizing efforts
- People of color have a limited and local point of view, while white people can see the broader picture
- The way to make change is through political influence, lobbying, advocacy, lawsuits, and the courts rather than mobilization and organizing
- The way to address environmental problems is to educate the public and change individual habits of consumption
- Power is located in the individual, not the collective
- Solutions must be market-based to be implementable and effective

To use a metaphor developed by social justice activists Victor Lewis and Hugh Vasquez, imagine the United States as a huge passenger ship.[7] The ruling class is in first class on the deck, enjoying all the amenities and thinking themselves protected from any hardship.

Most of us are in second, third, or fourth class. We may have moved down a class during the recent recession, but we are still getting by. Some of us are in fifth and sixth class and literally struggle to keep our heads above water. And many low-income people of color are at the very bottom of the boat in steerage, along with low-income white people, cleaning the rooms, preparing the food, serving and doing the laundry for those at the top.

The ship has a big hole in it, and those in steerage are living in water to their waist, struggling to stay alive. People higher in the ship may think they are immune to the water (pollution, climate change, natural disasters) pouring into the hole. But when the ship sinks—we all go down. Power and privilege may mitigate or postpone the impacts of environmental devastation, but ecologically all life is connected and interdependent.

The people at the bottom of the ship know the ship is sinking and have been organizing to save their communities, to fix the hole, and redistribute the resources on the ship. The people at the top also know it is sinking, but they don't want to publicize the fact. They are clearly benefiting from the way things are set up; they fear exposing their incompetent leadership and corruption and losing their wealth and power by riling up the rest of the passengers. They continue to mishandle the ship (for example, the Gulf Oil disaster), to drive too fast through dangerous waters, refusing to slow down or alter course (encouraging new deep-water oil drilling). Their actions contribute directly to the hole in the ship getting bigger.

Most of the rest of us are willing to go along with the ruling class. We don't give credibility to the voices at the bottom of the ship, or even if we do, we think we can either rely on those in power to take care of us or for advances in science and technology to fix things. Perhaps we are just in denial, minimizing the danger and assuming we'll be unaffected by what is happening. But increasing cancer rates, larger-scale natural disasters, constant war for control of declining oil fields, and contaminated air, food, and water belie the danger we're all in.

Today, Native Americans and Indigenous peoples are at the fore-front of environmental struggles to stop fossil fuel and mineral extraction, to preserve cultural and sacred sites, and to defend the natural environment from further degradation. Indigenous Peoples hold ancestral rights to around 65% of the planet. They play a critical role as environmental stewards and as political actors on the global stage. The 2016 Standing Rock Sioux encampment and non-violent protests in North Dakota are only the most visible of the attempts by Native peoples to defend the plants, animals, lakes, and forests we depend on for water, air, and food. Indigenous peoples such as the Maya Q'eqchi in Guatemala, Mapuche in Chile and Argentina, Wixarika (Huichol) in Mexico, Navajo at Black Mesa, Arizona, U'Wa in Colombia, Miskitu in Nicaragua, Wampis Nation in Peru, Munduruku in Brazil, Cree in James Bay, Canada, and literally hundreds more are leading the struggle to protect and heal the Earth from the ravages of corporations and ruling elites.[8] We have a responsibility and an obligation to stand with them in these struggles to build a world that will be habitable for all life on Earth.

5.8. Questions and Actions: Environmental Justice

1. Are you concerned by US wars in the Middle East over control of oil?
2. Have you and your family been affected by contaminants in the food you eat, the air, the water, or the toys your children play with?
3. Do you know anyone who has died of cancer or other pollution-related illness?
4. Do you know anyone who has died of heart disease, diabetes, or other illness related to lack of access to healthy food?
5. Do you acknowledge to yourself and others how serious this crisis is?

6. How is the health and well-being of communities of color in your area being impacted by environmentally related hazards?

7. How are they organizing around environmental issues?

8. How would you characterize the responses to environmental crises so far by corporations, the government, and the media?

9. What solutions are being proposed? Are they adequate?

10. What powerful groups are resisting or sabotaging these solutions?

11. Do you support any environmental organizations? Are they mostly white? Is their leadership mostly white?

12. What kinds of solutions are they working for? Who is being left out of those solutions?

13. What are you doing to support systematic institutional policies that change the way our society consumes, pollutes, and relates to the environment?

14. What are you doing to listen to communities of color, support their leadership and organizations, and work with them to sustain the planet and all life?

PART VI

Democratic, Anti-Racist Multiculturalism

Democratic, Anti-Racist Multiculturalism

I ENVISION A SOCIETY where each person is valued regardless of gender, race, cultural background, sexual orientation , ability or disability, or access to wealth.

This society would provide adequate shelter, food, education, recreation, health care, security, and well-paying jobs for all. The land would be respected and sustained, and justice and equal opportunity would prevail.

Such a society would value cooperation over competition, community development over individual achievement, democratic participation over hierarchy, and control and interdependence over either dependence or independence.

The only way to actualize such a vision is to create a democratic, anti-racist, multicultural society in which no one is left out and no one is left behind.[1]

Any fourth-grade US history textbook will tell you living in a Western democracy commits one to a common set of legal rights and responsibilities that are supposed to apply equally to all people. All people means *all people*.

Beyond these rights and responsibilities, our differences are infinite. In fact, our diversity makes our nation strong, dynamic, and creative. We are not all the same. Other people do not look like you, think like you, cook like you, eat like you, or act like you. For many of us, this is hard to accept. We are most comfortable when things are done in familiar ways.

Being a multicultural nation does not mean we all fit together easily, or that our differences complement each other. We should expect conflict and get good at it! Individually and as a nation, we need to develop tools for dealing with conflict without resorting to violence. The phrase *multicultural democracy* describes a process in which we all participate in making the decisions that affect our lives. It is a strategy toward full inclusion, participation, and justice.

When any strategy is turned into practice, however, it can fuel greater inequality or it can fuel further progress toward ending racism. What does it mean for an *organization* to be democratic, anti-racist, and multicultural? At a minimum, the membership, staff, administration, and board of directors would all have to reflect the ethnic, gender, economic, religious, and other diversity of the larger community. The organization would have to serve the needs of a broad-based section of the community. What the organization does, how decisions are made, and who is served would have to reflect an inclusive and democratic process.

- *How would it make a difference in your interactions with other people if you always assumed there was a cooperative solution possible that would benefit all parties?*

The assumption of *competition* built into Western thinking strongly influences our interactions with each other. Boys are particularly well trained by academic competition, sports, and the military to find competitive solutions to problems. We talk of winners and losers, champs and chumps, bullies and wimps. We don't teach people to negotiate, compromise, or work out creative solutions. Instead, particularly for men, aggression becomes the best defense. Action precedes discussion.[2]

We need innovative ways of embracing diversity, complexity, and cooperation. Some people have suggested we adopt a *both/and* way of thinking. In this framework, we assume the needs and perspectives of different parties are not necessarily in conflict. Using this approach allows us to embrace the perspectives of both sides and draw up a solution including elements of each. This kind of thinking shifts the emphasis from fighting to negotiating.

People who employ both/and thinking understand that truth is not absolute. Truth comes from the understanding, traditions, and experience of the people whose lives are involved. Different people have different experiences, and what is true for one person or culture may not be true for another. Although there may be simple truths in science (and even many of those are hotly debated), social reality is much more complex. One mark of a mature person is the ability to accept differing opinions and ideas respectfully and without attack.

Beyond either/or and both/and thinking is *inclusiveness*. In a democratic, multicultural process, everyone is included, each person's opinions are respected, and each community's needs are taken into account. Democratic, anti-racist multiculturalism requires time and more complex decision-making processes than most of us are used to. Such processes necessarily take time because each person must have the opportunity to be heard. We need to refine consensus models, systems of proportional representation, and other group processes so we have more versatile decision-making tools than simple majority rule or majority take all.

Full inclusion can only occur if we don't throw anyone away. One common way we deal with conflict is to label some people as the problem and then try to make them disappear by locking them up, isolating them, or segregating their communities. For example, labeling students of color troublemakers and kicking them out of school (which can consign them to a future with little prospect for success) is a way of throwing them away rather than working to include them. Locking up young people for long prison terms casts them out of society. We cannot throw some people away and then claim we are being inclusive just because we have included everyone who is left.

A cardinal rule of conflict resolution is to attack the problem, not the person. More often we attack people and leave the problem unattended. We talk about the poor rather than about poverty, the unemployed rather than the lack of jobs, the homeless rather than homelessness, and women who are abused rather than male violence. The people who are suffering the effects of discrimination or violence become the objects of our discussion, but those people are not themselves participants in the discussion. Most of the solutions we come up with are based on blaming and then punishing the victims.

I don't think we can solve problems if we exclude the people who are experiencing those problems. Living and working together in a democratic, anti-racist, and multicultural society has to be based on radical inclusion.

Multicultural Competence

IN ORDER TO MAKE SURE everyone is not only present, but can also participate fully, we need to be what many people call culturally competent. *Cultural competency* is the ability to understand another culture well enough to communicate and work with people from that culture.

We are all culturally competent in our own culture. We know the language, the nuances, and the assumptions about how the world is defined and organized. We know where there are disagreements and differences and generally what the rules are for solving problems. Most of us know how to get around in our own cultural neighborhood. *Multicultural competence* is fluency in more than one culture, in whichever cultures are part of your surroundings.

Culture is a vague shorthand word to name the complex ways people who form a *community* (another vague shorthand word) interact with each other. There are usually cultural norms within a community, but cultural practices can change, can be contradictory, and usually overlap with practices of other cultures. Cultures form around specific identities, geographies, beliefs, and daily practices. Other factors besides our ethnicity and "race" influence the cultures we are a part of, our roles and experiences within them. Multiculturalism requires more than racial balance and inclusion. All members of the community must be competent to communicate with each other.

Learning to be sensitive to the cultural expressions of another group is not difficult, but does require time and energy. We must learn to observe, empathize, and appreciate other people's ways of doing things. Even beginning levels of such competency open doors to understanding different perspectives. People who are culturally competent in even one culture besides their own have a broader, richer, and more accurate view of the world. They are able to work with others as full and equal partners.

It is difficult for white people to become multiculturally competent because, for the moment, we are the mainstream culture; we are in the culture of power. Wherever we look, we see ourselves—our language, values, images, and history. We have learned how great European-based US culture is. Most of the heroes we studied were white men such as Shakespeare, Washington, Jefferson, and Lincoln. We were taught our values, form of government, literature, science, and athletic accomplishments are not only the best of all, but an entire level above any others. We have been trained to think other cultures are less literate, less civilized, less efficient, less practical. It is impossible to make a good-faith effort to respect and learn about other cultures when we hold a core assumption they are inferior to ours. Operating from that assumption, we naturally believe, even if at a very subtle level, that we, white people, are the ones who should be in control, who should make the important decisions.

Many white people—women, people with disabilities, people who are poor or working-class, white Jews and Muslims, lesbians, gays, bisexuals, or transgender—are already competent in two or more cultures. They understand mainstream US culture and are fluent in their own. Sometimes this understanding gives them the impetus to challenge the cultural assumptions of whiteness. It can give them insight into how the dominance of one culture oppresses and exploits people outside the mainstream. However, white cultural dominance puts pressure even on alternative cultures to be white. These cultures often accept white norms and fail to be inclusive.

Furthermore, the more economically privileged we are, the more racially isolated we tend to be. The people of color we do come in contact with are in less powerful roles or are in jobs that provide services for us. We are trained to value them less and to devalue the contributions of their cultures. Without a good understanding of how this literal white supremacy has set up a hierarchy of status and sense of entitlement, we don't have much incentive to value or understand other cultures.

US culture has drawn from many different traditions. We have valued them enough to appropriate their strengths and achievements. It is time explicitly and publicly to acknowledge these contributions. It is not a question of valuing diversity, but of acknowledging rather than exploiting the contributions of all people to our society.

If we are not careful, cultural competency can itself become a substitute for *full inclusion*. I previously mentioned the teaching profession is still overwhelmingly white. It is crucial every white teacher becomes multiculturally competent, but schools will remain fundamentally racist until people of color are full participants at all levels of the educational system. White educators who are anti-racist activists should be fighting for the training, hiring, and retention of teachers, counselors, and administrators of color because nothing can replace the understanding and experience they bring.

Part of being multiculturally competent is realizing the limits of your own understanding. This competency should make you less arrogant and more humble. It should provide you with skills for supporting the leadership of those from the cultures in which you are competent.

Making multicultural processes work is essential to our success as a 21st-century society. The United States faces complex social challenges. Diverse experience, complex approaches, and critical thinking are tremendous assets, essential to the vitality and strength of our society. Valuing diversity is not just a personal preference. Nor is it something we can choose not to do if we all are to survive and thrive. The goals of multicultural competency are increased understanding, respectful communication, and full inclusion of all people, not cultural competence by itself.

Anti-Racism

WHY DOES ANTI-RACISM and other anti-oppression activism have to be one of the components in a multicultural process? Isn't it enough we are inclusive and democratic, that we value diversity and are culturally competent?

If we were starting out today without 500 years of history, we might be able to ignore racism. However, when we come together in a multicultural environment, it is in a context of white, Christian-based racism and a ruling-class, neoliberal agenda based on racial exploitation. Even if we are all included; even if we listen, value, and respect each other; and even if we focus on the challenges we face, we still need to address this legacy. All too often, people who are proponents of multiculturalism refuse to acknowledge or address the persistent effects of racism on our ability to create an inclusive process.

Anti-racism is the process of actively and consistently confronting racism wherever it occurs through a commitment to using anti-racist analysis and action, decentering whiteness, and centering the leadership of people of color—those most impacted by racism.

Other dynamics of racism also make it difficult to achieve our goals. For instance, people of color, Muslims, and Jews carry varying levels of distrust, unease, and trauma from their prior experiences. In addition, there are the many levels of institutional racism that influence particular situations. Unless we pay explicit attention to the specific ongoing dynamics of racism, they will inevitably sabotage our efforts to build an inclusive, diverse, and just society.

Even if we disagree with or are violently opposed to homosexuality, for example, it is often more comfortable to talk about lesbian and gay rights such as marriage equality if we have created a white context. We define issues of disability, gender, class, and sexual orientation as white issues, not having to do with race. (Most of us would probably say these issues are racially neutral, but in a racist society, "neutral" means not taking into account the reality of racism and therefore is a code word for "white.") In trying to be so broadly inclusive, we end up excluding people of color. Without a strong and continuous focus on racism, we can end up with a group of heterosexual white men and women, white lesbians, white gay men, white people with disabilities, white Jews, and some people of color who "represent" their racial groupings. This setup perpetuates racism under a guise of multiculturalism. Inclusion should not become a substitute for dealing with white dominance. Without an analysis of power and decision-making, multiculturalism can camouflage the continuing dominance of white people.

The word *democracy* implies more than a cultural democracy where every culture is represented. We also need to be sure this multicultural agenda includes the goal of ending economic injustice. For example, we have already noted how sectors of the African American, Latinx, Asian American, and Jewish communities have been given economic opportunities in exchange for supporting the *status quo*. Without an economic analysis, we can continue to support injustice while appearing multicultural.

There are many ways inattention to the distribution of wealth can subvert our efforts at democracy. For instance, we might bring only middle- or professional-class people of color into the organizations we are involved with, and this will do little to redress the unequal participation of broad groups of poor and working-class people. We can become professionals, specializing in multicultural or diversity trainings, and not challenge the segregation in our schools, neighborhoods, and workplaces. Attention only to multiculturalism, diversity, integration, and individual choice strengthens the ruling class's neoliberal agenda, avoiding examination of ruling-class power. Multiculturalism then becomes a form of collusion among professionals, both white and of color, to take advantage of the movement to end racism.

You can become an advocate for democratic, anti-racist multiculturalism within an economic framework in every place you go. Pick a formal or informal group you are a part of, and use the following questions to sharpen your strategic thinking.

6.1. Questions and Actions: Anti-Racism

1. Describe the group you are thinking about in terms of composition, purpose, and decision-making process.
   a. Is it multicultural? Who is involved and who is excluded?
   b. Is it democratic? Who holds power and how are decisions made?
   c. Is it anti-racist? Is racism talked about and dealt with effectively within the group?
   d. Is it multi-class with strong participation from people who are poor and working-class?
2. What needs to change?
   a. Who needs to be brought into the group to make it more inclusive?
   b. How would the group need to change to be truly open to their participation?
   c. How could the group be more democratic?
   d. What forms of racism need to be dealt with?
   e. Who can you talk with about these challenges?
   f. Who might be allies in changing the dynamics of the group?
   g. What is one thing you will do to begin this process?
   h. What fears or concerns do you have about raising these issues?
   i. What will you and the group lose if you don't raise them?

Integration and Tokenism

MANY PEOPLE OF COLOR have expressed concern that multiculturalism has become a new form of integration and tokenism. That's certainly a valid concern.

Integration is based on the belief people of color have been segregated from the mainstream of US society and need to be incorporated into it, with full participation. Even before the *Brown v Board of Education* US Supreme Court decision in 1954, mainstream discussion about racial equality revolved around integration.

White people's stated belief in the importance of integration (often while acting to subvert it) is based on the assumption there is one mainstream, normal set of (white) values, practices, and procedures that other people can learn and adapt to. We assume people of color want to be included in the mainstream but have previously been excluded because of prejudice and discrimination (interpersonal racism).

There is real cause for concern about the exclusion of people of color from mainstream institutions in the United States. To a great extent, white people have segregated themselves and walled off people of color from their neighborhoods, schools, congregations, and social spaces. This is a tragedy of injustice, as the Supreme Court ruled in 1954.

Many people of color feel having to give up culturally specific ways of thinking, acting, and relating to others in order to "integrate" simply maintains white power and locks them into subordinate positions. Our question needs to be: "Integration into what, on whose terms?" Integration can only be a strategy for justice and equality, not a goal. As a goal, it too often leads to tokenism.

Tokenism, small or insignificant change in lieu of fundamental transformation, can play out in many ways. Under pressure from African Americans in the 1960s and 1970s, for example, white people and white-run institutions fiercely resisted integration physically, socially, economically, and politically. They blocked the desegregation of schools, hospitals, and other public facilities for decades. White people seldom voluntarily gave up control or willingly looked at how we resisted change. Even now, if people of color push hard enough, we slowly and reluctantly accept their participation. We meet each stage with cries of "We've already done so much, what more do they want?" or "They're so unappreciative of what we've done; they'll never be satisfied until they control everything" or "We're moving as fast as we can." All the tactics of denial, minimization, blame, and counterattack discussed in Part I are marshaled to justify a slow pace toward equal participation.

Under severe public pressure and with much initial resistance, the first and simplest stage of tokenism occurs when an organization "allows" a small and insignificant number of people of color to integrate a school or workplace. Or we add a few names and pictures of people of color to a textbook or a wall. People of color and their contributions become exceptional. People of color are extremely isolated in these situations and acutely vulnerable to personal abuse. They do not have much support and usually succeed only if they assimilate by thoroughly internalizing the white-dominant values of the majority. In addition, it's also possible white people have pre-selected for people of color who fit a certain mold or support the traditional values of an institution. People of color are accepted for their decorative role and to deflect concerns about discrimination or diversity, not as full participants.

This is also the stage where white people quote or point to particular, usually conservative, people of color in academia or politics (such as Clarence Thomas, Colin Powell, Condoleezza Rice, Michael Powell, Shelby Steele, Ana Chavez, Clarence Thomas, Elaine Chao, or

Thomas Sowell) to give a seal of approval to white-dominant policies and statements. This process creates the illusion of participation, but there is still no sharing of power.

This stage might be coupled with another form of tokenism that involves paying attention to racism only when people of color are in the room, outside the door, or in the streets. When they are not visibly present, it is business as usual. Racism is viewed as a problem for people of color and only of incidental concern to the main business of the organization.

If these tactics don't succeed in quelling protest, white people will give up some control, but only in special areas deemed culturally appropriate to people of color. We may allow them to teach in ethnic studies departments but not in the sciences, or to write about news in their community but not about mainstream events.

These are just some of the ways white people control the participation of people of color and prevent a democratic multiculturalism from developing. Each involves a *token form of integration*. This "If we are forced, you can join us, but we're going to keep control" form of integration does not deal with the fundamental inequalities of racism.[1]

We should be actively organizing to create a democratic, anti-racist multicultural process in our workplaces, schools, religious organizations, athletic clubs, unions, and city, state, and national governments. We must keep four key questions in mind:

1. Is this organization multicultural?
2. Is it democratic?
3. Is it anti-racist (and anti-sexist, etc.)?
4. What are you going to do about it?

Organizational Change and Accountability

I ROUTINELY GET REQUESTS for workshops on racism, diversity, and multiculturalism from diversity coordinators, members of a diversity team, or someone in the HR department of an independent school, community-based nonprofit, or institution of higher education.[1]

These requests are one result of the success of the Civil Rights Movement, although the person making the request is probably not aware of this. The existence of their job, and their access to the education enabling them to be credentialed to do the job were the result of the demand that institutions be integrated, responsive to the needs of communities of color, and their staff and those they serve be representative of the general population. Currently, I receive these calls because of the activism and organizing of the Movement for Black Lives and the unavoidable visibility of police terror and other forms of racism across the US. Many people once again feel a public pressure to address issues of racism in their organizations.

However, the legacy of cultural racism and the focus on interpersonal racism and rogue cops has led many to define racism superficially, reducing it to trainings and workshops, calls to have "hard conversations." The core issues of institutionalized white power; systemic racism; economic, political, and social disparities in opportunities and outcomes—the continuing existence of white privilege and racial injustice—are now denied, minimized, or even justified. Instead of receiving requests for information and training about how to achieve organizations with full participation and empowerment of people of color, dedicated to eliminating racism both in individual behavior and in the greater community, I receive requests for a one-day training on diversity. I could certainly fly in, take the money, and fly out. However, that would be unaccountable on my part because I know I would be colluding in a deception: the illusion that one talk, workshop, or training will shift how racism operates in an organization.

My first question to people who call is "Why do you want a one-day training on diversity/racism?" We proceed to have a conversation about what they want to accomplish. Their goals are usually quite circumscribed. They often want white people to be educated, more sensitive, more supportive of efforts to address racism. This is a small goal within an organization or institution founded to benefit white people or to "serve" people of color—an organization which has white people in control, has no deep organizational commitment to racial justice, and probably is unwilling to dedicate significant resources to eliminating racism within.

My experience has led me to conclude talks and trainings only make sense in an organization committed to serious organizational change. Otherwise they are window-dressing—ineffective and possibly even damaging to the cause of racial justice. One feel-good workshop can lead individual participants to believe they have done something. The organization can claim they are serious about racial justice. The public may have the illusion something has changed. But business continues as usual.

I am not interested in furthering the illusion of anti-racism work where it is not happening. Therefore, through a series of questions, I try to indicate what I think needs to be in place for a talk or training to make a difference:

1. How will the training relate to preceding and ongoing efforts to create a practice of racial justice within the organization?
2. Is there sustainable leadership at the highest levels for this effort?
3. Is a serious commitment to racial justice built into the core mission of the organization?
4. Is there a strategic plan for diversity within the organization at all levels, and/or is it an integral part of the overall strategic plan?

5. Is there an adequate, sustainable, and dedicated budget for long-term anti-racism work?

Basically I am asking "Is this organization serious and committed to working toward racial justice?" I am not willing to settle for a verbal assurance. I want to see concrete indications the money, commitment, leadership for the sustainability of the project are in place so it has some chance to succeed. If the organization is ready, then we can talk about trainings, hiring and retention practices, organizational culture, accountability to various communities served, allocation of resources, and leadership development.

Almost always when I ask these questions, I am met with a polite response indicating the person I am talking with had not thought about any of these things. They say something about taking this information back to their director/the diversity committee/the board— and I never hear from them again.

Few organizations are serious about anti-racism work in their organizations, which is why most remain toxic environments for people of color, providing them with limited opportunities to thrive and succeed. Opportunities that do exist come with an unacknowledged requirement to assimilate and be submissive within an impenetrable culture of whiteness. These organizations are unaccountable to communities of color and—no matter how much they claim to do on behalf of those communities—they leave the structural problems of racism unaddressed and white institutional power intact.

Since these organizations function within an extremely unequal economic hierarchy, and in an increasingly segregated and racially polarized society, they can only begin to answer these questions by analyzing the effects of their work on the communities of color they claim to serve.

Who Benefits from Our Work?

Many of us would have to admit our work may help some people have greater access to job and educational opportunities, promotions, and training and greater access to social services, but it does

6.2. Questions for Educators, Trainers, and Consultants

1. What is your role when the existence of racism is routinely denied or defended, violence against Muslims and immigrants is increasing, and women, trans, men, and young people of color are being blamed for a variety of social ills and harassed, locked up, and killed?
2. What is your role when large-scale unemployment, environmental degradation, deterioration of public services, and the deflation of the housing bubble have disproportionately devastated the jobs, housing, and living conditions of people of color?
3. How do you maintain the political integrity of this work within increasingly conservative and embattled organizational environments?
4. How are the participants in your trainings connected to social justice activism?
5. How much racial justice activism are you involved in through your work and in your daily lives?

not challenge the distribution of power, wealth, and resources maintaining the basic structure of inequality. Many of us work in the middle area of the pyramid, providing a buffer zone between the frustration, pain, and anger of the people at the bottom and the concentration of wealth and power at the top. We may keep people and their hopes alive, but without giving them enough information, material resources, and skills to seriously challenge the racial and economic hierarchy.[2]

We should not be surprised by this situation. The growth of a group of professionals who do multicultural and diversity trainings, as opposed to racial justice organizing, was partly a progressive response to incorporating grassroots demands for inclusion and diversity by the Civil Rights Movement, and partly a reactionary response to deflect further such demands. During the 1960s and 1970s, there was a more liberal social climate and more immediate grassroots pressure on institutions. Multiculturalists had more leverage to fight for changes within organizations.

More recently, the question of how we can all get along, work together, succeed as a team, and hear everyone's voice superseded the questions of who has power and how can it be shared more equitably. With less external social pressure, organizations were quick to take racism off the agenda and to put team building and celebrating diversity in its place. Today, in the second decade of the 21st century, teachers and trainers have even less leverage to challenge this backlash, although we do have some.[3]

Even from within large organizations and institutional structures, it is possible to work for social justice and serve the interests of people who are most marginalized in our society. But doing so is not without risk.

We each need to determine the amount we can risk financially against the spiritual and emotional costs we incur when we don't stand by our commitment to social justice. These are strategic decisions we cannot make in isolation from the inside of the organization(s) we work for. Our work is part of a much wider network of individuals and organizations working for justice on the outside. To make effective decisions about our own work, we need to be accountable to those groups and their actions and issues. This accountability[4] then becomes a source of connection that breaks down our isolation and increases our effectiveness.

I think there are three questions we need to ask ourselves in the current political context:

Who supervises my work?

I don't mean who employs us or funds us. Who are the grassroots activists of color who advise us, review our work and with whom we consult? I think it is particularly critical for those of us who are white to be accountable to people of color so our work doesn't inadvertently fuel the backlash or otherwise make it more dangerous for them. But regardless of our ethnicity or race, we need to be accountable to people who are on the front lines of struggles for racial justice and who have leadership positions in local communities of color.

Am I involved in community-based anti-racist struggle?

If we are not fighting for civil, human, and immigrant rights; against environmental dumping on Indigenous land or in communities of color; against police brutality; and for access to health care and for anti-racist policies and practices within our own institutions, what are we modeling? How are we learning? What informs our work? I don't think we can be accountable to communities of color if we are not politically involved ourselves in some aspect of anti-racist struggle.

Are current political struggles part of the content of what I teach?

Do we connect the participants in our networks, classes, and trainings to opportunities for ongoing political work? Do we give them tools and resources for getting involved in the issues people of color identify as most immediate for them, such as access to health care, jobs with living wages, quality education, affordable and healthy food, a clean and sustainable environment, and immigrant rights? When they leave the (class)room after our training or workshop can they connect what they just learned to the racism people of color experience in their lives? Are we developing white allies who are responsive to the demands of people of color for white support, resources, and action?

We may be discouraged about the possibility of doing effective anti-racist work in our current conservative times, but this is also a time of widespread organizing and resistance to injustice.[5] It can be a time for us to realign clearly with those organizing efforts and reclaim the original vision of racial justice and equality which brought our work into being. A focus on organizational and institutional change within a framework of accountable practice is essential to any progress toward racial justice.

Home and Family

ALTHOUGH YOUR FAMILY MEMBERS may all be white and your neighbors appear so, there may well be people of other cultures, people in interracial families, people of mixed heritage, or people who are passing as white among your friends. People of color may also be providing childcare, cleaning, maintenance, or health care services for you, your children, or other relatives. Our environment is seldom as white as we assume.

Our homes are less separable from the greater community than they have ever been. They are connected to the outside world via smart phones, TV, computer games, the internet, toys, CDs, radio, books and magazines. Each of these provides a vehicle by which racism can enter your home, just as they also give you opportunities to respond to it.

- *Do you talk about racism where you live?*
- *When you and other family members watch a movie, discuss the news, or talk about daily events, do you notice and discuss racism?*

Talking about racism is not easy for most of us to do. Few of us grew up in homes where racism or other difficult and emotional issues were mentioned. We come from backgrounds of silence, ignorance, or a false belief that to talk about racism is to further it. When talk about race did occur, some of us experienced conflict with family members because we disagreed over racial issues. We can acknowledge these past experiences and create an atmosphere in our own homes where we can openly and respectfully talk about issues of race, gender, and class.

It is challenging to raise white children in the highly racist society we live in. When babies are born, they are unaware of racial difference and attach no intrinsic value to skin color. We know they begin to notice racial differences and their effects between the ages of two and four.[1] Throughout their childhood, they are bombarded with stereotypes, misinformation, and lies about race. Without our intervention, they might not become members of extremist groups or commit hate crimes, but they may well become white people who accept the injustice, racial discrimination, and violence in our society and perpetuate racism through their collusion. That is why it is important to begin teaching young people at an early age to embrace differences and to become racial justice activists. We can start this process by assessing our home and family environment for evidence of racism.

- Do the calendars, pictures, and posters on your walls reflect the diverse society we live in?
- Are there books by women and people who are trans or gender-queer from many different cultures?
- Are there magazines from communities of color?

We don't get extra points if there are. Nor are we trying to create an ethnic museum. But paying attention to our environment broadens our perspective and counters the stream of negative racial stereotypes in our society.

It is even more important to discuss racism and to pay attention to our home if we live with young people. As responsible parents, we need to think about the toys, games, computer games, dolls, books, and pictures our young ones are exposed to. I am not recommending you purge your house of favorite games and toys or become fanatical about the racism you find in a child's life. Young people don't need to be protected from racism. They see it all the time. They need to be given critical thinking tools for recognizing, analyzing, and responding to the different forms it takes. Discussing the racism (or sexism) in a book or movie for young people, helping them think about the injustices of racism, and providing alternative anti-racist materials—these increase young people's awareness and their ability to respond to injustice.

Young people need opportunities to listen to the experiences of people of color.[2] Placing them in multicultural childcare settings, encouraging multiracial friendships, reaching out to coworkers and colleagues who are of diverse backgrounds, and choosing professionals like doctors and dentists who are people of color are all ways to broaden their experience. Our efforts can help them build relationships with people of color and introduce them to critical thinking about racism.

If our neighborhood or school is segregated, we can still introduce young people to a multicultural world experience. The best and often most accurate way is to read what people of color write about their lives. Many books for your people realistically portray the lives of adults and children who are African American. There are a substantial number of books about the lives of Latinx and Jews. Books by Native American, Arab American, Asian American, and Muslim writers may be harder to find, but there are some good ones available.[3] Many of us, especially if we live in or visit large cities, have access to photo exhibits, live musical performances, museums, and cultural centers where we can take young people if we have the means. Hearing and seeing examples of other people's diverse experiences is extremely valuable for them.

If we understand we live in a multicultural society, we will begin to question any situation where people of color are not present. For example, if our children are in a predominately or all-white Scout troop, sports team, Math Olympics team, or a religious school class, we will ask ourselves, "Why is this group all white? Are there any barriers keeping children of color out?" Then we might question the curriculum or program. "Is it multicultural? Does it reflect the diversity of the larger community? What values are being taught? Are issues of racism being addressed? Are other groups excluded, such as girls or queer youth?"

Young people notice differences in people and how they are treated. Many of us want to teach them not to judge others in biased and unkind ways, and therefore we may downplay the significance of differences. But this can sometimes lead them to conclude avoiding discrimination means avoiding differences. On the contrary, we want young people to notice differences *and* similarities in people and to notice when differences lead to people being treated unfairly. As early childhood teachers Ann Pelo and Fran Davidson discovered, "children who notice differences and who are comfortable with them can identify discrimination more clearly and can explore the unfairness that arises from biased understandings of difference. This is the beginning of activism."[4]

When adults notice and remark on the ways people are separated and treated differently, we validate our young people's own perceptions and encourage them to build a sharper awareness of how racism works. When my son was caught shoplifting many years ago, the store manager called me and released him to my care without calling the police and having him arrested. Of course, my son was scared when he was caught and was relieved that he was not taken to jail. He was fined and banned from the store, but did not get an arrest on his record. Afterwards, when we talked about this incident, I asked him how Charles, an African American friend of his, might have been treated if he had been the one caught shoplifting. I didn't tell him he would have been treated differently. I asked him what difference he thought it might make. We had a thoughtful discussion of what might have happened if the store had called the police, how his friend might have been treated, what it would have meant if he had an arrest record. I brought this up not to make my son feel guilty or lucky, but to give him practice in noticing that race makes a constant difference in how people are treated.

I think it is crucial we be honest with young people about racial inequality in the larger society. When we are answering their questions about poverty, homelessness, or AIDS, we can discuss the ways racism makes people of color more vulnerable to these problems and less able to access resources and support. We can point out how people of color are blamed for having these problems while the larger number of white people in the same situation are not blamed as much—or perhaps not at all. For instance, there are substantial numbers of white people on government assistance in the United States, but the media most often present images of those on assistance as mothers who are black, not white.

Biased representations of people of color reinforce the unstated belief white people are superior. In almost every interpersonal and institutional setting, the assumption is white is better because white people are in charge, white images are taken for granted, white history is taught in our schools, and white people receive more respect. This instills in white youth a sense they are entitled to respect, power, and inclusion, and can even justify disrespect for, violence toward, and exclusion of people of color. They need to hear from us that white is not superior, all white people are not smarter, nor do they work harder than people of color.

When we talk about homelessness, hunger, or poverty, for example, we can discuss job and housing discrimination. This will help young people understand the social roots of individual problems. Whether the issue is race, gender, economics, or disability, nothing is more important than to give them insight (at the level at which they can absorb it) into the systemic nature of power, violence, and blame. We do this not to excuse abusive or destructive behavior, but to put actions into context and to help them move beyond blaming individuals for social problems.

It empowers white youth when they see they have a role to play in ending racism and other forms of injustice. White people are participating in the struggle against hate crimes, police brutality, housing and job discrimination, and environmental racism. There are probably local people, possibly members of your extended family or community, who are models of white people who have been allies to people of color. We can give our youth models of white people (particularly young white people) who have resisted racism so they know *racism as a system* is the problem, not every white person.

At the same time, we can help white children recognize that white people in general have been resistant to acknowledging and ending racism. We need to be honest about our own role and the roles of our foreparents. Many of us have relatives who did not support the Civil Rights movement or the struggles for racial justice by Latinx and Native Americans. Adult whites, either actively or passively, are the biggest supporters of racism in the US. Some of us have family members who are today speaking out or acting against equal opportunity, immigrant rights, police accountability, and religious tolerance. These stories need to be told as well.

Young white people need to see they can choose to support racist policies or they can choose to become racial justice activists. Present all sides—the complex dimensions of white responses to racism—so young people can see they have moral choices to make. When they understand how racism is institutionalized, they will know they are not responsible for it, but they are responsible for how they respond to it. Will they stand for racial justice and equal opportunity? Will they stand with people of color? Their answers to these questions will begin to form through the ways we raise them.

You might want to initiate family discussions about racism by talking about this book and how you don't want your home to support racism. You could solicit young people's help in doing an assessment of your home and thinking about how different games, books, videos, or posters might be racist.

Let your children help decide what to do to make your home different. It is one thing to create an anti-racist, multicultural environment by yourself. It is an entirely different level of education and empowerment to include young people as valued participants in the process of acknowledging and celebrating the diversity of people and cultures in our society.

Obviously, this kind of assessment and interactive process should also address issues of gender, class, disability, sexual orientation, and religious and cultural difference. People of color are also women, poor or working-class, people with disabilities, LGBT, and/or Muslim, Buddhist, or Jewish. Our differences are complex. When dealt with in a context of social justice, young people are quick to develop principles of fair treatment and equality, eager to become co-participants in creating a healthier environment and challenging injustice. They may well end up inspiring and leading us with their readiness to challenge authority, take risks, and stand up for fairness.

6.3. Questions and Actions: Home and Family

1. Were people of color and racism talked about in your childhood home? Think about particular incidents when they were. Who initiated discussions and who resisted them? Was there tension around it; how was tension handled if there was any?

2. Were Jews, the Jewish holocaust, or anti-Jewish oppression talked about? Were Muslims or Islam, the war on terror, or the attacks on 9/11 talked about? What was the tone of the discussion?

3. Was there silence in your home on issues of racism or other forms of oppression? What did you learn from the silence?

4. Was there conflict within your family because of racism (over integration, interracial or interfaith dating, music, or busing)? Think of particular incidents. How was the conflict dealt with?

5. Were there people of color who cared for you, your parents, house, or yard? If so, how were they treated? How did their presence and your family's attitudes toward them influence you?

6. As a young person, what stories, TV shows, or books influenced you the most in your attitudes about people of color? About people who were not Christian? What do you carry with you from that exposure?

7. Talk with your partner, housemates, and friends about these issues. Notice the whiteness of your surroundings out loud to family and friends. This needn't be done aggressively or with anger. Ask questions, notice things

out loud, express your concerns, and give other people
room to think about and respond to what you say.

8. Bring up feelings or thoughts about reading this book at
   dinner or other family time. What is difficult or awkward
   about doing this? What is the response?

9. Do an assessment of your home including the following
   items:

   a. books
   b. posters
   c. cookbooks
   d. calendars
   e. paintings
   f. magazines
   g. newspapers
   h. videos
   i. games
   j. computer games
   k. toys
   l. art materials
   m. religious articles
   n. sports paraphernalia
   o. music

10. What would you like to remove?

11. What would you like to add? Try to go beyond the tokenism
    of putting up pictures of Martin Luther King, Jr. or LeBron
    James or adding a book or two to your children's collection.
    Explore the roles and contributions of people of color in
    areas where you and other family members share an inter-
    est—such as sports, science, music, books, or movies.

12. Are women well represented in the items in your home?
    Are poor and working-class people? Are people with
    disabilities? Are Muslims, Jews, and Buddhists? Are the
    creations of young people themselves included?

13. Do you employ people of color? How well are they paid?
    How well are they treated? How do your children respond
    and relate to them? How will you talk with your children
    about these relationships? How will you balance these
    relationships with friends and neighbors from different
    cultures who are not employees? Are your children exposed
    to professionals such as teachers, doctors, and dentists who
    are people of color? How could you increase such exposure?

6.4. Resource Suggestions for Parents and Teachers

General

Teaching for Change: The best selection of books and curricula for young people on racism and other topics. tfcbooks.org/best-recommended/booklist.

Asian American Curriculum Project: A project educating the public on the diversity of the Asian American experience. asianamericanbooks.com.

Facing History and Ourselves: Provides educational and professional resources for teachers. facinghistory.org.

Rethinking Schools: A curricula and magazine publisher and activist organization. rethinkingschools.org.

Zinn Education Project: Provides lessons and articles to introduce students to a more accurate, complex, and engaging understanding of US history. zinnedproject.org.

Teaching Tolerance: Provides classroom tools and resources to reduce prejudice, improve intergroup relations, and foster school equity. tolerance.org.

Magazines

Skipping Stones: An International Multicultural Magazine (for young people). skippingstones.org.

Rethinking Schools: rethinkingschools.org/archive/index/shtml.

Teaching Tolerance: tolerance.org/magazine/archives.

Blogs

Raising Race Conscious Children: raceconscious.org.

Embrace Race: embracerace.org.

All of the above resources: [online]. [cited April 23, 2017].

Articles

Bree Ervin. "6 Things White Parents Can Do to Raise Racially Conscious Children." Everyday Feminism, August 30, 2014 [online]. [cited January 8, 2017]. everydayfeminism.com /2014/08/raising-racially-conscious-kids.

Madeleine Rogin. "How to Talk to Kids About Race: What's Appropriate for Ages 3–8." InCultureParent, May 14, 2013 [online]. [cited January 8, 2017]. incultureparent.com/2013 /05/how-to-talk-to-kids-about-race-whats-appropriate -for-ages-3-8.

Katie Kissinger. "5 Things to Know About Talking to Children About Race." Creating Democracy, March 10, 2014 [online]. [cited January 8, 2017]. creatingdemocracy.org/parenting -for-c.

Kathi Valeii. "The 6-Step Guide to Raising Anti-Racist White Kids as a White Parent." Resist, December 31, 2016. [online]. [cited January 8, 2017]. resistmedia.org/2016 /12/31/6-step-guide-raising-antiracist-white-kids/.

Books

Louise Derman-Sparks and Julie Olsen Edwards. *Anti-Bias Education for Young Children and Ourselves*, 2nd rev. ed. National Association for the Education of Young Children, 2010.

Katie Kissinger. *Anti-Bias Education in the Early Childhood Classroom: Hand in Hand, Step by Step.* Routledge, 2017.

Enid Lee and Deborah Menkart, eds. *Beyond Heroes and Holidays: A Practical Guide to K-12 Anti-Racist, Multicultural Education and Staff Development*, 2nd ed. Teaching for Change, 2008.

Nancy Schneidewind and Ellen Davidson. *Open Minds to Equality: A Sourcebook of Learning Activities to Affirm Diversity and Promote Equity*, 4th ed. Rethinking Schools, 2014.

Paul Kivel. *Boys Will Be Men: Raising Our Sons for Courage, Caring and Community*. New Society, 1999.

Allan Creighton and Paul Kivel. *Helping Teens Stop Violence, Build Community and Stand for Justice*, 20th anniversary ed. Hunter House, 2011.

Deborah Menkart et al., eds. *Putting the Movement Back into Civil Rights Teaching*. Teaching for Change, 2004.

Beverly Tatum. *Can We Talk About Race: And Other Conversations in an Era of School Resegregation*. Beacon, 2008.

Maureen Reddy, ed. *Everyday Acts Against Racism: Raising Children in a Multiracial World*. Seal Press, 1996.

Ann Pelo, ed. *Rethinking Early Childhood Education*. Rethinking Schools, 2008.

Ann Pelo and Fran Davidson. *That's Not Fair!: A Teacher's Guide to Activism with Young Children*. Red Leaf, 2002.

Mara E. Sapon-Shevin. *Because We Can Change the World: A Practical Guide to Building Cooperative, Inclusive Classroom Communities*, 2nd ed. Corwin, 2010.

Mary Cowhey. *Black Ants and Buddhists: Thinking Critically and Teaching Differently in the Primary Grades*. Stenhouse, 2006.

Debra van Ausdale and Joe R. Feagin. *The First R: How Children Learn Race and Racism*. Rowman & Littlefield, 2001.

Daphne Muse. *The New Press Guide to Multicultural Resources for Young Readers*. New Press, 1997.

Other Resources

Family Diversity Projects: familydiv.org.

Syracuse Cultural Workers: syracuseculturalworkers.com.

Northern Sun: northernsun.com.

All of the above resources: [online]. [cited April 14, 2017].

For the Long Haul

RACISM IS NOT going to end tomorrow or next year. Every delay and setback saps our strength and strains our hope. It is easy to despair, easy to give up. How do we nurture and sustain ourselves for what may well be a lifetime struggle? How do we keep alive a vision of racial justice and multicultural democracy to guide our action?

The first step is to stop and think about how we are taking care of ourselves for the long term. Our guilt, desperation, anger, fear, the immediate pressure of events, or even our enthusiasm may make it difficult for us to think about how to keep going after this next action, campaign, or crisis.[1]

If we are not thinking about how to nurture ourselves in the coming years, we are probably also not thinking strategically about the future. We may have become bogged down reacting to everyday events. We may have lost sight of our goals, not noticed how the world is changing, and forgotten we must renew ourselves to remain effective.

We need to create time in our overworked, overcommitted lives to reflect on the future. Some of us do this best alone, others with friends and family. In either case, we must start with time for reflection.

- *Take a moment to think about how you center your energy or calm yourself amidst the pressures and stress of your daily routines. How could you strengthen this part of your life?*

Reflection is a spiritual practice for some of us. Any spiritual practice connecting us to a reality greater than our individual lives—that connects us to other people, to animal and plant life, and/or to a larger energy in the world—can increase our respect for life and our valuing of difference. It can renew and guide our pursuit for a better world. We each have, or can find, our own unique way to reflect and connect.

- *What activities help you connect to a greater reality?*
- *How could these activities support your work for social justice?*
- *How might you create more time for reflection in your life?*

We also need to take care of ourselves physically and emotionally. We need to live as if we wanted to be alive when our visions are realized. It goes without saying we need to eat, exercise, relax, have fun, play, enjoy, and smile, yet how many of us don't take these parts of our lives seriously until we can't continue our work because of exhaustion or poor health? How do we expect to continue in the struggle? What are we modeling for the young people around us?

People with a white Christian background may experience a big divide between work and leisure. Taking care of oneself, goofing off, and having fun may seem self-indulgent, even sinful. Some people can turn exercise and other forms of recreation into work, diminishing their value. These attitudes can also make it difficult to exult in the singing, dance, drama, and other celebratory rituals that can renew our lives so much.

Reclaiming or developing cultural rituals can heal and reinvigorate us. Rituals build community, connect people, and inspire new visions and strategies. Singing or going to hear music; writing, reading, or listening to a poem; participating in a holiday ritual; sharing a meal with friends—we need to allow ourselves cultural activities which nurture our souls.

Mainstream male, white, and Christian traditions push people to be rugged individuals. The message is "Go it alone." This assumes there is an individual path to salvation and people shouldn't make mistakes or ask for help. As a result of this message, we can easily become isolated and feel scared, confused, or lost. We may not know where to turn for support. Many of us find it easier to support others than to ask for help. We have to overcome our pride and fear to admit we can't fight racism alone. We can't create social justice by ourselves.

Friends, family members, and community networks keep us connected, supported, and inspired. They help us maintain perspective on who we are and what we can do. Working with others aids us in evaluating what we can or cannot take on, what our share is. Taking care of ourselves through healthy lifestyles, rituals, cultural activities, and support networks builds and sustains a large community of people dedicated to the struggle for social justice.

6.5. Questions and Actions: For the Long Haul

1. Who are family and friends you can talk with about doing racial justice work? Who will you talk with first?
2. Who are coworkers who might help you form a racial justice action/support network? Who will you talk with first?
3. Do you know or know of people of color who you want to talk with about fighting racism? List the one you will talk with first. Ask if they have time and are willing to do this with you.
4. Name one network, action committee, or support group you are going to join.
5. What kind of cultural events, rituals, or celebrations bring you together with others? Which ones renew your spirit?
6. How can you honor and celebrate the efforts of those who have preceded you?

Finally, we need to celebrate our successes, no matter how small; our victories, no matter how tenuous. Although racism is still a central constituent of society, we have made progress, and some things have changed. They have changed because multitudes of courageous people of color and white allies have fought, resisted, and refused to be overwhelmed by racism. They have changed because the human spirit is indomitable and we each share that spirit. We can only sustain our efforts by building on and celebrating the achievements of the people who have contributed to getting us as far as we are today.

Conclusion

MANY YEARS AGO, my colleagues at the Oakland Men's Project and I did a five-day workshop in Ohio in which we focused extensively on racism. Six months later, we were back for a two-day follow-up with the same participants. To start the workshop, we asked participants to talk about how the previous workshop had affected them.

I sat listening to several people describe how the workshop had changed their understanding of racism, how it had affected their relationships with coworkers, and how it had sensitized them to racial injustice in their community. I was pleased our work had a positive impact, but was a little uneasy without knowing why. Finally a white man, Mark, who works at a large social service agency, began to speak:

> That workshop has influenced me in more ways than I can say. But I think it made the biggest difference at work. This fall my agency needed to hire five new staff, and I made sure three of those five people were people of color because our staff has been mostly white until now.

"That's it," I said to myself, realizing what had been missing from the others' accounts.

It is important for us to unlearn prejudice, broaden our understanding of racism, and learn to recognize racist acts when we see them. But unless we are actively involved in the fight against racism, we haven't taken it far enough. Mark understood he needed to turn his awareness into concrete action. Mark changed his workplace. He didn't just try to get one person of color into the organization, because he knew one person would be isolated and probably not last long. He wanted to make a significant impact, so he focused on the difficult but reachable goal of making three of the five new hires people of color.

Mark was not a high-level manager or director. When I talked with him later, he described in more detail what he had done. It had taken him many discussions, both one-on-one and with the full staff, to convince his peers and supervisors how important it was to hire qualified people of color. He had prepared a staff presentation about racism, looking at the agency, its staff, policies, and clientele. He had lobbied long and hard, at some personal risk, to convince people they needed to address racism concretely in their hiring practices. He had helped with the job search and interviewing so qualified candidates would be found. Now he was supporting the new staff.

We don't always have the visible impact Mark had in fighting racism. Even if he had not been able to diversify the staff, he would have made a difference. By raising the issue of racism within the organization, he was questioning established patterns and expectations. He challenged everyone to rethink how hiring was done and what the implications were for the organization and for the community.

Sometimes change doesn't come in the first round, but in the second, third, or fourth. Change starts with one person questioning, challenging, speaking up, and doing something to make a difference. Leaders in the Movement for Black Lives have been asking for white people to step up and *break white silence* with our words, actions, organizing wherever we are. Don't wait until you know everything or are perfectly prepared. Don't wait until someone else gives you permission. Step up, take a risk. We will make mistakes, in which case we should pick up the pieces, apologize if needed, learn from our mistakes, and keep going. Don't let racism go unchallenged.

As Jewish poet Marge Piercy wrote at the end of her poem "The Low Road"

> ...it starts when you care
> to act, It starts when you do
> it again after they said no,
> it starts when you say *We*
> and know who you mean, and each
> day you mean one more.[1]

We can make a difference because each of us is already part of the community where racism exists and thrives. We are connected to neighborhoods, workplaces, schools, and religious organizations. Our connections, our relationships, our positions in these organizations give us leverage to change them. Every time we add another white ally to our network, we increase our leverage. And every time white people step up as allies to people of color, that leverage increases the possibility of achieving racial justice.

I end by returning to questions I asked at the beginning of this book:

- What do you stand for?
- Who do you stand with?
- Do you stand for the idea that all people are created equal?
- Do you stand for the idea that everyone deserves life, liberty, and the pursuit of happiness?
- Do you stand for the idea that no one should be discriminated against because of their race, religion, gender, sexual identity, sexual orientation, ability, or other factors?
- Do you stand for the idea that, as Dr. Martin Luther King, Jr. said, an injustice against one is an injustice against all?

And, more specifically:

- Do you stand with people of color who are still being discriminated against, marginalized, and excluded from jobs, housing and educational opportunities?
- Do you stand with people of color who are experiencing increasing levels of hate crimes, racial profiling, police brutality, and governmental surveillance and intervention?

- Do you stand with people of color who are still suffering and dying disproportionately from inadequate health care, toxic waste in their communities, violence, and governmental neglect?
- If you stand for justice and, if you stand with those who are under attack, then what are you doing about it?

Afterword

I CANNOT PREDICT the future, and you may be reading *Uprooting Racism* one, five, or ten years from when I'm writing it. Whenever you are reading this book, I'm pretty certain racism will still be alive and thriving, and there will still be much for you to do to work for racial justice. In 2014 Naomi Klein wrote in *This Changes Everything* that the problem at the root of global climate change is capitalism—we cannot seriously address our environmental crisis without fundamentally altering and democratizing our economic system. I completely agree with her. And I am also very clear we cannot address our economic system without addressing the fundamental role racism, sexism, and colonialism play in sustaining it.

Early in *Uprooting Racism*, I write about neoliberalism, the current stage of global capitalism. This is a system of power, wealth, and control by ruling elites currently centered in the US and Europe; neoliberals use exploitation, surveillance, and violence to maintain power. The neoliberal agenda of the US ruling class, beyond constantly working to concentrate more and more wealth and power in their own hands, is to roll back the 1930s gains of the working class (unions, hours of work, job safety, and social welfare benefits) and the 1950–70s gains in civil rights and access to education, voting rights, housing, and jobs won by African Americans, women, people with disabilities, people who are LGBTQ, and environmental activists. Using a vocabulary of "free" (i.e., unregulated) markets, privatization, personal responsibility, individual choice, race-neutral policy, testing, and assessment, the ruling class has been transforming what were *public* education, health care, housing, prison, and other systems into profit centers for multinational corporations. In this process, everything is "commodified" (meaning assigned a market price): land, people, information, food, air, genes, water. These things become affordable only to those who have the cash to pay for them.

Nothing in the 21st-century capitalist world is immune to market valuation and control. Nothing is sacred. This has led directly to a devastated environment and global climate change; a great recession in which millions lost their homes; poverty-level wages for many; lack of food, shelter, health care, inadequate schools; and the incarceration of large numbers of people of color. The ruling class has decimated poor, working-, and middle-class families and communities. Unfettered government-supported corporate power has limited US democracy, made us all vulnerable to high levels of personal surveillance, increased racial profiling, harassment and violence against those most vulnerable, and fuels endless war around the world, particularly in western Asia.

Neoliberalism is built on the exploitation of Native American land; women's unpaid and low-paid productive, reproductive, and caring labor; and the unpaid and super-exploited paid labor of people of color. This system would collapse without all three. It also depends on white complicity: our acceptance of racial exploitation and violence to our benefit; our assumptions of superiority and entitlement; our silence; our denial and minimization; and the scapegoating and blame we direct toward those most marginalized in our society.

There continues to be tremendous popular resistance to this agenda and large-scale organizing throughout the US and the rest world. In 2016 alone, there were massive movements within US prisons and deportation centers, on the streets, in the courts, and in the farms, fields, and factories. Some of the most visible of these struggles were the Movement for Black Lives, prison strikes, the fight for $15, environmental campaigns including fossil-fuel divestment, and notably the fight to stop the North Dakota Access Pipeline (NO DAPL) at Standing Rock.

With the election of Donald Trump to the presidency, the US is entering a new configuration of the political elite but not a new agenda for the ruling class. We must defend those under attack, consolidate the real gains we have made in the last few years, and organize on a broad and massive scale on all fronts for the long term. The people most under attack—particularly women and trans people, people with disabilities, people of color, Native Americans, immigrants, Muslims, poor and working-class white people—need to be in leadership. Those of us not on the front lines of grassroots struggle but understanding our mutual interest need to respond to their leadership and stand beside them as allies in the struggle. Anything less diminishes our humanity and in the long run will not protect us.

Resistance can be physical and cultural. Rejecting neoliberal values and building sustainable communities based on love, mutual respect, healing, inclusion, democratic processes, and interdependence with the natural environment is our only way forward.

Institutional racism is the way neoliberal policies get carried out in communities of color. Cultural racism is the way it is justified and normalized in white communities. Broad-based organizing and movement building is the way racism can be resisted. Now is the time to step up our efforts, amplifying the resistance and building a society which serves all of us.

Notes

Preface to the Fourth Edition

1. See the bibliography.
2. Catherine E. Shoichet. "Is Racism on the Rise?: More in America Say Racism Is a 'Big Problem.'" CNN, November 25, 2015. [online]. [cited November 27, 2016]. cnn.com/2015/11/24/us/racism-problem-cnn-kff -poll/index.html.
3. Janie Valencia. "Majority of White People Say There's Racism Every- where, but Not Around Them." *Huffington Post*, September 9, 2015. [online]. [cited November 27, 2016.] huffingtonpost.com/entry/white -people-racism-poll_us_55a91a4fe4b0c5f0322d17f2.
4. This transfer is estimated to be in the hundreds of billions of dollars: Amaad Rivera et al. *Foreclosed: State of the Dream 2008*. United for a Fair Economy, January 15, 2008. [online]. [cited May 4, 2017]. faireconomy.org/dream8.

A Note on Language

1. Tanisha Love Ramirez and Zeba Blay. "Why People Are Using the Word 'Latinx.'" *Latino Voices*, July 5, 2016 [online]. [cited October 25, 2016]. huffingtonpost.com/entry/why-people-are-using-the-term-latinx_us _57753328e4b0cc0fa136a159.

A Note to Readers Outside the US

1. The Parekh Report. *The Future of Multi-Ethnic Britain*. Profile, 2000.

Introduction

1. Ron Romanovsky and Paul Phillips. "Burning Angels" on *Let's Flaunt It!* Fresh Fruit Records, 1995.
2. Barry Glassner. *The Culture of Fear: Why Americans Are Afraid of the Wrong Things*. Basic, 1999, pp. xi–xxviii.

3. By *complicity* I mean the connections between interventionist US foreign policy, prior to 9/11, in Middle Eastern countries such as Iran, Iraq, Saudi Arabia, Afghanistan, Palestine, and Israel.

4. I use *anti-Jewish oppression* in place of the more common *anti-Semitism* for accuracy, clarity and to separate it from the recent use of *anti-Semitism* to describe critiques of policies of the State of Israel. Use of *anti-Semitic* to refer to Jewish oppression makes invisible the oppression of other Semitic people. It also misrepresents Jews because not all Jews are Semitic in geographic origin; the ancestors of many Jews converted to Judaism in other parts of the world. Anti-Jewish oppression is parallel to anti-Muslim oppression and so helps to highlight the common history of systemic attack Muslims and Jews have experienced within Christian-dominated Europe and the US.

5. Quoted in Chris Crass. "Answering the Call: White People Showing Up for Racial Justice." The Good Men Project, June 18, 2015. [online]. [cited January 3, 2017]. goodmenproject.com/featured-content/answering-the-call-white-people-showing-up-for-racial-justice-hesaid.

6. Unlearning racism refers to "unlearning" the lies, myths, and stereotypes about people of color and white people that foster racial prejudice.

7. This quote and others of Braden's can be found at: Kentucky Women in the Civil Rights Era. "Pictures and Quotes." [online]. [cited April 15, 2017]. kywcrh.org/projects/kchr-hall-of-fame/braden/picturesquotes.

Part I: What Color Is White?
"I'm Not White"

1. Kathleen McGinnis and Barbara Oehlberg. *Starting Out Right: Nurturing Young Children as Peacemakers*. Crossroad, 1988; Louise Derman-Sparks and Julie Olsen Edwards. *Anti-Bias Education for Young Children and Ourselves*, 2nd rev. ed. Stenhouse, 2010.

2. Annie S. Barnes. *Everyday Racism: A Book for All Americans*. Sourcebooks, 2000, p. 38.

3. For a more detailed discussion about how racism is lived in our bodies, see George Yancy. *Black Bodies, White Gazes: The Continuing Significance of Race in America*, 2nd ed. Rowman & Littlefield, 2016.

"I'm Not Racist"

1. Sarah Smarsh. "Dangerous Idiots: How the Liberal Media Elite Failed Working-class Americans." *Guardian*, October 13, 2016. [online].

[cited on November 7, 2016.] theguardian.com/media/2016/oct/13
/liberal-media-bias-working-class-americans.

What is Racism?

1. Ruth Thompson-Miller et al. *Jim Crow's Legacy: The Lasting Impact of Segregation*. Rowman & Littlefield, 2014.
2. Catherine Y. Kim et al. *The School-to-Prison Pipeline: Structuring Legal Reform*. NYU Press, 2012.
3. Thompson-Miller, *Jim's Crow's Legacy*.
4. Quoted in Jane H. Hill. *The Everyday Language of White Racism*. Wiley-Blackwell, 2008, p. 19.
5. Ibid. p. 19.
6. David Nirenberg. *Anti-Judaism: The Western Tradition*. W. W. Norton and Company, 2014; Deepa Kumar. *Islamophobia and the Politics of Empire*. Haymarket Books, 2012.
7. There were and still are Jews of color in Europe, so not all Europe-descended Jews are white.
8. John Feffer. *Crusade 2.0: The West's Resurgent War on Islam*. City Lights Books, 2012, pp. 27–51.

What Is Whiteness?

1. James Carroll. *Constantine's Sword: The Church and the Jews*. Houghton Mifflin, 2001, pp. 374–5.
2. In some northern and western European countries, there are still strong patterns of racism against southern and eastern Europeans.
3. Quoted in Ronald Takaki. *Strangers from a Different Shore: A History of Asian Americans*, updated and rev. ed. Little Brown, 1989, p. 47.
4. This separation of white from Christian occurred officially in Virginia in 1667 when legislators passed a law that stipulated "The conferring of baptisme doth not alter the condition of the person as to his bondage or freedom." Quoted in Bill Bigelow and Bob Peterson, eds. *Rethinking Columbus: The Next 500 Years*, 2nd ed. Rethinking Schools, 1998, p. 26.
5. Thandeka. *Learning to Be White: Money, Race and God in America*. Bloomsbury, 1999, p. 43.
6. Stephen J. Gould. *The Mismeasure of Man*, rev. and expanded ed. Norton, 1996.
7. Ian Haney López. *White by Law: The Legal Construction of Race*, 10th anniversary ed. New York University, 2006.

8. Tomás Almaguer. *Racial Fault Lines: The Historical Origins of White Supremacy in California*. University of California, 1994, pp. 9–10, 54.

9. Sandra Harding, ed. "Science Constructs Race," section 2 of *The "Racial" Economy of Science: Toward a Democratic Future*. Indiana University, 1993.

10. Barbara A. Koenig. "Which Differences Make a Difference?: Race, DNA, and Health" in Hazel Rose Markus and Paula M. L. Moya, eds. *Doing Race: 21 Essays for the 21st Century*. Norton, 2010, p. 165.

11. Marcus W. Feldman. "The Biology of Ancestry" in Markus and Moya, p. 151.

12. Ibid., p. 144.

13. There are no medical conditions or vulnerabilities that are exclusive to one "race" although there are medical conditions that people within specific genetic subgroupings are more likely to experience: Koenig. "Which Differences Make a Difference?," pp. 160–184.

14. See Sholomo Sands. *The Invention of the Jewish People*. Verso, 2009, particularly pp. 256–280, for a historical account of the creation of the story that Jews are a racial or biological grouping.

15. See Steven Fraser, ed. *The Bell Curve Wars: Race, Intelligence and the Future of America*. Basic, 1995; Richard Lewontin, et al. *Not in Our Genes: Biology, Ideology and Human Nature*, 2nd ed. Haymarket, 2017; Stephen J. Gould. *Ever Since Darwin: Reflections in Natural History*. Norton, 1977, and Gould. *The Mismeasure of Man*.

16. Leslie Picca and Joe Feagin. *Two-Faced Racism: Whites in the Backstage and Frontstage*. Routledge, 2007, p. 12.

17. See, for health care workers, Janice A. Sabin et al. "Physicians' Implicit and Explicit Attitudes about Race by MD Race, Ethnicity, and Gender." *Journal of Health Care for the Poor and Underserved* 20 (2009): 896–913; for law enforcement officers, Joshua Correll et al. "Across the Thin Blue Line: Police Officers and Racial Bias in the Decision to Shoot." *Journal of Personality and Social Psychology* 92 (2007): 1006–1023; for judges, Jeffrey J. Rachlinski et al. "Does Unconscious Racial Bias Affect Trial Judges?" *Notre Dame Law Review* 84 (2009): 1195–1246.

18. The section is drawn from Cheryl Staats. "Understanding Implicit Bias: What Educators Should Know." *American Educator*, Winter 2015–2016. [online]. [cited November 7, 2016]. aft.org/ae/winter2015-2016/staats. You can take an implicit bias test on race at the Harvard.edu website: implicit.harvard.edu/implicit/takeatest.html.

19. Bernard Glassman. *Anti-Semitic Stereotypes Without Jews: Images of the Jews in England 1290–1700*. Wayne State University, 1975.

20. *Roma* is the name of those European peoples commonly referred to as gypsies, a racially derogatory term.

21. Joshua Muravchik. "Facing Up to Black Anti-Semitism." Discoverthe networks.org: A Guide to the Political Left; originally published in *Commentary*, December 1995. [online]. [cited March 29, 2017]. discoverthenetworks.org/Articles/FacingUpToBlackAntiSemitism JoshuaMuravchik.html.

22. I will not use *American* except in this context because the word refers to people from anywhere in the Americas; the term has been racially appropriated by white people in the US.

23. There was anti-German and anti-Italian sentiment during the war, and some people from both groups were harassed, discriminated against, or attacked.

24. Nathan Lean. *The Islamophobia Industry: How the Right Manufactures Fear of Muslims*. Pluto Press, 2012.

25. See the chapter "Recent Immigrants" in Part IV for more discussion of this and similar anti-immigrant legislation.

26. See the chapter "Exotic and Erotic" in Part II, especially pages 105–109.

27. See Allan Creighton and Paul Kivel. *Helping Teens Stop Violence, Build Community and Stand for Justice*. Hunter House/Turner, 2011; Allan Creighton and Paul Kivel. *Young Men's Work: Stopping Violence & Building Community*. Hazelden, 1998; Paul Kivel. *Boys Will Be Men: Raising Our Sons for Courage, Caring, and Community*. New Society, 1999.

Words and Pictures

1. John Tehranian. *White Washed: America's Invisible Middle Eastern Minority*. New York University, 2009, p. 75.

2. Fred Pfeil. *White Guys: Studies in Postmodern Domination and Difference*. Verso, 1995.

3. For an extended discussion of how white people are generally portrayed in movies as moral heroes with beautiful bodies while people of color are portrayed as dangerous, immoral, or marginalized, see Hernan Vera and Andrew M. Gordon. *Screen Saviors: Hollywood Fictions of Whiteness*. Rowman & Littlefield, 2003.

White Benefits, Middle-Class Privilege

1. See the important work on privilege done by Peggy McIntosh. *White Privilege and Male Privilege: A Personal Account of Coming to See Correspondences Through Work in Women's Studies*. Wellesley College, Center for Research on Women, 1988, as well as material from Creighton and

Kivel. *Helping Teens Stop Violence*, and George Lipsitz. *The Possessive Investment in Whiteness: How White People Profit from Identity Politics*, rev. and expanded ed. Temple University, 2006.

2. In 2014 black families earned 59 cents, Latino families earned 72 cents, for every dollar in income earned by a white family. Nationally, Asian American income was $1.23 but was highly variably based on geography and ethnicity: Bernadette D. Proctor et al. *Income and Poverty in the United States: 2015*. United States Census Bureau, issued September 2016. [online]. [cited March 27, 2017]. census.gov/content/dam/Census /library/publications/2016/demo/p60-256.pdf.

3. Pew Research Center."Demographic Trends and Economic Well-being." Social & Demographic Trends, June 2016. [online]. [cited October 19, 2016]. pewsocialtrends.org/2016/06/27/1-demographic -trends-and-economic-well-being.

4. Mariko Lin Chang. "Fact Sheet: Women and Wealth in the United States." Distributed by Sociologists for Women in Society, Spring 2010. [online]. [cited November 19, 2016]. socwomen.org/wp-content /uploads/2010/05/fact_2-2010-wealth.pdf.

5. Forbes. "Forbes 400: The Wealthiest in America." *Forbes*, n.d. [online]. [cited January 12, 2017]. forbes.com/forbes-400/list/?ss=forbes400.

6. For an extended history of the relationship between the white working-class and workers of color, see David R. Roediger. *The Wages of Whiteness: Race and the Making of the American Working Class*, new ed. Verso, 2007.

White Benefits? A Personal Assessment

1. Bristow Hardin. "Race, Poverty and the Militarized Welfare State." *Poverty & Race* (January/February 1999). [online]. [cited December 14, 2016]. prrac.org/full_text.php?text_id=193&item_id=1862&newsletter _id=42&header=Search%20Results. There were few women of any color who were eligible for veterans' benefits, although women served in many capacities vital to the war effort. Many white women and men and women of color were, in fact, displaced from manufacturing, clerical, and sales jobs after the war by affirmative action programs for white men.

2. For more on the disproportionate impact of the GI Bill, see Chapters 1 and 8 in Edward Humes. *Over Here: How the GI Bill Transformed the American Dream*. Houghton Mifflin Harcourt, 2006.

3. Eric Foner. "Hiring Quotas for White Males Only." *Nation*, June 26, 1995, p. 24.

4. Dalton Conley. *Being Black, Living in the Red: Race, Wealth, and Social Policy in America*, 10th anniversary ed. University of California, 1999, p. 36.

5. Melvin L. Oliver and Thomas M. Shapiro. *Black Wealth/White Wealth: A New Perspective on Racial Inequality*. Routledge, 1997, p. 39.

6. Lipsitz. *The Possessive Investment in Whiteness*, p. 6.

7. Oliver and Shapiro. *Black Wealth/White Wealth*, p. 151.

8. Legacy admissions were started in the 1920s by elite eastern schools to give the children of old monied white families preference over the children of Jewish and other recent immigrants who were outscoring them on entrance exams. As recently as the late 1980s, legacies were three times more likely to be accepted to Harvard than non-legacies, and on average, 20% of Harvard's freshmen class were legacy admissions. At Yale the ratio was two times more likely to be accepted, and Dartmouth admitted 57% of its legacy applicants, compared to 27% of non-legacies. The University of Pennsylvania even has a special office of alumni admissions that actively lobbies for alumni children. Legacy admissions are clearly preferences for less academically qualified students. The Office of Civil Rights found that the average admitted legacy at Harvard between 1981 and 1988 was significantly less qualified than the average admitted non-legacy: John Larew. "Who's the Real Affirmative Action Profiteer?" *Washington Monthly*, June 1991, reprinted in Nicolaus Mills, ed. *Debating Affirmative Action: Race, Gender, Ethnicity, and the Politics of Inclusion*. Delta, 1994, pp. 247–258. For up-to-date information and arguments against legacy admissions, see Richard D. Kahlenberg, ed. *Affirmative Action for the Rich: Legacy Preferences in College Admissions*. Century Foundation, 2010. Kahlenberg argues in part that legacy admissions are white admissions.

9. Michael Eric Dyson. *I May Not Get There With You: The True Martin Luther King Jr.* Free Press, 2000, pp. 60–61.

10. This generational advantage of affirmative action is quite common. The Los Angeles Survey of Urban Inequality, for instance, indicates white homebuyers are twice as likely to receive family assistance in purchasing a home as blacks: Oliver and Shapiro. *Black Wealth/White Wealth*, p. 145.

11. This checklist works well as an exercise in a workshop or other group situation. As each item is read by a facilitator, all the people in the

group to whom the item applies stand up or, if physically unable to stand, raise their hands silently for a moment, then sit down (or lower their hands) before the next item is read. Discussion in pairs or as a whole group can follow.

12. Percentages are from 2013 and drawn from Edward N. Wolff. "Household Wealth Trends in the United States, 1962–2013: What Happened Over the Great Recession?" National Bureau of Economic Research Working Paper 20733, 2014. [online]. [cited December 6, 2016]. marineconomicconsulting.com/w20733.pdf.

13. Ariane Hegewisch and Asha DuMonthier. "The Gender Wage Gap: 2015; Annual Earnings Differences by Gender, Race, and Ethnicity." Institute for Women's Policy Research, September 2016. [online]. [cited December 14, 2016]. iwpr.org/publications/pubs/the-gender-wage -gap-2015-annual-earnings-differences-by-gender-race-and-ethnicity.

14. Stephen J. Rose and Heidi I. Hartmann. *Still a Man's Labor Market: The Long-Term Earnings Gap*. Institute for Women's Policy Research Report #C355, 2004. [online], [cited December 14, 2016]. iwpr.org/publications /pubs/still-a-mans-labor-market-the-long-term-earnings-gap.

The Economic Pyramid

1. Numbers are from Wolff. "Household Wealth Trends in the United States."

2. Michael Goldfield. *The Color of Politics: Race and the Mainsprings of American Politics*. New Press, 1997. The movie *Free State of Jones* (2016) tells the powerful story of a group of poor white Southerners seceding from the Confederacy because they didn't want to fight and die for the slave-owning class.

The Costs of Racism to People of Color

1. For an interactive exercise in the form of a race that illustrates disparities between white people and people of color, see Paul Kivel. "Examining Class and Race." Paul Kivel, 2002 [online]. [cited December 14, 2016]. paulkivel.com/resource/examining-class-and-race.

2. See Ellis Cose. *The Rage of a Privileged Class*. HarperCollins, 1993; Joe R. Feagin and Vera Hernan. *White Racism: The Basics*, 2nd ed. Routledge, 2000; Barnes. Everyday Racism; Philomena Essed. *Understanding Everyday Racism: An Interdisciplinary Theory*. Sage, 1991.

3. Jane Elliot. Posted December 31, 2015. [online]. [cited November 28, 2016]. youtube.com/watch?v=w7SCgNjPMq4.

The Culture of Power

1. Paul Kivel. *Living in the Shadow of the Cross: Understanding and Resisting the Power and Privilege of Christian Hegemony*. New Society, 2013, pp. 109–130.

Cultural Appropriation

1. Susan Scafidi, author of *Who Owns Culture? Appropriation and Authenticity in American Law*, quoted in Nadra Kareem Nittle. "What Is Cultural Appropriation and Why Is It Wrong." Racerelations.about.com, updated November 14, 2016. [online]. [cited December 9, 2016]. racerelations.about.com/od/diversitymatters/fl/What-Is-Cultural-Appropriation-and-Why-Is-It-Wrong.htm.

2. The Doctrine of Discovery. "The Bull Romanus Pontifex (Nicholas V) January 8, 1454." [online]. [cited April 22, 2017]. doctrineofdiscovery.org/.

3. Jarune Uwujaren. "The Difference Between Cultural Exchange and Cultural Appropriation?" Everyday Feminism, September 30, 2013. [online]. [cited November 2, 2016]. everydayfeminism.com/2013/09/cultural-exchange-and-cultural-appropriation/.

4. Ibid.

5. Ibid. Also check out The White Noise Collective's collection of resources on cultural appropriation. [online]. [cited December 8, 2016]. conspireforchange.org/?page_id=4#cultural-appropriations; Susanna Barkataki. "How to Decolonize Your Yoga Practice." *Huffington Post*, March 2, 2015. [online]. [cited December 9, 2016]. huffingtonpost.com/susanna-barkataki/how-to-decolonize-your-yo_b_6776896.html; George Tinker. *American Indian Liberation: A Theology of Sovereignty*. Orbis Books, 2008; Chapter 5 "Belonging and Appropriation" in Shelly Tochluk. *Living in the Tension: The Quest for a Spiritualized Racial Justice*. Crandall, Dostie & Douglass Books, 2016, pp. 126–170.

The Costs of Racism to White People

1. For examples of this process, see Thandeka. *Learning to Be White*.

2. For a more extended discussion of the costs of oppression to the oppressors, see Derald Wing Sue. *Microaggressions in Everyday Life: Race, Gender and Sexual Orientation*. Wiley, 2010, pp. 128–33.

3. Original version copyright the Oakland Men's Project, 1990. Adapted from Creighton and Kivel, *Helping Teens Stop Violence*. Reprinted with permission.

Retaining Benefits, Avoiding Responsibility

1. Ward Churchill. *Indians Are Us? Culture and Genocide in Native North America*. Common Courage, 1994, p. 35.
2. *Crash*. Lion's Gate Entertainment, 2005. For excellent discussions of the film, see Michael Benitez Jr. and Felicia Gustin, eds. *Crash Course: Reflections on the Film Crash for Critical Dialogues About Race, Power and Privilege*. Institute for Democratic Education and Culture—Speak Out, 2007.
3. Matthew J. Breiding et al. "Prevalence and Characteristics of Sexual Violence, Stalking, and Intimate Partner Violence Victimization." US Centers for Disease Control, National Intimate Partner and Sexual Violence Survey, United States, 2011. CDC 63(SS08) pp. 1–18, September 5, 2014. [online]. [cited November 28, 2016]. cdc.gov/mmwr/preview/mmwrhtml/ss6308a1.htm?s_cid=ss6308a1_e; Alanna Vagianos. "30 Shocking Domestic Violence Statistics That Remind Us It's an Epidemic." *Huffington Post*, February 13, 2015. [online]. [cited November 28, 2016]. huffingtonpost.com/2014/10/23/domestic-violence-statistics_n_5959776.html.
4. Michael S. Kimmel. "'Gender Symmetry' in Domestic Violence: A Substantive and Methodological Review." *Violence Against Women*, Vol. 8 #11 (November 2002), pp. 1332–1363. [online]. [cited March 24, 2017]. xyonline.net/sites/default/files/Kimmel, Gender symmetry in dom.pdf.

White Fragility and White Power

1. Robin DiAngelo. "White Fragility." *International Journal of Critical Pedagogy*, 3(3), 2011. [online]. [cited November 28, 2016]. libjournal.uncg.edu/ijcp/article/view/249/116.

"Thank You for Being Angry"

1. Tim Wise. *Speaking Treason Fluently: Anti-Racist Reflections from an Angry White Male*. Soft Skull, 2008, p. 82.
2. Bianca DiJulio et al. "Survey of Americans on Race." Kaiser Family Foundation/CNN, November 2015. [online]. [cited November 28, 2016]. files.kff.org/attachment/report-survey-of-americans-on-race.

It's Good to Talk about Racism

1. Federal Safety Net. "U.S. Poverty Statistics." US Census Bureau, released September 2016. [online]. [cited November 28, 2016]. federalsafetynet.com/us-poverty-statistics.html.

2. Tim Worstall. "The Average US Welfare Payment Puts You in the Top 20% of All Income Earners [in the world]." *Forbes*, May 4, 2015. [online]. [cited November 28, 2016]. forbes.com/sites/timworstall /2015/05/04/the-average-us-welfare-payment-puts-you-in-the-top -20-of-all-income-earners/#283b757b9d8f.

3. Global Research and Washington's Blog. "Non-Muslims Carried Out More than 90% of All Terrorist Attacks in America." Centre for Research on Globalization, May 2013. [online]. [cited November 19, 2016]. globalresearch.ca/non-muslims-carried-out-more-than-90-of-all -terrorist-attacks-in-america/5333619.

Who Is a Victim?

1. Marianne Bertrand, Sendhil Mullainathan. "Are Emily and Greg More Employable than Lakisha and Jamal? A Field Experiment on Labor Market Discrimination." National Bureau of Economic Research Working Paper 9873, July 2003. [online]. [cited November 19, 2016]. nber.org/papers/w9873.pdf.

Part II: The Dynamics of Racism
The Enemy Within

1. Drew Desilver. "U.S. Income Inequality, on Rise for Decades, Is Now Highest Since 1928." Pew Research Center, December 5, 2013. [online]. [cited March 30, 2017]. pewresearch.org/fact-tank/2013/12/05/u-s -income-inequality-on-rise-for-decades-is-now-highest-since-1928.

2. For a more detailed analysis of how the US economic system works: Paul Street. *They Rule: The 1% vs. Democracy*. Paradigm, 2014; Mike Lofgren. *The Deep State: The Fall of the Constitution and the Rise of a Shadow Government*. Penguin, 2016.

Fear and Danger

1. Richard Slotkin. *Gunfighter Nation: The Myth of the Frontier in Twentieth-Century America*. Atheneum, 1992, pp. 14–15.

2. United States Census Bureau. "FFF: American Indian and Alaska Native Heritage Month: November 2015." Release Number: CB15-FF.22, November 2, 2015. [online]. [cited November 29, 2016]. census.gov /newsroom/facts-for-features/2015/cb15-ff22.html. Racially motivated government policies exclude Hispanics and African Americans with Native American ancestry from current estimates, so all current demographic figures are highly contested.

3. The life expectancy at birth for United States white males is 76.5 years and for black males is 72.2: Ashley Welch. "Life Expectancy for White Women Falls Slightly in U.S."CBS News, April 20, 2016. [online]. [cited November 29, 2016]. cbsnews.com/news/life-expectancy-for-white -women-falls-slightly-in-u-s/.

4. Jane Mayer. *Dark Money: The Hidden History of the Billionaires Behind the Rise of the Radical Right*. Anchor, 2017.

5. National Sexual Violence Resource Center. "Statistics about Sexual Violence." Info & Stats for Journalists, 2015. [online]. [cited November 19, 2016]. nsvrc.org/sites/default/files/publications_nsvrc_factsheet _media-packet_statistics-about-sexual-violence_0.pdf.

6. Megan Burke and Gloria Penner. "False Rape Accusation Furthers Institutionalized Racism." KPBS, October 1, 2010. [online]. [cited December 15, 2016]. kpbs.org/news/2010/oct/01/false-rape-accusation -furthers-institutionalized-r.

7. US Census figures in 2015 gave a figure of 38.4% for people of color and 61.6% for the white population: United States Census Bureau, QuickFacts, 2015. [online]. [cited December 15, 2016]. census.gov /quickfacts/.

The Geography of Fear

1. John A. Tures. "Are Most Killings Really Interracial?" *Huffington Post*, updated February 2, 2015. [online]. [cited March 30, 2017]. huffington post.com/john-a-tures/are-most-killings-really-_b_6264370.html.

2. Tracy Jan. "Harvard Professor Gates Arrested at Cambridge Home." *Boston Globe*, July 20, 2009. [online]. [cited December 15, 2016]. archive.boston.com/news/education/higher/articles/2009/07/20 /harvard_professor_gates_arrested_at_cambridge_home/.

Exotic and Erotic

1. The eroticization of difference is amply documented in the images of women of color, Jewish and Muslim women in thousands of TV shows, movies, books, advertising, video games, and historical documents.

2. Angela Y. Davis. *Women, Race & Class*. Random House, 1981, pp. 184–187; Elizabeth Pleck. *Rape and the Politics of Race*, 1865–1910. Working Paper No. 213. Wellesley College, Center for Research on Women, 1990.

3. One common crime for which African American men were arrested during the Jim Crow period was "reckless eyeballing."

4. Davis. *Women, Race & Class*, pp. 110–126.

5. Ibid.; bell hooks. *Ain't I a Women: Black Women and Feminism*. South End, 1981.

6. INCITE! Women of Color Against Violence. "Stop Law Enforcement Violence." [online]. [cited December 15, 2016]. incite-national.org /page/stop-law-enforcement-violence.

7. Davis. *Women, Race & Class*, p. 195.

8. See "Disloyal to Civilization: Feminism, Racism, Gynephobia" in Adrienne Rich, *On Lies, Secrets and Silence: Selected Prose, 1966–1978*. Norton, 1979; Ann Braden. "A Second Open Letter to Southern White Women." *Southern Exposure*, Vol 4 #4 (Winter 1977).

The Myth of the Happy Family

1. During slavery, most white people in the US viewed the issue as "a family affair" and viewed white people as parents and enslaved African Americans as children not capable of independence. Public debate was often not over the legitimacy of slavery but whether slave owners were cruel or benevolent masters. In the 20th century, citizens of the Philippines and countries in Central and South America were described as not yet properly raised children; white people had a Christian and parental responsibility to *civilize* them. For a representative sample of images of people of color as children (focusing on the Philippine-American War), see Abe Ignacio et al. *The Forbidden Book: The Philippine-American War in Political Cartoons*. T'boli Publishing, 2004.

What's in a Name?

1. Renaming was seldom documented except in personal and family histories. For the example of the missionary practice of renaming boarding school children: Lisa Gitelman and Geoffrey B. Pingree, eds. *New Media: 1740-1915*. Massachusetts Institute of Technology, 2003, p. 79.

2. It has been well documented that many white people claim a tolerant and color-blind persona when in public and much more freely engage in negative racial talk when they perceive themselves to be in white-only space: for example, see Picca and Feagin. *Two-Faced Racism*.

3. It is disrespectful to our fellow Americans throughout the hemisphere to claim the word *American* to refer only to people in the US.

Separatism

1. For hundreds of examples: James W. Loewen. *Sundown Towns: A Hidden Dimension of American Racism*. Touchstone, 2005.
2. For more on this topic, see Beverly Daniel Tatum. *Why Are All the Black Kids Sitting Together in the Cafeteria: And Other Conversations About Race*, rev. ed. Basic Books, 2003.

Part III: Being Allies
Mutual Interest

1. Showing Up for Racial Justice. "About." [online]. [cited March 29, 2017]. showingupforracialjustice.org/about.
2. My appreciation to Victor Lewis and Hugh Vasquez for the boat metaphor which is developed more fully in Part V.

Getting Involved

1. Adapted from Paul Kivel. *Men's Work: How to Stop the Violence that Tears Our Lives Apart*, rev. ed. Hazelden/Ballantine, 1998.
2. For examples, see Claudia Rankine. *Citizen: An American Lyric*. Graywolf, 2014; Ta-Nehisi Coates. *Between the World and Me*. Spiegel & Grau, 2015; Philomena Essed. *Understanding Everyday Racism: An Interdisciplinary Theory*. Sage, 1991.

An Ally Educates, Mobilizes, and Organizes Other White People

1. Showing Up for Racial Justice (SURJ) website.
2. Ibid. "Affiliated Groups and Local Contacts." [online]. [cited March 29, 2017]. showingupforracialjustice.org/affiliated_groups_local_contacts.

An Ally Makes a Commitment

1. For an overview of the struggle to eliminate Indian mascots: C. Richard King, ed. *The Native American Mascot Controversy: A Handbook*. Rowman & Littlefield, 2015.

It's Not Just a Joke

1. For the research and an analysis of what has been labeled *backstage racism*, see Picca and Feagin. *Two-Faced Racism*.
2. See Jane Hill's discussion of what she calls "the folk theory of racism": Jane H. Hill. *The Everyday Language of White Racism*. Wiley-Blackwell, 2008, p. 180.
3. Paul Kivel. *Living in the Shadow of the Cross*, pp. 115–22.

Tips for Talking with White People about Racism

1. Much of this material is adapted from Showing Up for Racial Justice—SURJ. "SURJ Thanksgiving Toolkit: Bringing Justice Home." Showing Up for Racial Justice—SURJ, November, 2016. [online]. [cited December 1, 2016]. showingupforracialjustice.org/thanksgiving?splash=1; and Jewish Voice for Peace. "A Guide to Difficult Conversations about Israel and Palestine." Jewish Voice for Peace, updated November 2016. [online]. [cited December 1, 2016]. https://jewishvoiceforpeace.org/conversations.

Allies, Collaborators, and Agents

1. For a demonstration of how this reasoning applies to the massive incarceration of African American men, see: Michelle Alexander. *The New Jim Crow: Mass Incarceration in the Age of Colorblindness*. New Press, 2010, p. 235.

A Web of Control

1. For extensive documentation of the impact of racist practices on communities of color, see Dorothy Roberts. *Shattered Bonds: The Color of Child Welfare*. Basic Books, 2002.
2. National Fair Housing Alliance. "Where You Live Matters: 2015 Fair Housing Trends Report." National Fair Housing Alliance, 2015. [online]. [cited December 1, 2016]. nationalfairhousing.org/LinkClick.aspx?fileticket=SYWmBgwpazA%3d&tabid=3917&mid=5321.
3. "Social Capital Is the Intangible Good Produced by Relationships Among People, as Distinguished from the Tangible Skills, Resources, and Knowledge that Constitute Human Capital." James S. Coleman. *Foundations of Social Theory*. Harvard, 1990, p. 98.
4. Taiaiake Alfred. *Peace, Power, Righteousness: An Indigenous Manifesto*. Oxford, 1999, p. 73.

Part IV: The Effects of History
People of Mixed Heritage

1. The US Census Bureau found that in 2013 nine million people—or about 2.9% of the population—identified as two or more racial categories. The Pew Research Center suggests that, based on the racial background of parents and grandparents, up to 6.9% of the population could more accurately be considered multiracial. Pew Research Center. "Multiracial in America: Proud, Diverse and Growing in Numbers."

Pew Research Center Social & Demographic Trends, June 11, 2015. [online]. [cited February 8, 2017]. pewsocialtrends.org/2015/06/11 /multiracial-in-america/.

2. Fouad Zakharia, et al. "Characterizing the Admixed African Ancestry of African Americans." *Genome Biology*, 2010:R141 (2009). [online]. [cited February 18, 2011]. genomebiology.com/2009/10/12/R141.

3. A majority (55%) of those polled in the Pew survey cited in footnote #1 above say they have been subjected to racial slurs or jokes.

4. Loving v. Virginia, 388 U.S. 1 (1976). [online]. [cited April 6, 2017]. law.cornell.edu/supremecourt/text/388/1.

5. Marcia P. P. Root, ed. *Racially Mixed People in America*. Sage, 1992, pp. 217 and 251.

6. Pew Research Center. "Multiracial in America."

Native Americans

1. M. Annette Jaimes, ed. *The State of Native America: Genocide, Colonization, and Resistance*. South End, 1992, pp. 23–53.

2. US Census Bureau. "FFF: American Indian and Alaska Native Heritage Month."

3. Churchill. *Indians Are Us?*, pp. 28–38.

4. Robert A. Williams, Jr. *The American Indian in Western Legal Thought: The Discourses of Conquest*. Oxford, 1990, pp. 78–81.

5. John Ahni Schertow. "Indigenous in Americas Just Say NO to Papal Bull." *Intercontinental Cry*, August 14, 2006. [online]. [cited March 31, 2017]. intercontinentalcry.org/indigenous-in-americas-just-say-no-to -papal-bull.

6. Pelican Network. "Salinan Nation: People of the Coast." [online]. [cited March 31, 2017]. pelicannetwork.net/salinan.htm.

7. Churchill. *Indians Are Us?*, pp. 309–316.

8. Bigelow and Peterson. *Rethinking Columbus*, p. 56.

9. Churchill. *Indians Are Us?*, pp. 309–316.

10. Ibid., p. 343; Jaimes. *The State of Native America*, pp. 31–34.

11. Jack Weatherford. *Indian Givers: How the Indians of the Americas Transformed the World*. Fawcett/Columbine, 1988, pp. 133–150.

12. Sally Roesch Wagner. *The Untold Story of the Iroquois Influence on Early Feminists*. Sky Carrier Press, 1996.

13. *Avatar*, directed by James Cameron (2009; 20th Century Fox Home Entertainment, 2010) DVD; Stephanie Meyer. *The Twilight Saga*; *The*

Twilight Saga Five-Movie Collection, directed by Catherine Hardwicke (2013).

14. Sorgorea-te' Land Trust. "Shuumi Land Tax." [online]. [cited March 31, 2017]. sogoreate-landtrust.com/.

15. Liza Minno Bloom and Berkley Carnine. "Towards Decolonization and Settler Responsibility: Reflections on a Decade of Indigenous Solidarity Organizing." Counterpunch, October 3, 2016. [online]. [cited November 15, 2016]. counterpunch.org/2016/10/03/towards -decolonization-and-settler-responsibility-reflections-on-a-decade-of -indigenous-solidarity-organizing/.

African Americans

1. Ronald Takaki. A Different Mirror: A History of Multicultural America. Little Brown, 1993, p. 54.

2. Ibid., p. 67.

3. Howard Zinn. A People's History of the United States. Harper, 1980, p. 29.

4. The devastating effects on African societies have been well documented in such books as Walter Rodney. How Europe Underdeveloped Africa. Howard University Press, 1982.

5. Zinn. A People's History, p. 186.

6. National Museum of African American History and Culture. [online]. [cited March 31, 2017]. nmaahc.si.edu.

7. Davis. Women, Race & Class; Paula Giddings. When and Where I Enter: The Impact of Black Women on Race and Sex in America. Bantam, 1985.

8. James T. Patterson. "Moynihan and the Single-Parent Family: The 1965 Report and Its Backlash." Education Next, Vol. 15 #2 (Spring 2015) [online]. [cited April 7, 2017]. educationnext.org/moynihan-and-the -single-parent-family.

9. James Baldwin. Note of a Native Son. Beacon Press, 1984, p. 25.

10. Nancy Vogt. "African American News Media: Fact Sheet." Pew Research Center, State of the News Media, June 2016. [online]. [cited November 20, 2016]. journalism.org/2016/06/15/african-american -media-fact-sheet/.

11. Black Lives Matter. "About the Black Lives Matter Network." blacklivesmatter.com/about. [cited November 15, 2016].

12. Guardian. "The Counted: People Killed by Police in the US." Guardian, 2016 [online]. [cited January 13, 2017]. theguardian.com/us-news/ng -interactive/2015/jun/01/the-counted-police-killings-us-database.

13. The full document can be found here: The Movement for Black Lives. *Platform*. [online]. [cited November 15, 2016]. policy.m4bl.org /platform/.

Asian Americans

1. Gary Y. Okihiro. *Margins and Mainstreams: Asians in American History and Culture*. University of Washington, 1994, p. 53.
2. Ibid., pp. 8–9.
3. Ibid., Chapter 2; Takaki. *A Different Mirror*, pp. 202–204.
4. Yen Le Espiritu. *Asian American Panethnicity: Bridging Institutions and Identities*. Temple University, 1992, p. 135.
5. Robert Gooding-Williams, ed. *Reading Rodney King, Reading Urban Uprising*. Routledge, 1993, p. 201.
6. Ibid., pp. 196–211.
7. Espiritu. *Asian American Panethnicity*, pp. 141–143.
8. Lowen Liu. "Just the Wrong Amount of American: Wen Ho Lee's 1999 Arrest Taught Chinese Americans that Their Country May Never Trust Them." *Slate*, September 11, 2016. [online]. [cited December 17, 2016]. slate.com/articles/news_and_politics/the_next_20/2016/09/the_case _of_scientist_wen_ho_lee_and_chinese_americans_under_suspicion _for.html.
9. Average family income figures for Asian Americans hide large dispar-ities in the distribution of wealth. Substantial groups of Asian Ameri-cans live in poverty. Generalizations about average income lump together different communities, some long established and some very recent, as well as covering over gender and class differences in income and opportunity: Meizhu Lui, et. al. *The Color of Wealth: The Story Be-hind the U.S. Racial Wealth Divide*. New Press, 2006, pp. 209–15.
10. Nearly all the Japanese in the western US, over 120,000 people, were interned in ten concentration camps around the country. They lost their land, homes, possessions, jobs—everything that they couldn't carry with them on short notice. For moving accounts of the Japanese experience of internment, see: Lawson Fusao Inada. *Only What We Could Carry: The Japanese American Internment Experience*. Heyday, 2000.

Latinx

1. Renee Stepler and Anna Brown. "Statistical Portrait of Hispanics in the United States." Pew Research Center: Hispanic Trends, April 19,

2016 [online]. [cited December 2, 2016]. pewhispanic.org/2016/04/19/statistical-portrait-of-hispanics-in-the-united-states-key-charts.

2. Renee Stepler and Mark Hugo Lopez. "U.S. Latino Population Growth and Dispersion Since the Onset of the Great Recession." Pew Research Center: Hispanic Trends, September 8, 2016. [online]. [cited December 2, 2016]. pewhispanic.org/2016/09/08/latino-population-growth-and-dispersion-has-slowed-since-the-onset-of-the-great-recession.

3. Takaki. *A Different Mirror*, p. 176.

4. Zinn. *A People's History*, pp. 306–310.

5. Denis Lynn Daly Heyck. *Barrios and Borderlands: Cultures of Latinos and Latinas in the United States*. Routledge, 1994, p. 6.

6. Almaguer. *Racial Fault Lines*, pp. 54–56.

7. Ibid., pp. 7–9.

8. Gooding-Williams. *Reading Rodney King*, p. 122.

Arab Americans

1. Saud Joseph. "Against the Grain of the Nation: The Arab" in Michael W. Suleiman, ed. *Arabs in America: Building a New Future*. Temple, 1999, p. 260.

2. Tehranian. *White Washed*, pp. 57–59.

3. Arab American Institute Foundation. "Quick Facts About Arab Americans." Arab American Institute. [online]. [cited December 17, 2016]. aaiusa.org/demographics.

4. Suleiman. *Arabs in America*, p. 7.

5. At that time Arabs and Muslims were treated as the same in the legal system. Khaled A. Beydoun. "America Banned Arabs Long Before Donald Trump." *Washington Post*, August 18, 2016. [online]. [cited April 7, 2017]. washingtonpost.com/opinions/trumps-anti-muslim-stance-echoes-a-us-law-from-the-1700s/2016/08/18/6da7b486-6585-11e6-8b27-bb8ba39497a2_story.html?utm_term=.c076c6414432. For more on the political disenfranchisement of Arab Americans, see: Alia Malek. *A Country Called Amreeka: Arab Roots, American Stories*. Free Press, 2009.

6. Quoted from the *Globe and Mail* and cited in Karim H. Karim. *Islamic Peril: Media and Global Violence*, rev. ed. Black Rose, 2003, p. 152.

7. Jillian Kestler-D'Amours and Zena Tahhan. "Man in US Killed in Suspected 'Anti-Arab Hate Crime.'" *Aljazeera*, August 18, 2016 [online]. [cited December 17, 2016]. aljazeera.com/news/2016/08/man-killed-suspected-anti-muslim-hate-crime-160816191517636.html.

9. This information is culled from various issues of the Southern Poverty Law Center's "Intelligence Report." For more information on the nearly 900 hate groups in the US, consult their website and magazine: [online]. [cited December 18, 2016]. splcenter.org/hate-map.

Muslims

1. Information on these events is from Deepa Iyer. *We Too Sing American: South Asian, Arab, Muslim, and Sikh Immigrants Shape Our Multiracial Future*. New Press, 2015, pp. 169–70.
2. Michael Lipka. "Muslims and Islam: Key Findings in the U.S. and Around the World." Pew Research Center Fact Tank, July 22, 2016. [online]. [cited December 18, 2016]. pewresearch.org/fact-tank/2016/07/22/muslims-and-islam-key-findings-in-the-u-s-and-around-the-world.
3. I use the word *claim* rather than the more common *reclaim* intentionally because Christians had no more historical right to control these areas than Muslims did. Crusades were waged by Christians against Moors, Slavs, dissident Christian groups such as the Cathars, and even against individual secular Christian leaders over a period of 600 years.
4. As part of this whitening process, Western Christianity transformed images of God and Jesus into light-skinned European.
5. The *limpieza de sangre* statute was passed in 1449.
6. Anouar Majid. *We Are All Moors: Ending Centuries of Crusades Against Muslims and Other Minorities*. University of Minnesota, 2009, p. 62.
7. Ibid., p. 63.
8. Ibid., p. 71.
9. Samuel S. Hill et al. *Encyclopedia of Religion in the South*. Mercer University, 2005, p. 394.
10. See the previous chapter on Arab Americans. Many Arab Christians claimed immigration rights as white people. Although not all these claims were upheld by the courts, a significant number of Christian Lebanese, Palestinians, and Syrians successfully entered the US.
11. Pew Research Center. *Muslim Americans: Middle Class and Mostly Mainstream*. May 22, 2007. [online]. [cited August 10, 2010]. pewresearch.org/files/old-assets/pdf/muslim-americans.pdf.
12. American Civil Liberties Union. "Nationwide Anti-Mosque Activity." ACLU, 2015. [online]. [cited December 18, 2016]. aclu.org/map/nationwide-anti-mosque-activity.

13. Iyer. *We Too Sing American*. See this detailed report on the Islamopho-
    bia industry: Matthew Duss, et al. "Fear, Inc. 2.0: The Islamophobia
    Network's Efforts to Manufacture Hate in America." Center for Ameri-
    can Progress, February 11, 2015 [online]. [cited December 8, 2016].
    americanprogress.org/issues/religion/reports/2015/02/11/106394
    /fear-inc-2-0.
14. Mona Chalabi. "How Anti-Muslim Are Americans? Data Points to
    Extent of Islamophobia." *Guardian*, December 8, 2015. [online]. [cited
    December 2, 2016]. theguardian.com/us-news/2015/dec/08/muslims
    -us-islam-islamophobia-data-polls.
15. Ibid.
16. Sarah Lazare. "On Both Sides of the Atlantic Muslims Organizing to
    'Reject Dehumanization.'" *Common Dreams*, December 21, 2015. [on-
    line]. [cited October 25, 2016]. commondreams.org/news/2015/12/21
    /both-sides-atlantic-muslims-organizing-reject-dehumanization.

Jewish People

1. Paul Lawrence Rose. *German Question/Jewish Question: Revolutionary
   Antisemitism in Germany from Kant to Wagner*. Princeton, 1990, p. 3.
2. Rosemary Radford Ruether. *Faith and Fratricide: The Theological Roots of
   Anti-Semitism*. Seabury, 1974, pp. 184–204.
3. A good map summarizes banishments between 1100–1500 CE: Florida
   Center for Instructional Technology. "Map of Jewish Expulsions and
   Resettlement Areas in Europe." *A Teacher's Guide to the Holocaust*,
   2005. [online]. [cited February 24, 2011]. fcit.usf.edu/holocaust/gallery
   /expuls.htm.
4. Foundation for the Advancement of Sephardic Studies and Culture.
   "The Edict of Expulsion of the Jews." [online]. [cited May 2, 2017].
   sephardicstudies.org/decree.html.
5. Evyatar Friesel. *Atlas of Modern Jewish History*. Oxford, 1990; Martin
   Gilbert. *Atlas of Jewish History*. Morrow, 1992.
6. For further information on the Khazarian Jews, see: Arthur Koestler.
   The Thirteenth Tribe: The Khazar Empire and Its Heritage. Last Century
   Media, 1976; Scholmo Sands. *The Invention of the Jewish People*. Verso,
   2009; Eran Elhaik. "The Missing Link of Jewish European Ancestry:
   Contrasting the Rhineland and the Khazarian Hypotheses." *Genome
   Biology & Evolution*, Vol. 5 #1 (2012). [online]. [cited December 3, 2016].
   oxfordjournals.org/content/early/2012/12/14/gbe.evs119.full.pdf.

7. Rose. *German Question/Jewish Question*, p. 7.
8. David G. Singer. "From St. Paul's Abrogation of the Old Covenant to Hitler's War Against the Jews: The Response of American Catholic Thinkers to the Holocaust, 1945–76," in David A. Gerber, ed. *Anti-Semitism in American History*. University of Illinois, 1987, p. 386.
9. Chris Martin. "7 Questions Asked on an Application to Be a Member of the KKK." *Independent Journal Review*, February 2016. [online]. [cited December 4, 2016]. ijr.com/2016/02/545602-7-questions-asked-on-an -application-to-be-a-member-of-the-kkk.
10. Diane Tobin, et. al. *In Every Tongue: The Racial & Ethnic Diversity of the Jewish People*. Institute for Jewish and Community Research, 2005, p. 24. For more on diversity in the Jewish community, see also Melanie Kaye/Kantrowitz. *The Colors of Jews: Racial Politics and Radical Diasporism*. Indiana, 2007.

Recent Immigrants

1. Grace Chang. *Disposable Domestics: Immigrant Women Workers in the Global Economy*. South End, 2000, p. 2.
2. Aviva Chomsky."*They Take Our Jobs!": And 20 Other Myths About Immigration*. Beacon, 2007, pp. 5–7.
3. For a detailed description of how this process works over several job sectors, see Chang. *Disposable Domestics*.
4. For detailed accounts of how immigrants of color were treated, see Takaki. *A Different Mirror*, especially chapters 10 on Asian Americans and 12 on Latinx.
5. Chang. *Disposable Domestics*, pp. 3–4.
6. Sen with Mamdouh. *The Accidental American: Immigration and Citizenship in the Age of Globalization*. Berrett-Koehler, 2008, p. 160.
7. Southern Poverty Law Center. "The Immigrants: Myths and Reality." *Intelligence Report*, Issue 101 (Spring, 2001), p. 12.
8. Lisa Christensen Gee et al. "Undocumented Immigrant's State and Local Tax Contributions." Institute on Taxation & Economic Policy, updated February 2016. [online]. [cited November 26, 2016]. itep.org /pdf/immigration2016.pdf.
9. Statement of the Honorable Mark W. Everson, Commissioner, Internal Revenue Service, Testimony Before the House Committee on Ways and Means, July 26, 2006.
10. Sen with Mamdouh. *The Accidental American*, pp. 58–9, 140–1.

11. For more on Arizona SB1070, see Randal C. Archibold. "Arizona Enacts Stringent Law on Immigration." *New York Times*, April 23, 2010. [online]. [cited February 24, 2011]. nytimes.com/2010/04/24/us/politics /24immig.html?_r=0.

Part V: Fighting Institutional Racism
Land and Housing

1. For a detailed history and current legal examples of the use of this doctrine, see: Steven T. Newcomb. *Pagans in the Promised Land: Decoding the Doctrine of Christian Discovery*. Fulcrum, 2008.

2. Trina Williams. *The Homestead Act: A Major Asset-Building Policy in American History*. Community-wealth.org Working Paper 00-9. [online]. [cited April 6, 2017]. community-wealth.org/content/home stead-act-major-asset-building-policy-american-history-working -paper-00-9.3.

3. This information is drawn from: Michael Riley. "Feds Settle Suit over Mismanagement of Indian Trust Land." *Denver Post*, December 8, 2009. [online]. [cited December 18, 2016]. denverpost.com/2009/12 /08/feds-settle-suit-over-mismanagement-of-indian-trust-land; Joel Dyer. "Billions Missing from US Indian Trust fund." *Albion Monitor*, August 15, 1996. [online]. [cited February 26, 2011]. albionmonitor.com /free/biatrustfund.html.

4. Ibid.

5. Jane Herrings. "The Indian Casino Myth." A.I.R. Policy Center, January 19, 2016. [online]. [cited December 3, 2016]. airpi.org/the-indian -casino-myth.

6. For a full description of several racial cleansings, see: Elliot Jaspin. *Buried in the Bitter Waters: The Hidden History of Racial Cleansing in America*. Basic, 2007. For information on Forsyth County, see pp. 6–7 and 125–151.

7. Tom Cohen and Alyse Shorland. "Government Settles Lawsuit with Native American Farmers." CNN, October 20, 2010. [online]. [cited December 18, 2016]. cnn.com/2010/US/10/19/lawsuit.native.farmers.

8. Jess Gilbert et al. *Who Owns the Land? Agricultural Land Ownership by Race/Ethnicity in Rural America*. Economic Research Service/USDA Newsletter, Vol 17 #4 (Winter 2002). See: Farmland Information Center. [online]. [cited April 6, 2017]. farmlandinfo.org/who-owns-land -agricultural-land-ownership-raceethnicity.

9. Inada. *Only What We Could Carry*.

10. Loewen. *Sundown Towns*, p. 12.

11. Eduardo Bonilla-Silva. *Racism Without Racists: Color-Blind Racism and the Persistence of Racial Inequality in the United States*, 2nd ed. Rowman & Littlefield, 2006, p. 11.

12. For a detailed account of the dumping of garbage and toxic and environmentally damaging waste in poor communities of color, see: Robert D. Bullard. *Dumping in Dixie: Race, Class, and Environmental Quality*, 3rd ed. Westview, 2000; Robert D. Bullard and Benjamin Chavis Jr. *Confronting Environmental Racism: Voices from the Grassroots*. South End, 1999.

13. For a detailed analysis of anti-gentrification strategies, see: [Boston, MA] Metropolitan Area Planning Council. "Managing Neighborhood Change: Selected Anti-Displacement Strategies in Practice." MAPC, updated October 2011 [online]. [cited December 18, 2016]. mapc.org /sites/default/files/MAPC_LitReview_AnnotatedBibliography.pdf.

Public Policy

1. Movement for Black Lives. *Platform*.

Reparations

1. For detailed information about these and many other reparations processes, consult Pablo De Greiff, ed. *The Handbook of Reparations*. Oxford, 2008.

2. Some of this information comes from: Salim Muwakkil. "Why American Blacks Deserve Reparations." *Chicago Tribune*, February 5, 2001. [online]. [cited April 13, 2017]. articles.chicagotribune.com/2001-02 -05/news/0102050176_1_slavery-americans-african.

3. Ibid.

4. Yana Kunichoff and Sarah Macaraeg. "Black and Blue: Chicago Tries a New Way to Heal." *Yes!* Vol. 81 (Spring 2017), pp. 8–13.

5. Iyer. *We Too Sing American*, p. 54.

6. Jeanne Sahadi. "The Richest 10% Hold 76% of the Wealth." CNN Money, August 18, 2016. [online]. [cited November 20, 2016]. money .cnn.com/2016/08/18/pf/wealth-inequality/.

7. Matt Bruenig. "The Top 10% of White Families Own Almost Everything." *Demos Policyshop*, September 5, 2014. [online]. [cited November 25, 2016]. demos.org/blog/9/5/14/top-10-white-families-own-almost -everything.

8. These suggestions are from: Donald L. Bartlett and James B. Steele. *America: Who Really Pays the Taxes?* Simon & Schuster, 1994.

Voting

1. John Henley. "White and Wealthy Voters Gave Victory to Donald Trump, Exit Polls Show." *Guardian*, November 9, 2016. [online]. [cited November 25, 2016]. theguardian.com/us-news/2016/nov/09/white -voters-victory-donald-trump-exit-polls.

2. David Brion Davis. "The Central Fact of American History." *American-Heritage*, Vol. 65 #1 (February/March 2005). [online]. [cited December 19, 2016]. americanheritage.com/content/central-fact-american -history; David R. Roediger. *How Race Survived U.S. History: From Settlement and Slavery to the Obama Phenomenon*. Verso, 2008, pp. 50–51.

3. Lara Merling and Dean Baker. "In the Electoral College White Votes Matter More." Center for Economic and Policy Research, November 13, 2016. [online]. [cited November 26, 2016]. cepr.net/blogs/beat-the -press/in-the-electoral-college-white-votes-matter-more.

4. Adam Liptak. "Smaller States Find Outsize Clout Growing in Senate." *New York Times*, March 11, 2013 [online]. [cited December 19, 2016]. nytimes.com/interactive/2013/03/11/us/politics/democracy-tested .html?_r=0#/#smallstate.

5. Steven Hill. "Why Progressives Lose: Affirmative Action for Conservatives." Center for Voting and Democracy, June 2003. [online]. [cited December 19, 2016]. archive.fairvote.org/articles/progressivepopulis .htm.

6. Quoted in US Supreme Court. Harmon v Forsennius 380 U.S. 528 (1965). [online]. [cited April 12, 2017]. supreme.justia.com/cases /federal/us/380/528/case.html.

7. Laura Conaway and James Ridgeway. "Democracy in Chains." *Village Voice*, November 28, 2000. [online]. [cited December 19, 2016]. villagevoice.com/news/democracy-in-chains-6417114.

8. It is important to note that states where people of color are disenfranchised or where they receive the lowest wages are often the same states in which poor and working-class whites are disenfranchised and paid the lowest wages as well.

9. The information following is adapted from: Manning Marable. "Stealing the Election: The Compromises of 1876 and 2000." *Standards* Vol. 7 #2 (Spring-Summer 2001). [online]. [cited December 19, 2016]. colorado.edu/journals/standards/V7N2/FIRST/marable.html.

386   NOTES TO PAGES 263-266

10. A common provision introduced in the South after the reconstruction period: only those whose grandfathers could vote could themselves vote, eliminating almost all blacks from voting rolls.

11. Prison Policy Initiative. "Felon Disenfranchisement: Jim Crow Redux." Last updated June 12, 2005. [online]. [cited December 19, 2016]. prisonpolicy.org/articles/prisonindex_jimcrow.pdf.

12. Katie Rose Quandt. "1 in 13 African-American Adults Prohibited from Voting in the United States." Moyers & Company, March 24, 2015. [online]. [cited November 20, 2016]. billmoyers.com/2015/03/24/felon -disenfranchisement. Although rules vary state by state, the United States is the only industrialized country that denies former prisoners, who have completed their sentences and are fully integrated into the community, the vote.

13. Nicholas Thompson. "Locking Up the Vote." Washington Monthly, January 2001 [online]. [cited December 19, 2016]. ic.galegroup.com /ic/suic/MagazinesDetailsPage/MagazinesDetailsWindow?zid=f4 a13c9262622bc6a05904dcffc6e22a&action=2&catId=&documentId =GALE%7CA69795097&userGroupName=inglewood&jsid=c82ed fa738a6075aec4c313dd34a28e0.

14. Bob Wing. "White Power in Election 2000." ColorLines, March 15, 2001. [online]. [cited December 19, 2016]. colorlines.com/articles/white -power-election-2000.

15. Brennan Center for Justice. "New Voting Restrictions in Place for 2016 Presidential Election." Updated September 12, 2016. [online]. [cited November 20, 2016]. brennancenter.org/voting-restrictions-first-time -2016.

16. Brennan Center for Justice. "Voting Problems Present in 2016, but Further Study Needed to Determine Impact." Brennan Center for Justice, November 15, 2016. [online]. [cited November 20, 2016]. truth-out. org/news/item/38382-voting-problems-present-in-2016-but-further -study-needed-to-determine-impact.

17. David A. Love. "2010 Census Undercount Could Spell Disaster for Blacks, Latinos." TheGrio, May 24, 2012, [online]. [cited April 12, 2017]. thegrio.com/2012/05/24/2010-census-undercount-could-spell -disaster-for-blacks-latinos.

Affirmative Action

1. See the affirmative action timeline: Marquita Sykes. The Origins of Affirmative Action. National Organization of Women, 1995. [online].

[cited December 19, 2016]. thenewcom.com/pdf/Origins_of_Affirma tive_Action.pdf.

At Work

1. David R. Roediger. *The Wages of Whiteness: Race and the Making of the American Working Class*. Verso, 2007.
2. Michael Reich. *Racial Inequality: A Political-Economic Analysis*. Princeton, 1981, quoted in Victor Perlo. *Economics of Racism II: The Roots of Inequality, USA*. International, 1996, p. 159.
3. Perlo. *Economics of Racism II*, p. 171. I have been unable to find more recent calculations of the cost to workers of color from super-exploitation.

At School

1. Kevin K Kumashiro. "When Billionaires Become Educational Experts." AAUP, May-June, 2012. [online]. [cited October 31, 2016]. aaup.org/article/when-billionaires-become-educational-experts; Tim Walker. "The Well-Funded Echo Chamber That Is Attacking Public Education." NEAToday, April 28, 2016. [online]. [cited October 31, 2016]. neatoday.org/2016/04/28/the-money-behind-education -reform.
2. Linda Darling-Hammond. "Structured for Failure: Race, Resources, and Student Achievement," in Markus and Moya. *Doing Race*, p. 300.
3. Alana Semuels. "Good School, Rich School; Bad School, Poor School: The Inequality at the Heart of America's Education System." *Atlantic*, August 25, 2016. [online]. [cited November 25, 2016]. theatlantic.com /business/archive/2016/08/property-taxes-and-unequal-schools /497333.
4. Emily Deruy. " Student Diversity Is up but Teachers Are Mostly White." American Association of Colleges for Teacher Education, nd. [online]. [cited November 20, 2016]. aacte.org/news-room/aacte-in-the-news /347-student-diversity-is-up-but-teachers-are-mostly-white.
5. Amine Ouazad. *Assessed by a Teacher Like Me: Race, Gender, and Subjective Evaluations*. Centre for the Economics of Education, 2008, quoted in Markus and Moya. *Doing Race*, pp. 67–8.
6. F. Crosby, S. Bromley, and L. Saxe. "Recent Unobtrusive Studies of Black and White Discrimination and Prejudice: A Literature Review." *Psychological Bulletin*, 87 (1980), quoted in Lisa Delpit. *Other People's Children: Cultural Conflict in the Classroom*. New Press, 1995, p. 115.

7. Martin Bernal. *Black Athena: The Afroasiatic Roots of Classical Civilization*. Rutgers, 1987.

8. Bernal. *Black Athena*; Weatherford. *Indian Givers*; Ivan Van Sertima, ed. *Blacks in Science: Ancient and Modern*. Transaction, 1986.

9. Seyyed Hossein Nasr. *Islamic Science: An Illustrated Study*. World of Islam Festival Publishing, 1976, pp. 75–88.

10. The average SPP [School Performance Profile] score for traditional public schools was 77.1, while for charter schools it was 66.4, and cyber-charter schools came in at a low 46.8. Seventy is considered the minimally acceptable score: Valerie Strauss. "A Dozen Problems with Charter Schools." *Washington Post*, May 20, 2014. [online]. [cited November 16, 2016]. washingtonpost.com/news/answer-sheet/wp/2014/05/20/a-dozen-problems-with-charter-schools.

11. David C. Berliner. "Effects of Inequality and Poverty vs. Teachers and Schooling on America's Youth" quoted in Bree Picower and Edwin Mayorga, eds. *What's Race Got to Do with It: How Current School Reform Policy Maintains Racial and Economic Inequality*. Peter Lang, 2015.

Health Care

1. Much of the following information was summarized in an article by Neil Rosenberg. "Separate and Unequal: U.S. Practices a System of Medicine that Shortchanges Minorities and Women." *Milwaukee Journal Sentinel*, April 16, 2001. See also Ruqaiijah Yearby. "Sick and Tired of Being Sick and Tired: Putting an End to Separate and Unequal Health Care in the United States 50 Years After the Civil Rights Act of 1964." *Health Matrix*, Vol. 25 #1 (2015) [online]. [cited December 21, 2016]. scholarlycommons.law.case.edu/healthmatrix/vol25/iss1/3.

2. W. Michael Byrd and Linda A. Clayton. *An American Health Dilemma: A Medical History of African Americans and the Problem of Race: Beginnings to 1900*. Routledge, 2000, p. 29.

3. James Macinko and Irma T. Elo. "Black-White Differences in Avoidable Mortality in the United States, 1980–2005." *Journal of Epidemiology and Community Health*, April 2009. [online]. [cited December 19, 2016]. ncbi.nlm.nih.gov/pubmed/19364760.

4. US Centers for Disease Control and Prevention. *Health, United States, 2009*. Publication #DHHS 2010-1232, January 2010. [online]. [cited December 19, 2016]. cdc.gov/nchs/data/hus/hus09.pdf.

5. For an in-depth look at racial disparities in health care, see Brian D.

Smedley et al. *Unequal Treatment: Confronting Racial and Ethnic Disparities in Health Care*. National Academies, 2003. [online]. [cited December 19, 2016]. nap.edu/read/10260/chapter/1.

6. The examples in this chapter are taken from Jordi Martorell. "Drug Companies Putting Profits Before Millions of People's Lives." March 9, 2001. [online]. [cited December 19, 2016]. marxist.com/drugs-companies-profits090301.htm.

7. Pierre Chirac and Els Torreele. "Global Framework on Essential Health R&D." *Lancet*, Vol. 367 (May 13, 2006), pp. 1560–1561. [online]. [cited February 28, 2011]. dndi.org/images/stories/pdf_scientific_pub/2006/chirac_lancet05132006.pdf.

8. Martorell. "Drug Companies Putting Profits Before Millions."

The Police

1. See the chilling account of a police attack on a private party: Mandisa-Maia Jones and Valerie Willson Wesley. "Anatomy of a Party Gone Wrong: When Police Brutality Hits Home." *Essence*, December 1991. [online]. [cited December 19, 2016]. connection.ebscohost.com/c/articles/9112230380/anatomy-party-gone-wrong.

2. Christopher Ingraham. "You Really Can Be Pulled Over for Driving While Black, Federal Statistics Show." *Washington Post*, September 9, 2014. [online]. [cited October 31, 2016]. washingtonpost.com/news/wonk/wp/2014/09/09/you-really-can-get-pulled-over-for-driving-while-black-federal-statistics-show.

3. Elizabeth Preza. "Cops Violently Arrest Black Man Suspected of Stealing Car—That Turns Out to Be His Own." *Raw Story*, January 13, 2017 [online]. [cited February 8, 2017]. rawstory.com/2017/01/watch-cops-violently-arrest-black-man-suspected-of-stealing-car-that-turns-out-to-be-his-own.

4. Aarti Shahani. "Social Network Nextdoor Moves to Block Racial Profiling Online." *NPR: All Tech Considered*, August 23, 2016. [online]. [cited November 22, 2016]. npr.org/sections/alltechconsidered/2016/08/23/490950267/social-network-nextdoor-moves-to-block-racial-profiling-online.

5. Jonathan Capehart. "PostPartisan: It's Tamir Rice's Fault." *Washington Post*, March 2, 2015. [online]. [cited April 11, 2017]. washingtonpost.com/blogs/post-partisan/wp/2015/03/02/its-tamir-rices-fault/?utm_term=.af4c7240ed07.

6. Sue. *Microaggressions in Everyday Life*, p. 6.

7. Charlene Muhammad. "The High Cost of Police Brutality." *New America Media*, February 27, 2009. [online]. [cited February 28, 2011]. surrealworld.wordpress.com/2009/02/25/millions-paid-out-in -judgments-for-abusive-officers-as-cities-cut-services-furlough -workers.

8. Julia Craven. "More Than 250 Black People Were Killed by the Police in 2016." *Huffington Post*, updated January 1, 2017 [online]. [cited January 10, 2017]. huffingtonpost.com/entry/black-people-killed-by -police-america_us_577da633e4b0c590f7e7fb17; *Guardian*. "The Counted."

9. Matt Ferner and Nick Wing. "Here's How Many Cops Got Convicted for Murder Last Year for On-Duty Shootings: There's Something Strange about This Picture." *Huffington Post*, January 13, 2016 [online]. [cited January 10, 2017]. huffingtonpost.com/entry/police-shooting -convictions_us_5695968ce4b086bc1cd5d0da.

10. Michael Sallah et al. "Stop and Seize." *Washington Post*, September 6, 2014. [online]. [cited November 1, 2016]..washingtonpost.com/sf /investigative/2014/09/06/stop-and-seize/?tid=a_inl.

11. American Civil Liberties Union Foundation. "War Comes Home: The Excessive Militarization of American Policing." ACLU Foundation, 2014. [online]. [cited November 1, 2016]. aclu.org/sites/default/files /assets/jus14-warcomeshome-report-web-rel1.pdf.

12. Bill Yousman. *Prime Time Prisons on U.S. TV: Representation of Incarceration*. Peter Lang, 2009, pp. 41–44.

13. Community policing refers to the practice of assigning police to specific neighborhoods so they can get to know the area and the people.

The Criminal Justice System

1. Feagin and Hernan. *White Racism*, p. 189.

2. Douglas A. Blackmon. *Slavery by Another Name: The Re-Enslavement of Black Americans from the Civil War to World War II*. Anchor, 2008.

3. Investors Watch Blog. "These 7 Household Names Make a Killing off of the Prison-Industrial Complex." September 1, 2015. [online]. [cited April 11, 2017]. investmentwatchblog.com/these-7-household-names -make-a-killing-off-of-the-prison-industrial-complex.

4. The Leadership Conference. *Justice on Trial: The Racial Disparities in the American Criminal Justice System*. [online]. [cited December 21, 2016].

civilrights.org/publications/justice-on-trial/; Center for Children's Law and Policy. "Racial and Ethnic Disparities Resources." [online]. [cited December 21, 2016]. cclp.org/racial-and-ethnic-disparities -resources.

5. Danielle Kaeble et al. "Correctional Populations in the United States, 2014." Bureau of Justice Statistics Publication # NCJ 249513, December 2015. [online]. [cited November 27, 2016]. bjs.gov/content/pub/pdf /cpus14.pdf.

6. John Schmitt et al. "The High Budgetary Cost of Incarceration." Center for Economic and Policy Research, June 2010. [online]. [cited December 21, 2016]. cepr.net/documents/publications/incarceration-2010 -06.pdf.

7. Martha C. White. "Locked-in Profits: The U.S. Prison Industry, by the Numbers." NBC News, November 2, 2016. [online]. [cited December 24, 2016]. nbcnews.com/business/business-news/locked-profits-u-s -prison-industry-numbers-n455976.

8. Prison/industrial complex can be defined as "the overlapping interests of government and industry that use surveillance, policing, and imprisonment as solutions to economic, social, and political problems." Marc Lamont Hill. Nobody: Casualties of America's War on the Vulnerable, from Ferguson to Flint and Beyond. Atria Books, 2016, p. 150.

9. Sally Kohn. "The Danger Society Doesn't Talk About." CNN Opinion, updated March 27, 2015. [online]. [cited December 4, 2016]. cnn.com /2015/03/19/opinions/kohn-young-white-men/index.html.

10. US National Association for the Advancement of Colored People. "Criminal Justice Fact Sheet." NAACP, 2016. [online]. [cited November 20, 2016]. naacp.org/criminal-justice-fact-sheet.

11. Harry G. Levine et al. "Arresting Blacks for Marijuana in California: Possession Arrests, 2006–08." Drug Policy Alliance, October 2, 2010. [online]. [cited January 15, 2017,]. drugpolicy.org/resource/arresting -blacks-marijuana-california-possession-arrests-2006-08.

12. David Scharfenberg. "Blacks Are Still More Likely Than Whites to Be Arrested for Marijuana." Boston Globe, October 6, 2016. [online]. [cited October 31, 2016]. bostonglobe.com/metro/2016/10/06/report-finds -sharp-racial-disparities-marijuana-arrests/VKB2BB3Oqn1RdoMHiX hFRN/story.html.

13. Women's Prison Association, Institute on Women and Criminal Justice. Quick Facts: Women and Criminal Justice—2009. [online]. [cited

January 15, 2017]. wpaonline.org/wpaassets/Quick_Facts_Women_and_CJ_2009_rebrand.pdf.

14. Correctional Association of New York. "Women and the Criminal Justice System." [online]. [cited November 16, 2016]. correctionalassociation.org/issue/women.

15. George S. Bridges and Sara Steen. "Racial Disparities in Official Assessments of Criminal Offenders: Attributional Stereotypes as Mediating Mechanisms." *American Sociological Review*, Vol. 63 (August 1998). [online]. [cited April 12, 2017]. academicroom.com/article/racial -disparities-official-assessments-juvenile-offenders-attributional -stereotypes-mediating-mechanisms.

16. National Council on Crime and Delinquency. "And Justice for Some: Differential Treatment of Youth of Color in the Justice System." January 2007. [online]. [cited December 21, 2016]. nccdglobal.org/sites /default/files/publication_pdf/justice-for-some.pdf.

17. Richard Morin. "Unconventional Wisdom: Justice Isn't Blind." *Washington Post*, September 3, 2000, p. B05 [online]. [cited December 21, 2016]. washingtonpost.com/archive/opinions/2000/09/03/un conventional-wisdom/671a7fbe-446f-4005-bdf3-0345f1c691cf/?utm _term=.f70f8fad5b0c.

18. Manning Marable. "Halt the Machinery of Death." *ColorLines*, February 2000. [online]. [cited April 12, 2017]. alternet.org/story/246/along_the _color_line%3A_halt_the_machinery_of_death.

19. Amnesty International. "Death Sentences and Executions in 2015." AI Document # ACT 50/3487/2016, April 6, 2016. [online]. [cited November 20, 2016]. amnesty.org/en/documents/act50/3487/2016/en.

20. US Department of Labor, Bureau of Labor Statistics. "Police and Detectives." Occupational Outlook Handbook. December 17, 2015. [online]. [cited November 20, 2016]. bls.gov/ooh/protective-service/police-and -detectives.htm.

21. Manning Marable. "Race-ing Justice: The Political Cultures of Incarceration." *Souls*, Vol. 2 #1 (Winter 2000), p. 10.

22. Marisa Franco and Paromita Shaw. "The Department of Homeland Security: The Largest Police Force Nobody Monitors." *Guardian*, November 19, 2015. [online]. [cited February 9, 2017]. theguardian.com /commentisfree/2015/nov/19/the-department-of-homeland-security -the-largest-police-force-nobody-monitors.

23. Brian Kincade. "The Economics of the American Prison System."

SmartAsset.com, March 2016. [online]. [cited November 20, 2016]. smartasset.com/insights/the-economics-of-the-american-prison -system.

24. Federal Register. "Annual Determination of Annual Cost of Incarcer-ation." Prisons Bureau, March 9, 2015. [online]. [cited December 4, 2016]. federalregister.gov/documents/2015/03/09/2015-05437/annual -determination-of-average-cost-of-incarceration.

25. Schmitt et al. *The High Budgetary Cost of Incarceration.*

26. Prisoner Hunger Strike Solidarity. Prisoner Demands, April 3, 2011. [online]. [cited December 21, 2016]. prisonerhungerstrikesolidarity .wordpress.com/education/the-prisoners-demands-2/; Democracy Now! "Hunger Strikes, Marches & Work Stoppages: Unprecedented National Prison Strike Enters Third Week." *Democracy Now*, Sep-tember 28, 2016 [online]. [cited December 21, 2016]. democracynow .org/2016/9/28/hunger_strikes_marches_work_stoppages_unprece dented.

27. To find out how to become a pen pal to a prisoner, contact humanrightspenpals.org.

Religion

1. See, for example: Papal Bull *Romanus Pontifex*, (Nicholas V), January 8, 1455. [online]. [cited December 22, 2016]. nativeweb.org/pages/legal /indig-romanus-pontifex.html.

2. There are many accounts of Christian churches (orders such as the Franciscans) and Christian universities (such as Georgetown Univer-sity) owning slaves. For an account of the slave-owning Presbyterian churches of Virginia: Jennifer Oast. "'The Worst Kind of Slavery': Slave-owning Churches in Prince Edward County, Virginia." *Journal of Southern History*, Vol. 76 #4 (November 1, 2010). [online]. [cited Decem-ber 22, 2016]. https://www.jstor.org/stable/27919282?seq=1#page_scan _tab_contents. For information about Christian-run boarding schools and their impact: Ward Churchill. *Kill the Indian, Save the Man: The Geno-cidal Impact of American Indian Residential Schools*. City Lights, 2004.

3. For a detailed account of the active involvement of one particular Christian institution, the family, in US foreign and domestic policy: Jeff Sharlet. *C Street: The Fundamentalist Threat to American Democracy*. Little Brown, 2010.

4. Lillian Smith. *Killers of the Dream*. Norton, 1994, p. 84.

5. For a detailed look at the history and dynamics of Christian dominance and resistance to it: Paul Kivel. *Living in the Shadow of the Cross: Understanding and Resisting the Power and Privilege of Christian Hegemony*. New Society, 2013.

Foreign Policy

1. For an extended discussion of this chosen people metaphor and its influence on colonial policy and subsequently on US law, see: Newcomb. *Pagans in the Promised Land*.

2. Godfrey Hodgson. *The Myth of American Exceptionalism*. Yale, 2009, p. 10.

3. Danios. "America Has Been at War 93% of the Time—222 out of 239 Years—Since 1776." Washington's Blog, written 2011, posted February 20, 2015. [online]. [cited December 22, 2016].washingtonsblog.com /2015/02/america-war-93-time-222-239-years-since-1776.html.

4. Veterans for Peace. "Total Cost of War Since 2001." Home page. [online]. [cited December 22, 2016]. veteransforpeace.org.

5. Madeleine Albright on *60 Minutes*, May 12, 1996. [online]. [cited December 23, 2016]. youtube.com/watch?v=FbIX1CP9qr4. In 2012 Albright said she was sorry for having said that killing a half million Iraqi children was worth it, but not for having participated in the war that led to their deaths.

6. I borrow this phrase from Peggy Pascoe. *Relations of Rescue: The Search for Female Moral Authority in the American West*, 1874–1939. Oxford, 1990.

7. For example: Michael Chossudovsky. *The Destabilization of Haiti*. Centre for Research on Globalization, February 29, 2004. [online]. [cited December 23, 2016]. globalresearch.ca/articles/CHO402D.html.

8. In January 2017, the answer was seven: Afghanistan, Iraq, Libya, Pakistan, Somalia, Syria, and Yemen.

Environmental Justice

1. Robert D. Bullard. *Environmental Justice in the 21st Century*. Environmental Justice Resource Center at Clark Atlanta University, September 2001. [online]. [cited December 23, 2016]. courses.arch.vt.edu /courses/wdunaway/gia5524/bullard.pdf. See the endnotes for extensive documentation of environmental racism and its health effects.

2. Researcher Harvey L. White stated: "nonwhite workers are 50% more likely to be exposed to hazards in the workplace..." Harvey L. White.

"Race, Class, and Environmental Hazards." California Environmental Protection Agency, 2003. [online]. [cited December 23, 2016]. calepa .ca.gov/files/2016/10/EnvJustice-Documents-2003yr-Appendices -AppendixB.pdf.

3. For example, the phrase *food deserts* has been coined to describe urban areas where people of color don't have access to healthy and affordable food because of corporate decisions to relocate grocery stores from city centers to the suburbs. US Centers for Disease Control. "A Look Inside Food Deserts." last updated September 24, 2012. [online].[cited April 12, 2017]. cdc.gov/features/FoodDeserts/index.html.

4. Worldwatch Institute. "The State of Consumption Today." [online]. [cited November 27, 2016]. worldwatch.org/node/810.

5. International Peace Bureau. *The Military's Impact on the Environment: A Neglected Aspect of the Sustainable Development Debate*. August 2002. [online]. [cited December 23, 2016]. sdissues.net/SDIN/uploads/Mil -Envir%20JOBURG%20version.doc.

6. Jean Hardisry. *Hurricane Katrina and Structural Racism: A Letter to White People*. October 2005. [online]. [cited December 23, 2016]. jeanhardisty.com/errant-thoughts/hurricane-katrina-and-structural- racism-a-letter-to-white-people/; Lee Sustar. "Hurricane Katrina Exposes Racism and Inequality." Countercurrents.org, September 1, 2005. [online]. [cited December 23, 2016]. countercurrents.org/cc -sustar010905.htm.

7. Personal communication.

8. Staff, *Intercontinental Cry* Magazine. "Fifteen Indigenous Struggles You Need to Know About." October 22, 2016. [online]. [cited October 25, 2016]. truth-out.org/news/item/38064-fifteen-other-indigenous -struggles-you-need-to-know-about.

Part VI: Democratic, Anti-Racist Multiculturalism
Democratic, Anti-Racist Multiculturalism

1. My appreciation to Nell Myhand and Allan Creighton for this phrase.

2. For a discussion of male training, see: Paul Kivel. *Men's Work: How to Stop the Violence that Tears Our Lives Apart*, 2nd ed. Hazelden, 1998.

Integration and Tokenism

1. For a detailed account of the resistance of elite educational institutions to respond to demands for racial justice and the pressure on people of color to assimilate to them: Richard L. Zweigenhaft and G. William

Domhoff. *Blacks in the White Establishment?: A Study of Race and Class in America*. Yale, 1991, chapters 2–4.

Organizational Change and Accountability

1. I do not work for corporations or the military because I don't think systemic change can come from organizations whose mission is inimical to social justice.
2. For more on these dynamics, see my article "Social Service or Social Change?" in *Incite!* Women of Color Against Violence, ed. *The Revolution Will Not Be Funded: Beyond the Non-profit Industrial Complex*. South End, 2007, pp. 129–150. [online]. [cited April 13, 2017]. paulkivel.com /resource/social-service-or-social-change/.
3. For more on the history of this work, see: "Part I: The Rise of the Non-Profit Industrial Complex." in *Incite! The Revolution Will Not Be Funded*.
4. Resources on accountability: Bonnie Berman Cushing et al. *Accountability and White Anti-Racist Organizing: Stories from Our Work*. Crandall, Dostie, and Douglass Books, 2010; Clare Land. *Decolonizing Solidarity: Dilemmas and Directions for Supporters of Indigenous Struggles*. Zed Books, 2015; Jen Margaret. *Working as Allies: Supporters of Indigenous Justice Reflect*. AWEA, 2013; Lynne Davis. *Alliances: Re/envisioning Indigenous-non-Indigenous Relationships*. University of Toronto, 2010.
5. You can find contact information for a variety of social justice organizations in the Other Resources section at the back of this book.

Home and Family

1. For example: Debra Van Ausdale and Joe R. Feagin. *The First R: How Children Learn about Race and Racism*. Rowman & Littlefield, 2001.
2. The following paragraphs are adapted from my book *Boys Will Be Men*.
3. One useful resource to begin with: Daphne Muse, ed. *The New Press Guide to Multicultural Resources for Young Readers*. New Press, 1997.
4. Ann Pelo and Fran Davidson. *That's Not Fair! A Teacher's Guide to Activism with Young Children*. Red Leaf, 2000, p. 31.

For the Long Haul

1. Useful resources on taking care of ourselves spiritually as well as physically include: Claudia Horowitz. *The Spiritual Activist: Practices to Transform Your Life, Your Work, and Your World*. Penguin, 2002; Shelly

Tochluk. *Living in the Tension: The Quest for a Spiritualized Racial Justice*. Crandall, Dostie, and Douglass Books, 2016; angel Kyodo-Williams et al. *Radical Dharma: Talking Race, Love, and Liberation*. North Atlantic Books, 2016; Laura Van Dernoot Lipsky and Connie Burk. *Trauma Stewardship: An Everyday Guide to Caring for Self While Caring for Others*. Berrett Koehler, 2009.

Conclusion
1. Marge Piercy. "The Low Road" from *The Moon Is Always Female*. Knopf, 1980. For a powerful reading of this poem, see Staceyann Chin, July 23, 2013. [online]. [cited December 23, 2016]. youtube.com/watch?v=5lnI7 -iib7U.

Bibliography

The author and publisher have decided to lower the cost of this book and to keep the resources up-to-date by providing an online bibliography and other resources for the reader at paulkivel.com. Below is a sample of what you will find there:

Alexander, Michelle. *The New Jim Crow: Mass Incarceration in the Age of Colorblindness*. New Press, 2010.

Alfred, Taiaiake. *Peace, Power, Righteousness: An Indigenous Manifesto*. Oxford, 1999.

Coates, Ta-Nehisi. *Between the World and Me*. Spiegel and Grau, 2015.

Crass, Chris. *Towards the "Other America": Anti-Racist Resources for White People Taking Action for Black Lives Matter*. Chalice Press, 2015.

Dunbar-Ortiz, Roxanne. *An Indigenous Peoples' History of the United States*. Beacon, 2015.

Iyer, Deepa. *We Too Sing America: South Asian, Arab, Muslim and Sikh Immigrants Shape Our Multiracial Future*. New Press, 2015.

Lopes, Tina and Barb Thomas. *Dancing on Live Embers: Challenging Racism in Organizations*. Between the Lines, 2006.

Pilgrim, David. *Understanding Jim Crow: Using Racist Memorabilia to Teach Tolerance and Promote Social Justice*. PM Press, 2015.

Van Ausdale, Debra and J. R. Feagin. *The First R: How Children Learn About Race and Racism*. Rowman and Littlefield, 2001.

Other Resources

Magazines
Against the Current: solidarity-us.org/atc
Bitch: bitchmedia.org
Black Scholar: theblackscholar.org
Briarpatch: briarpatchmagazine.com
Colorlines: colorlines.com
Dollars & Sense: dollarsandsense.org
In Motion Magazine (online only): inmotionmagazine.com
Indian Country Media Network (online only):
    indiancountrytodaymedianetwork.com
Mother Jones: motherjones.com
Ms.: msmagazine.com
The Nation: thenation.com
Rethinking Schools: rethinkingschools.org
Skipping Stones-An International Multicultural Magazine:
    skippingstones.org
Teaching Tolerance: tolerance.org
Tikkun: tikkun.org
YES!: yesmagazine.org
Z magazine: zcomm.org/zmag

Film Distributors and Resources
Bullfrog Films: bullfrogfilms.com
California Newsreel: newsreel.org
Groundspark: groundspark.org
Making Change Media: makingchangemedia.org
Media Education Foundation: mediaed.org
New Day Films: newday.com

Third World Newsreel: twn.org

Women Make Movies: wmm.com

The Working Group: theworkinggroup.org

World Trust Educational Services, Inc.: world-trust.org

Organizations and Websites offering Information and Resources for Racial Justice

ACLU Racial Justice Program: aclu.org/racial-justice

American-Arab Anti-Discrimination Committee (ADC): adc.org

Alternet: alternet.org

AWARE-LA: awarela.org

Asian Americans Advancing Justice: advancingjustice-aajc.org

Audre Lorde Project: alp.org

Bend the Arc: bendthearc.us

Black Commentator: blackcommentator.com

Black Lives Matter: blacklivesmatter.com

Black Mesa Water Coalition: blackmesawatercoalition.org

Black Youth Project 100: byp100.org

Campaign for America's Future: ourfuture.org

Catalyst Project: collectiveliberation.org

Center for Economic and Policy Research: cepr.net

Center for Genetics and Society: geneticsandsociety.org

Center for Media Justice: centerformediajustice.org

Center for Popular Economics: populareconomics.org

Centre for Research on Globalization: globalresearch.ca

Center for Story Based Strategy (formerly Smart Meme): storybasedstrategy.org

Center for Third World Organizing: ctwo.org

Center for Voting and Democracy: fairvote.org

Challenging White Supremacy Workshops: cwsworkshop.org

Civil Rights Project: civilrightsproject.ucla.edu

Color of Change: colorofchange.org

Columbia Journalism Review: cjr.org

Common Cause: commoncause.org

Common Dreams News Center: commondreams.org

Cosecha: lahuelga.com

Council on American-Islamic Relations (CAIR): cair.com

Countercurrents: countercurrents.org

Counterpunch: counterpunch.org

Critical Resistance: criticalresistance.org

Crosspoint Anti Racism: magenta.nl/crosspoint

Democracy Now!: democracynow.org

Demos: demos.org/

Desis Rising Up and Moving (DRUM), South Asian Organizing Chapter:
    drumnyc.org

Dignity in Schools: dignityinschools.org

Drug Policy Alliance: drugpolicy.org

Engaging Schools: engagingschools.org

Facing Race: facingrace.org

Fairness and Accuracy in Reporting: fair.org

Fight for $15: fightfor15.org

Hand in Hand—The Domestic Employers Network:
    domesticemployers.org

The Hapa Project: kipfulbeck.com/the-hapa-project

Highlander Research and Education Center: highlandercenter.org

Human Rights Watch: hrw.org

Idle No More: facebook.com/IdleNoMoreCommunity

INCITE: Women of Color Against Violence: incite-national.org

Independent Media Center: indymedia.org

Indigenous Environmental Network: Ienearth.org

Insight Center for Community Economic Development: insightcced.org

Institute for Policy Studies: ips-dc.org

Institute for Women's Policy Research: iwpr.org

Institute on Race and Policy: irpumn.org

Jewish Voice for Peace: jewishvoiceforpeace.org

Jews for Racial and Economic Justice (JFREJ): jfrej.org

Jobs With Justice: jwj.org

The Labor/Community Strategy Center: thestrategycenter.org

Leadership Conference: civilrights.org

Levy Economics Institute of Bard College: levy.org

Media Action Grassroots Network: mag-net.org

Midwest Academy: midwestacademy.com

Mijente: mijente.net

Movement for Black Lives: policy.m4bl.org

Movement Generation Justice & Ecology Project:
    movementgeneration.org

Movement Strategy Center: movementstrategy.org

Muslim Public Affairs Council: mpac.org

National Association for the Advancement of Colored People: naacp.org
National Coalition Building Institute: ncbi.org
National Council on Crime and Delinquency: nccdglobal.org
National Day Laborer Organizing Network (NDLON): ndlon.org/en
National Domestic Workers Alliance: domesticworkers.org
National Fair Housing Alliance: nationalfairhousing.org
National Network for Immigrant and Refugee Rights: nnirr.org
National Network of Arab American Communities (NNAAC): nnaac.org
Northern Sun: northernsun.com
#Not1More: notonemoredeportation.com
Organizers for America: organizersforamerica.org
Pacifica Radio: pacifica.org
People's Institute for Survival and Beyond: pisab.org
Pew Research Center: pewforum.org
Political Research Associates: politicalresearch.org
PolicyLink: policylink.org
Poverty & Race Research Action Council: prrac.org
Presente: Presente.org
Prison Policy Initiative: prisonpolicy.org
Project Censored: projectcensored.org
Project South: Institute for the Elimination of Poverty and Genocide:
    projectsouth.org
Race Forward: The Center for Racial Justice Innovation: raceforward.org
Race, Racism and the Law: racism.org
Racial Equity Tools: racialequitytools.org
Responsible for Equality and Liberty (R.E.A.L.): realcourage.org
Rethinking Schools: rethinkingschools.org
School of Unity & Liberation (SOUL): schoolofunityandliberation.org
Showing Up for Racial Justice (SURJ): showingupforracialjustice.org
Sins Invalid: sinsinvalid.org
SisterSong—Women of Color Reproductive Justice Collective: sistersong.
    net
SpeakOut: Institute for Democratic Education and Culture:
    speakoutnow.org
South Asian Americans Leading Together (SAALT): saalt.org
Southern Poverty Law Center: splcenter.org
Southerners on New Ground (SONG): southernersonnewground.org
Southwest Organizing Project: swop.net
Southwest Research and Information Center: sric.org

Syracuse Cultural Workers: syracuseculturalworkers.com
Teachers for Social Justice: t4sj.org
Teaching for Change: teachingforchange.org
Teaching Tolerance: tolerance.org
Transgender, Gender/Variant and Intersex Justice Project: tgijp.org
Transgender Law Center: transgenderlawcenter.org
Truthout: truth-out.org
United for a Fair Economy: faireconomy.org
Urban Institute: urban.org
War Resisters League: warresisters.org
Western States Center: westernstatescenter.org
Z Communications: Zcomm.org
Zinn Education Project: zinnedproject.org

Conferences

Allied Media Conference: alliedmedia.org/amc
Creating Change: creatingchange.org
Facing Race: facingrace.raceforward.org
National Association for Multicultural Education: nameorg.org
National Conference on Race and Ethnicity in Higher Education:
    ncore.ou.edu
White Privilege Conference: whiteprivilegeconference.com

Full bibliography and other resources available at paulkivel.com

Index

About the Author

PAUL KIVEL, social justice educator, activist, and writer, has been involved in racial justice work for over 50 years. He is an accomplished trainer and speaker on men's issues, racism and diversity, challenges of youth, teen dating and family violence, raising boys to adulthood, and the impact of class and power on daily life. His work gives people the understanding to become involved in social justice work and the tools to become more effective allies in community struggles to end oppression and injustice and to transform organizations and institutions.

Kivel is the author of numerous books and curricula including *Men's Work, Making the Peace, Helping Teens Stop Violence, Build Community, and Stand for Justice, Boys Will Be Men, I Can Make My World a Safer Place, You Call This a Democracy?* and most recently *Living in the Shadow of the Cross: Understanding and Resisting the Power and Privilege of Christian Hegemony.*

Kivel may be contacted via his resource-filled website: paulkivel.com.

ABOUT NEW SOCIETY PUBLISHERS

New Society Publishers is an activist, solutions-oriented publisher focused on publishing books for a world of change. Our books offer tips, tools, and insights from leading experts in sustainable building, homesteading, climate change, environment, conscientious commerce, renewable energy, and more—positive solutions for troubled times.

We're proud to hold to the highest environmental and social standards of any publisher in North America. This is why some of our books might cost a little more. We think it's worth it!

- We print all our books in North America, never overseas

- All our books are printed on **100% post-consumer recycled paper**, processed chlorine-free, with low-VOC vegetable-based inks (since 2002)

- Our corporate structure is an innovative employee shareholder agreement, so we're one-third employee-owned (since 2015)

- We're carbon-neutral (since 2006)

- We're certified as a B Corporation (since 2016)

At New Society Publishers, we care deeply about *what* we publish—but also about *how* we do business.

New Society Publishers
ENVIRONMENTAL BENEFITS STATEMENT

For every 5,000 books printed, New Society saves the following resources:[1]

44	Trees
3,990	Pounds of Solid Waste
4,391	Gallons of Water
5,727	Kilowatt Hours of Electricity
7,254	Pounds of Greenhouse Gases
31	Pounds of HAPs, VOCs, and AOX Combined
11	Cubic Yards of Landfill Space

[1] Environmental benefits are calculated based on research done by the Environmental Defense Fund and other members of the Paper Task Force who study the environmental impacts of the paper industry.

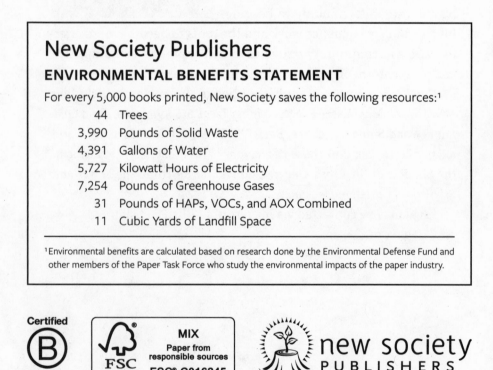